Environmental Issues and Social Welfare

Edited by
Michael Cahill and Tony Fitzpatrick

Blackwell
Publishers

© 2002 by Blackwell Publishers Ltd
a Blackwell Publishing company

First published as a special issue of *Social Policy & Administration* Vol. 35, No. 5, December 2001

Editorial Offices:
108 Cowley Road, Oxford OX4 1JF, UK
Tel: +44 (0)1865 791100
Osney Mead, Oxford OX2 0EL, UK
Tel: +44 (0)1865 206206
350 Main Street, Malden, MA 02148-5018, USA
Tel: +1 781 388 8250
Iowa State University Press, a Blackwell Publishing company, 2121 S. State Avenue,
Ames, Iowa 50014-8300, USA
Tel: +1 515 292 0140
Blackwell Munksgaard, Nørre Søgade 35, PO Box 2148, Copenhagen, DK-1016, Denmark
Tel: +45 77 33 33 33
Blackwell Publishing Asia, 54 University Street, Carlton, Victoria 3053, Australia
Tel: +61 (0)3 347 0300
Blackwell Verlag, Kurfürstendamm 57, 10707 Berlin, Germany
Tel: +49 (0)30 32 79 060
Blackwell Publishing, 10, rue Casimir Delavigne, 75006 Paris, France
Tel: +331 5310 3310

First published 2002 by Blackwell Publishers Ltd

Reprinted 2004

Library of Congress Cataloging-in-Publication Data has been applied for

ISBN 0-631-23552-3

A catalogue record for this title is available from the British Library.

Set in Hong Kong by Graphicraft Limited
Printed and bound in Great Britain by MPG Books Ltd, Bodmin, Cornwall

For further information on Blackwell Publishers visit our website:
www.blackwellpublishers.co.uk

ENVIRONMENTAL ISSUES AND SOCIAL WELFARE

CONTENTS

NOTES ON CONTRIBUTORS

David Barling is Senior Lecturer at the Centre for Food Policy, Thames Valley University.

John Barry is Reader in Politics at Queen's University, Belfast.

Michael Cahill is Reader in Social Policy at the University of Brighton.

Martin Caraher is Reader in Food and Social Policy at the Centre for Food Policy, Thames Valley University.

Hartley Dean is Professor of Social Policy at the University of Luton.

Brian Doherty is Lecturer in Politics in the School of Politics, International Relations and the Environment at Keele University.

John Ferris is Director, Community Policy Research Ltd, Nottingham.

Tony Fitzpatrick is Lecturer in Social Policy at the University of Nottingham.

Jo Guiver is a PhD student at the Institute for Transport Studies, University of Leeds.

Paul Hoggett is Professor of Politics and Director of the Centre for Psycho-Social Studies at the University of the West of England.

Meg Huby is Lecturer in Social Policy at the University of York.

Juliet Jain is a PhD student at the Centre for Science Studies, Department of Sociology, Lancaster University.

Tim Lang is Professor of Food Policy at the Centre for Food Policy, Thames Valley University.

Carol Norman is a freelance garden consultant and former teacher and occupational therapist.

Joe Sempik is an independent environmental researcher.

Douglas Torgerson is Director of the Centre for the Study of Theory, Culture and Politics, and a Professor in the Political Studies Department, the Environmental and Resource Studies Program, and the Cultural Studies Program at Trent University, Canada.

CHAPTER 1

Editorial Introduction

The World Summit on Sustainable Development to be held in Johannesburg in September 2002—the follow-up conference to the 1992 Rio Earth Summit—will be, in part, an assessment of the progress made on sustainable development in the last decade. This special issue of *Social Policy & Administration* examines a wide variety of themes and topics which link the environment with social policy and welfare. First, though, it is timely to assess where we have reached in the greening of social policy.

In the UK the environmental consciousness of the 1970s which produced the Club of Rome *Limits to Growth* report and the pressure groups, Friends of the Earth and Greenpeace, did not mean that environmental issues were included on the agenda of most social scientists. Fred Hirsch's *Social Limits to Growth* was a notable exception (Hirsch 1977). The subject area of Social Policy and Administration ignored the environmental agenda.

By the late 1980s this had changed. The green consciousness of the late 1980s which resulted in a vote of 15 per cent for the Green Party at the 1989 European Elections, the green consumer movement and the first ever government White Paper on the environment was reflected in contributions to the *Social Policy Review 1990–1* where under the heading of the "Greening of Social Policy" there were four contributions (Manning 1991).

Looking back, it can be said that the Earth Summit of 1992 was important in putting sustainability on the global agenda. The Agenda 21 document produced at Rio declared that humankind should share wealth and opportunities more fully between the northern and southern hemispheres, between countries, and between different social groups within each country, with special emphasis on the needs and rights of the poor and disadvantaged. Local Agenda 21—the local strategy for sustainable development—stimulated a diverse range of research and action on the ways in which sustainability could be operationalized. After Rio UK social science became involved. The Economic and Social Research Council Global Environmental Change programme was an important result of the changed perception of environmental issues, and in 1995 one of the Council's research themes became environment and sustainability. Other research funders have followed including the Rowntree Foundation's programme entitled "Reconciling Environmental and Social Concerns".

Social scientists of many persuasions have responded to the challenge of Rio. Among academic journals there has been the launch of *Environmental*

Politics, Environmental Values and *Local Environment.* Work on environmental issues by social scientists has been published by pressure groups and think tanks of various persuasions. Parallel to this there has been a mushrooming of work on the social economy—the creation of Local Employment Trading Schemes, community environmental initiatives, credit unions, community gardening—exploring the diverse ways in which needs can be met at the local and community level by local people.

Local Agenda 21 has been enthusiastically adopted by many local authorities often working in concert with these projects, and they have begun to focus on issues which flow from the concept of social sustainability: accessibility, community participation, anti-poverty strategies.

It is our contention that, for Social Policy and Administration, the environment is not another topic that can be added to those which constitute the welfare state: personal social services, health, housing, education and social security. Rather, all these areas have an environmental dimension and, as Agenda 21 claimed, are part of what we mean by sustainability. Similarly, a focus upon environmental issues forces us to rework our notions of welfare. Are we merely discussing human welfare? Can we speak intelligibly of the welfare of the planet? How do we rank the welfare of future generations compared with our own? Equally, ecologism—or "greenism" as it is sometimes called—is not simply another political ideology which merits a chapter in the textbooks but is rather a fundamental challenge to mainstream political and social thought.

The 1990s were an extremely productive decade in the engagement of social scientists with environmental issues. The essays in this special issue are from scholars working in a number of different disciplines within the social sciences. They are united by a belief in the importance of environmental themes and by a commitment to working on the diverse implications of taking the environment seriously in a number of policy areas. Together with the work contained in our forthcoming book *Greening the Welfare State* (Fitzpatrick and Cahill 2002), we consider that these essays demonstrate that sustainability issues are now being seriously addressed in Social Policy and Administration.

Three themes are pursued in this issue. The first is the nature of green political and social theory. The nature of politics itself is examined in the essay by Douglas Torgerson setting out a model of politics which adds to the traditional distinction between reformism and radicalism in green politics a third dimension—the performative—using Hannah Arendt's work which has the potential to connect the formal and informal aspects of a green economy. Hartley Dean reviews the ways in which the term green citizenship has been employed, noting that an ethic of environmental obligation has remained within the confines of academic texts. He outlines a taxonomy of moral discourse on citizenship, comparing the conventional with the ecological, before outlining his own *eco-socialist* version of citizenship which is based upon co-responsibility and an ethic of care. Tony Fitzpatrick, drawing upon recent work in political philosophy on social justice and sustainability, proposes a meta-generational theory which attempts to weigh the claims of the poor in the present against those in the future.

The second theme features policy areas where environmental considerations are paramount. Focusing upon the developing world Meg Huby outlines the conflicts inherent in sustainable development in relation to energy and water. Given the growing involvement of private sector companies in utilities in the poor world there is an obvious need for governments to act as regulators and to protect goals of sustainable development. Tim Lang, David Barling and Martin Caraher present a model of ecological health food policy in the context of successive food scandals and an inadequate regulatory system. Their model gives equal weight to how people eat and how their diet is produced and distributed. In so doing they note the ways in which adverse environmental consequences of our food system are linked to deleterious health and social impacts. In a related paper John Ferris, Carol Norman and Joe Sempik review the community gardening movement. They report on community gardening initiatives in the United States and propose that they are important in the development of sustainable urban policy.

The environmental case against the car is well known and proven but the social inequalities it has generated are not so widely recognized. Juliet Jain and Jo Guiver argue that the car is such a divisive technology that its use needs to be regulated and restricted within the context of a wider debate on the nature of mobility and access which can promote social inclusion.

Pathways to sustainability constitute the third theme. John Barry and Brian Doherty offer an upbeat assessment of the contribution made by green social movements to thinking about social policy and produce a categorization of their approaches to the state. They conclude by formulating a green social policy position on key questions of inequality and welfare. Paul Hoggett sketches an ecowelfare model of relationships which should underpin the transition to a sustainable society. He draws the conclusion that extensive democratization is key to this process. Finally, Michael Cahill explores the implications of consumerism for the prospects of a transition to a sustainable society.

The ten papers presented in this collection are evidence enough of the scholarship that is in progress on the key questions concerning the realignment of social policy to confront environmental issues. They present a challenging socio-environmental agenda for social policy.

Michael Cahill and Tony Fitzpatrick

References

Fitzpatrick, T. and Cahill, M. (eds) (2002), *Greening the Welfare State*, London: Palgrave.
Hirsch, F. (1977), *Social Limits to Growth*, London: Routledge.
Manning, N. (ed.) (1991), *Social Policy Review 1990–1*, Harlow: Longman.

CHAPTER 2

Rethinking Politics for a Green Economy: A Political Approach to Radical Reform

Douglas Torgerson

Abstract

Because the process of achieving a green economy is bound to be political, it is important how politics is understood. This essay employs a three-dimensional model of politics (functional, constitutive, performative) in developing an approach to radical reform that accentuates political potentialities—understood in terms of debate, open exchanges of differing opinions. By exploring a central tension between the formal economy (associated with administrative and policy arenas in modern society) and the informal economy (associated with the enhancement of community), the argument concludes that achieving a green economy involves a key role not simply for the rational economic individual or the cooperative community member, but also for the citizen.

Keywords

Green economy; Politics; Community; Social policy; Administration; Guaranteed income; Citizen

Introduction

A central tension marks thought about prospects for a green economy. Should effort focus on altering the operations of the formal economy or on developing and expanding the informal economy? The question, translated into political terms, is whether a functional politics of system adjustment and adaptation is the right path or whether a green economy depends on a constitutive politics aimed at creating a system that is altogether different.

Although it makes sense for particular groups and individuals to focus their practical efforts on either the formal or the informal economy, it is theoretic- ally inadequate to try to conceptualize potential change without examining the relationship between the two. That relationship is examined here as part of an effort to conceptualize a political approach to radical reform for a

Address for correspondence: *Douglas Torgerson, Centre for the Study of Theory, Culture and Politics, Trent University, Peterborough, Ontario, Canada K9J 7B8. E-mail: dtorgerson@trentu.ca*

green economy. This approach does not rely on a rationalistic, comprehensive strategy formulated by a unified agent, but on a political process involving a multiplicity of agents whose efforts are expected to conflict as well as coalesce.

How might we adequately conceptualize such a political approach to radical reform? The contention here is that a needed step is to rethink politics. The essay thus follows a model, arguably already implicit in green political practice, that identifies *three dimensions of politics: functional, constitutive,* and *performative* (see Torgerson 1999, 2000).

The first two dimensions are actually quite familiar and relate to the opposition between reformism and radicalism. Functional politics can be described as involving the interplay of policy inputs and outputs that are needed in the operations of a socioeconomic system. This is the typical domain of reform-oriented green politics. Constitutive politics, in contrast, involves the very foundation of a socioeconomic order—establishing, maintaining or changing it. This is the primary domain of radical green politics and its agenda of transforming the existing order and its alignments of power.

Distinguishing explicitly between functional and constitutive dimensions of politics helps focus attention on possible relationships between the two. Either/or thinking might then be avoided and the relationships between reformism and radicalism, better understood. But it is also important not to ignore the third dimension of politics: the performative.

While the functional and constitutive dimensions of politics are both instrumental—that is, concerned about getting results—the performative dimension is concerned with the value of process. In particular, political debate—the public interchange of differing opinions—acquires a value in itself (see, e.g., Arendt 1958, 1968). The performative dimension of politics is of course not everything there is to politics, but it is something that needs to be recognized even if we retain a predominantly instrumental focus.

The tripartite model provides for an open exchange of differing opinions as something significant not only in the performative dimension of politics, but also in the instrumental dimensions: in the functional context of the policy process and in the constitutive domain of contests over the alignment of power. These dimensions of politics all have their places, as we shall see, in a political process of radical reform populated not only by rational economic individuals or cooperative community members, but also by citizens.

Formal and Informal: A Central Tension of Modernity

The opposition between formal and informal economies in green thought[1] corresponds to a central tension of modernity. To focus on the formal economy draws attention to the question of how operations of the market and of public and private bureaucracies can be modified to produce green outcomes. The hope of this orientation is perhaps best captured in the idea of ecological modernization (see Christoff 1996). A focus on the informal economy, in contrast, draws attention to the potential of developing economic life outside and against those abstract, anonymous forces of modernity that often seem irresistible and uncontrollable. This orientation is pinned to the idea of a green community.

5

The formal domain has not existed since time immemorial, but emerged clearly in the eighteenth and nineteenth centuries through a historical process that Karl Polanyi called "the great transformation" (Polanyi 1957; cf. Booth 1994). The rise of the formal economy was central to a disembedding of human relationships that tore apart the fabric of integrated communities to produce the fragmented world of modern society. The more community came apart, the more it became possible for "the economy" to stand apart as a largely distinct, formalized, anonymous set of relationships. The informal economy in today's world recalls the image of community as a domain of integrated, personalized life activity. It is this image that inspires radical hopes of centring economic life in green communities.

To understand the difference—and relationship—between the formal and the informal, it is helpful to revisit a key contrast in social theory, particularly as formulated by Ferdinand Tönnies in his famous opposition between "community" and "society"—*Gemeinschaft* and *Gesellschaft* (Tönnies 1957). This contrast is not merely a typology, but registers a pattern of historical change whereby the informal relationships of community increasingly give way, with the advent of modernity, to the formal relationships of society.

Jürgen Habermas (1984/1987) offers a contemporary reformulation of much the same opposition. Yet here we find a bifurcation of two worlds in which the "system", through the anonymous media of market exchange and administrative power, colonizes the "lifeworld" domain of mutual recognition and understanding. Although there are border disputes and opportunities for communicative action in the "public sphere" to influence the operations of the system (Habermas 1992), no prospect appears for realigning the terms of the opposition. Tönnies's idea, in contrast, is of prevailing tendencies rather than an either/or opposition, and he is able to imagine the possibility of historical shifts favouring community relationships.

Max Weber's account of the rationalization of the modern world, emerging along with Tönnies's contribution in the context of classical German sociology, provides much of the foundation for Habermas's analysis. Weber holds out little if any prospect, however, for the shifts toward community that Tönnies can imagine or even for the possibility, à la Habermas, of the system coming under the influence of the lifeworld by virtue of a revitalized public sphere. If anything, Weber looks with grim resignation to the future of his disenchanted world (e.g., Weber 1978, vol. 2: 992).

Weber's resignation is less significant here than the centrepiece of his analysis. He portrays modern administration as instrumentally rational, a tool well suited to achieving the ends to which it is directed (Weber 1978, vol. 1: 24–6). Yet this instrumental rationality requires the shaping of social institutions into something predictable (1978, vol. 2: 975) and thus depends on a formal rationality that casts human behaviour "in numerical, calculable terms" (vol. 1: 85). Weber is under no illusion that the calculability and predictability of collective human behaviour is something simply given in the nature of things. Like Hobbes, he knows that such order depends on the creation of a social artifice (Torgerson 1990b). For Weber, as for Hobbes, moreover, the basic building block of this artifice is a particular model of the individual.

In elaborating this aspect of Weber's analysis, Alfred Schutz draws attention to what he sees as a key feature of the lifeworld: its structure depends on how individual actors regard one another. In Schutz's terms, individual conduct depends on the recognition of particular "action types" involving characteristic courses of action (Schutz 1967). These action types vary in the extent to which they are either *abstract and anonymous* or *concrete and personal*—to the extent, in other words, that they are either formal or informal. The formal economic and organizational relationships of the modern world (what Habermas calls the system) thus depend on a particular structuring of the lifeworld, not on being somehow detached from it.

The model of the rational economic actor—the "possessive individual" (Macpherson 1964)—looms large here as that particular action type which is quintessentially abstract and anonymous. As community comes apart with the emergence of modern society, order—as well as calculability and predictability—comes to depend on the salience of the formal relationships that obtain among abstract and anonymous actors. This tendency becomes so pronounced, indeed, that vast analytic enterprises depend on presupposing the model of the possessive individual—even consecrating this otherwise rather peculiar action type as the essence of humanity—rather than recognizing its prevalence as a historical and cultural artefact.[2]

From Hobbes to Bentham, indeed, social order comes to depend on this type of actor (Halévy 1955), an individual predictably manipulated by fear and anxiety. Weber understood the historical specificity of a social order dependent on this type of individual (Schutz 1964), and Foucault has more recently provided detailed analyses of how the disciplinary and governmental modalities of modern society shape the individual (Foucault 1980, 1991). The abstract and anonymous individual becomes central to the system—the basic unit of the mechanism, so to speak—and even comes to define the limit of human possibility.

Approaches to a green economy that focus on the formal economy generally remain within this horizon of possibility. The key question, accordingly, is how to change the character of incentives confronting possessive individuals in order to promote more environmentally friendly outcomes (e.g. Freeman *et al.* 1973; cf. Victor 1979). There is no questioning of the way the formal economy has become disembedded, populated by abstract, anonymous actors. To focus on the informal economy, in contrast, means throwing into question dramatically the prevailing horizon of possibility and promoting more concrete and personal forms of human interaction.

In the terms Tönnies sets out, enhancing the informal economy would mean accentuating community-like modes of interaction in order to alter the historical trend that saw society displace community. At best, in Habermas's more bifurcated version of the central tension of modernity, the lifeworld—via the public sphere—makes its claims on the system from without. What this formulation neglects, however, is what Schutz's commentary on Weber reveals: the lifeworld remains at the heart of the system. The real question is what action types come to predominate in actual economic and administrative relationships.

At an extreme of anonymity and abstraction, it perhaps makes sense to say that systemic operations come to cancel out lifeworld interactions, but such hyperbole risks reifying the central institutions of modern societies as essentially alien and impenetrable. To believe that this extreme has actually been realized in contemporary society would mean being misled by a caricature, simply accepting the rationalistic self-image that the system characteristically projects of itself.

This self-image, though undoubtedly significant to the behaviour of the system, obscures crucial modes of interaction that depend on significantly concrete and personal action types—indeed, on vagaries and complexities of communication that have become increasingly noted, promoted, and celebrated in contemporary organization theory (e.g. Morgan 1986; cf. Crozier and Friedberg 1980). It is important to look beyond the streamlined image of the system to grasp the nature and significance of the administrative sphere.

Although the image of a self-regulating market mechanism is currently central to the conceptualization of the formal economy, today's actually existing market depends on promotion and coordination by an administrative sphere consisting of a complex of organizations that includes both state agencies and private corporations (Torgerson 1990a). Market relationships are not self-regulating, that is, but are managed through this complex, which is by no means some neutral mechanism. To identify such a complex is not to suggest a homogeneous entity operating according to fixed imperatives. The sphere is ambivalent, exhibiting features that are simultaneously cohesive and fragmented, cooperative and conflictual. Nothing guarantees an easy ride for the administrative sphere.

Its different actors—state and corporate, domestic and international—face a host of pressures, and it is by no means obvious that this complex can effectively deal with the dysfunctions of industrialism (e.g. environmental problems) that the complex itself serves to generate (Torgerson 1999: 135–45). Despite rationalistic imagery, moreover, the administrative sphere is a domain of functional *politics*, complete with the rough and tumble of political reality and the complex vagaries of human communication. This sphere is at least the inescapable backdrop for any effort to promote a green economy and, at the same time, furnishes the key arenas for any effort focusing on the reform of the formal economy.

The importance of the administrative sphere, obvious in market-based approaches to a green economy such as neoclassical environmental economics (Victor 1979; Gowdy and Olsen 1994), also appears in ecological economics, although this approach challenges conventional conceptions of the formal economy. Here the market is displaced as non-human nature takes centre stage along with human interactions: "Ecological economics deals with the interactions between humans and the natural world, interactions which themselves are ever evolving as the very interactions impact upon the ecosystem and alter it, and as perceptions of the environment also change" (Faber *et al.* 1996: 15). The key point is to move beyond market models in order to develop ecological models of human/nature interactions.

By shattering the idea of the self-enclosed market as the central figure of analytic attention, ecological economics represents an at least tentative step toward re-embedding economic relationships. Although consistent in this respect with a strengthening of the informal economy, the approach still

8

largely assumes an institutional base centred within the administrative sphere (e.g. Duchin 1996; cf. May and Pastuk 1996). Ecological economics does not take a decisive step toward strengthening the informal economy and rooting it in green communities.

Prospects for a Green Community: A Return to the Informal?

The image of community stands in opposition to the anonymity and abstraction of modern society and its formal economy. Community is a place of human scale where economic relationships have no status as a separate domain, but are themselves part of a larger ensemble of relationships rooted in a common ethos. Economic relationships do not constitute a mechanism that rules the community, but are themselves guided by principles constituting the community.

This image of community inspires much green thinking (see Eckersley 1992, ch. 7; Dobson 1995, chs 3–4). The green community, characterized by freedom and equality among human beings as well as respect for non-human nature, is imagined as breaking free of the formal economy in favour of a self-sufficient informal economy. This image, however utopian, is based on the insight that it is profoundly misleading to restrict the idea of economic activity to the formal economy.

How do human beings effect an interchange with the rest of nature so as to provide for their collective livelihood? If that is taken as the key economic question, then the range of economic activity extends well beyond the formal domain. Serge Latouche focuses in this regard on economic life where the formal economic system has broken down. Especially in areas of the so-called underdeveloped third world, Latouche finds, people often fend for themselves through "networks of solidarity", informal spaces of production and exchange (Latouche 1993: 146). The logic of his argument points to a re-embedding of economic relations: "The basis for the very existence of the informal, and for its viability, is its reinsertion of the economic within the larger social texture of life, to the point that sometimes the economic is completely absorbed within this texture" (1993: 127).

Latouche's argument further suggests the possibility of a reversal of position between the formal and the informal. Even to regard the informal as a particular economic sector is mistaken, he claims, for the informal "is often present at the very heart of the formal economy and functions in close association with it" (Latouche 1993: 127). Marginalized in both theory and practice, informal economic activity thus seems potentially capable of a comeback, of regaining a place at the centre of things.

Although Latouche's attention focuses very much on the margins of the formal economy, his perspective remains relevant to its centre. His view that the informal can be found at the heart of the formal also coincides with a key feminist idea: that "women's work"—traditionally most of what has been understood as the reproduction of labour power—constitutes a type of informal economic activity needed for the formal economy to be constructed and maintained (Mellor 1995). The very rise of industrialism in the context of the capitalist market, moreover, drew of necessity upon informal norms of cultural solidarity, even though modernity was to take that culture apart and was increasingly to codify those norms—as they were needed for business— in a formal legal system that would allow for calculability and predictability.

Green initiatives to promote the informal economy envision community self-reliance and self-determination at the local level (Young 1997; Barry 1999: 160–2). The chief accent here is on various forms of cooperation, both old and new.[3] Along with community economic development strategies, we find a focus on the importance of both consumer and producer cooperatives. Perhaps the most significant recent innovation is what have been called "cooperation circles" (Offe and Heinze 1992; Gorz 1999), more commonly known as "local employment and trading systems" or simply "LETS" (e.g. Williams 2000). The key environmental rationale for this local focus is to relax the intensive reliance of the formal economy on long-distance transportation networks. These networks involve heavy demands on energy and other resources along with the generation of pollution. Such intensive reliance upon transportation also creates certain vulnerabilities, such as a tendency to transform local agri-cultural disease outbreaks into widespread epidemics. At the same time, a local focus in economic activity draws upon local knowledge for understandings and designs attentive to the ecological particularities of a given locale.

The accent on cooperation at the local level points toward a re-embedding of economic activity in a green community. However, this different accent, even if significantly developed, would still be a long way from a return to community and a central reliance on the informal economy. What this accent mainly signals, rather, is cultural change in the way identities are shaped. To enhance economic activity oriented to cooperation rather than to the competition characteristic of the formal economy is to promote an alternative to the abstract and anonymous action type prevailing in the for-mal economy. Dominating the scene, patterns of rational economic activity shape individual identities, strategies, and expectations in a way that gives interaction in the formal economy a particularly anxious and alienating texture. The cooperative alternative suggests—and partially realizes—the potential for patterns of interaction that confirm individuals in a sense of collective security and reinforce among them relations of mutual recognition and support. The possessive individualism of the rational economic actor is displaced by the cooperative spirit of the community member.

In the quest for a green economic community, the critique of industrialism and the formal economy at times becomes a straightforward rejection. Visions are advanced of a frugal, communal type of life in which human solidarity as well as the value, meaning and dignity of work are reaffirmed (for surveys, see Dobson 1995: 104–12; Eckersley 1992: 163–7). When greens endorse the value of work, however, they seem at times, strangely, to echo the authoritar-ian celebration of the work ethic that is central to industrialism. Of course, the rationale is quite different. A context is envisioned in which the value of meaningful work—now experienced by a rather privileged few—could be more generally enjoyed. In the actual contemporary context, nonetheless, green endorsements of the value of work too often neglect how they resonate with the prevailing discourse.

This neglect proceeds from a utopianism that counsels a flat abandonment of industrialism and the administrative sphere. Sacrifice is moralistically exalted, as indeed it would have to be in an economic context where avoiding privation demands significant contributions of labour by all. Here the idea of a green community not only breaks with the formal economy of industrialism, but also reinforces forms of identity and expectation that were central to preindustrial modes of domination.

Whatever the potential of communities, their actual history has not been idyllic. With the subordination of women a frequent feature, communities have often been sites of hierarchy and oppression. Even without hierarchy, the shared identity characteristic of community promotes unity and consensus, tending thereby to marginalize or exclude difference and dissidence. Community in this sense celebrates the cooperative member, not the citizen, and diminishes the potential for politics as an open exchange of differing opinions.

Changing Dynamics of the Formal Economy: Guaranteed Income?

Communitarian visions typically involve moral exhortations to adopt a green lifestyle. Yet it is hard to imagine how such lifestyle change, even if coupled with collective resistance to the prevailing order, could amount to constitutive change unless individuals, on a large scale, also gained greater opportunity to plan and direct their lives apart from the systemic pressures of both production and consumption. This is the key point in the strategic orientation advanced by Helmut Wiesenthal: "Central to Wiesenthal's strategy for ecological reform", as John Ferris puts it, "is the idea that there must be societal structural reforms to make it possible for people to live in ecologically responsible ways. Both current values and structural mechanisms 'lock' people into unsustainable 'lifestyles'" (Ferris 1993: 19).

Much the same idea has been advanced from the perspective of ecological economics (Duchin 1996: 296): "Will people living in different kinds of households be interested in imagining—and experimenting with—lifestyles that could be comfortable and satisfying but that put less stress on the environment than those of today's affluent classes? Could less work, less consumption, and more leisure be more attractive than the 'work and spend' cycle?" This question envisions the possibility of designing "incentive systems of various sorts" (Duchin 1996: 297) to promote the adoption of environmentally friendly lifestyles.

Such an orientation clearly involves functional politics, interventions particularly into the operations of the formal economy. This is the starting point for green social policy. However, green social policy proposals tend to connect also with the constitutive, thus linking the dimensions of functional and constitutive politics (cf. Fitzpatrick 1998). This is particularly the case with the idea of a guaranteed basic income, which has been portrayed as the quintessential green social policy (Dobson 1991; Fitzpatrick 1999: 201). As it was first proposed in an environmental context, the idea of a guaranteed basic income is based on the view that work, as part of the economic system of advanced industrial society, has become environmentally destructive: "We work too much" (Johnson 1973: 179).[4]

The guaranteed basic income has been advocated from a variety of perspectives, including ones that are far from socially radical (see Fitzpatrick 1999; Van Parijs 1992a). The proposal can appear as simply a marginal adjustment of social welfare policy to help the system adapt to unemployment problems engendered by the growth of automation. The scheme might thus be seen from a radical green perspective as nothing but a way of streamlining the big industrial machine as it heads for the abyss. Nonetheless, basic income has emerged as a central element of proposals for radical reform generally and, notably, of green realist strategy, particularly as advanced by Wiesenthal (1993: 184). If adopted, a basic income could be a significant development in the functional politics of advanced industrial societies, potentially helping to tilt the terms and conditions of environmental policy discourse in a manner more favourable to green initiatives. Such functional change also suggests possibilities for change at a constitutive level, for the change would involve a dynamic central to the formal economy.

Proposals to seek transformation by rejecting the formal economy may be necessary, but they are not sufficient: by themselves, they lead to a dead end. A decisive break with the prevailing economic system cannot simply leave its central dynamics untouched (cf. Helleiner 1996). In other words, such a pattern of historical change would (albeit perhaps paradoxically) have to involve politics in its functional as well as its constitutive dimension. This need is addressed by green thinking that, questioning the purpose of work in advanced industrial society, recognizes the potential for guaranteed income initiatives to promote at least some alteration in the dynamics of the formal economy.

The continuous drive for technological development under industrial capitalism systematically promotes unemployment by making machines cheaper to employ than people. With unemployment a persistent problem, there is the question of how to distribute income in a manner that is fair, that smooths over the hard times of the business cycle, and that generates growth to promote job creation. The great social challenge thus becomes not one of maintaining adequate production, but of producing enough jobs to keep the bulk of the population working.

Provisions for social welfare have been the key policy response. Such provisions are supposed to offer (some) fairness by providing a general safety net for the population; at the same time, welfare state policies are meant to help secure social order and support the level of effective demand in the economy. What the policies are emphatically not meant to do, however, is to promote any diminution of the work ethic and the willingness to work. To this end, the policies seek as far as possible to keep the distribution of income tied to actual or potential performance in the workplace, a general inclination that has been accentuated with conservative shifts in social policy since the 1980s.

With the connection between employment and livelihood carefully maintained, social welfare policy typically offers a modicum of social security, but not too much. There is certainly not enough security to lessen the anxieties and acquisitive impulses of the possessive individual that continue to be aroused by concerns about future livelihood. The possessive individual is moved not, as often assumed, just by a senseless drive to acquire and consume more, but also—perhaps more fundamentally—by the anxiety and uncertainty individuals typically face in a competitive world that does not owe them a living.

Proposals for a guaranteed basic income advance a social policy innovation that could systematically loosen the connection between employment and livelihood. The basic income scheme would, of course, like other social welfare measures, serve to support levels of effective demand in the economy. However, a systematic loosening of connections between the livelihood of individuals and their uncertain prospects for employment would tend to reduce the scope and intensity of motives for growth—that is, those pressures that often undercut the potential for serious public deliberation about economic alternatives and environmental costs (Offe 1992: 70–1; Fitzpatrick 1999: ch. 9; Van Parijs 1992b).

By promising to loosen the link between employment and livelihood, basic income initiatives represent a challenge unsettling for any strong attachment to the work ethic, especially when the attachment is part of unquestioned industrialist presuppositions. For individuals, such initiatives promise greater opportunity in planning for both their livelihood and life activity beyond paid employment (Offe 1992: 75–6; Offe *et al.* 1996: 216–17). At a collective level, basic income not only promises a context more hospitable to environmental policy initiatives, but also sets the stage for a broader and more effective airing of green perspectives on the meaning and purpose of economic life.

Guaranteed income proposals invariably provoke opposition on behalf of self-discipline, initiative and the intrinsic rewards of meaningful work. This celebration of work and personal responsibility, however, typically appears as more than a little disingenuous, as but an effort to reinforce the social discipline required to maintain a system in which human creative potential is generally degraded by the demands of meaningless toil in an authoritarian workplace.

What are the chances for a guaranteed basic income in the prevailing political context of advanced industrial societies? There have been occasions when the prospects seemed good. At the moment, however, the chances generally appear rather dim. Of course, the present context is one in which the problem of unemployment has not lately been intense. If this problem should substantially intensify, the guaranteed income scheme could again emerge on the policy agenda for serious consideration.

In any consideration, design or implementation of a guaranteed income policy, there would be at least two key issues of contention: (1) the level of income to be guaranteed, and (2) whether the guarantee should be unconditional or should depend on some type of work or work-related performance. Although both of these issues would of course be important, the question of conditionality is particularly significant. Here resides the issue of whether the key link between work and livelihood is to be maintained or broken.

The prospects for unconditionality seem especially dim. Even greens have strongly opposed it.[5] The overall situation is such, according to A. B. Atkinson, that "to secure political support, it may be necessary for proponents of basic income to compromise" on the question of "unconditional payment" (Atkinson 1995: 301). However much some greens might maintain that "we work too much" for our environmental good—and that the productive capacity of modern technology has eliminated the real need for an unrelenting work requirement—it is still widely believed that the well-being of society depends on enhancing productive capacity. Hence the world does not—and should not—owe anyone a living. This position is one that now often seems to be advanced as much by the moderate left as by the extreme right wing (Grover and Stewart 2000; Atkinson and Elliott 2001).

It would thus be naive to envision a policy of unconditional guaranteed income suddenly springing on to the scene. It is not unreasonable, though, to anticipate the possibility of social policy initiatives that would move towards some guaranteed income scheme, particularly if unemployment problems should become intense. Such a move would primarily be a matter of functional politics, centred in the administrative sphere and concerned with the operation of the formal economy. Moving beyond that to a policy of unconditional basic income would have constitutive implications, and this no doubt is one reason why the step to unconditionality tends to be strongly resisted.

We thus seemingly enter a quandary in terms of a green approach to radical reform that would include as a central element an unconditional, guaranteed basic income. That measure seems blocked at the outset as entirely unrealistic in the present political context. Anything we might realistically expect would be a modest and highly qualified move in the direction of a guaranteed income scheme. Almost certainly, there would be some kind of condition—a requirement, if not for work, at least for a surrogate such as training or community service.

With such a requirement, though, the scheme could not work automatically. There would have to be some kind of policing mechanism that would bring its own costs and difficulties. We can also be confident that the design and implementation of any such guaranteed income measure would be the result only of a complex political process involving an array of different and no doubt often conflicting interests and perspectives. As we shall see, this political character of the process carries a significant potential for radical reform.

The Political Connection

Green thinking need not consider formal and informal economies to be either/or alternatives. The two can be seen as potentially complementary aspects of a complex, political process of radical reform beyond the control of any single agent responsible for achieving a green economy. With the process involving two divergent if not antagonistic institutional worlds, politics (both functional and constitutive) would be the point of connection.

Self-interested and acquisitive impulses would be sure to persist as salient features of human behaviour with any historical change emerging from the present cultural context. The possessive individual, who is not suddenly going to disappear through legislation or moral condemnation, needs to be acknowledged. Still, a central question is how to diminish the cultural impact of this action type.

One obvious step would be to encourage citizenship through opportunities and invitations to participate in political life. Neither the formal nor the informal economy offers much in the way of such encouragement, but we can find a potential for citizenship in the relationship between these two institutional worlds.

Visions of a return to the informal economy express hope for a mode of human interaction that radically departs from the kind of interchanges typical of possessive individuals. These visions anticipate that the cooperative, community-spirited potentialities of people will come to prevail. The accent on harmonious cooperation in community life serves to accentuate an image of active, creative people working together. However, this image neglects politics and the significance of the citizen as another kind of counter to the possessive individual (see Sagoff 1988: 51–3).

Michael Kenny has advanced an especially pertinent critique of "the *gemeinschaft* metaphor at the heart of many communitarian arguments" (Kenny 1996: 27). He does not altogether reject community, but indicates that what is crucial is how community is understood—how, that is, community serves as a *metaphor* to shape identities and interactions. Kenny particularly stresses that "the *gemeinschaft* logic of ecological communitarianism" (1996: 22) tends "to conjure up a utopian future" in which "competing interests and power relationships have disappeared", in which indeed they "have no place" (1996: 23). As continually reiterated "in some green circles", this particular metaphor of community "encourages the belief that power relationships can be transcended once humans and nature are operating harmoniously" (1996: 23).

Kenny highlights the significance of difference for green communities. For one thing, there can be no such thing as a green community in the singular, but only green communities existing in a context of other green communities. To suppose otherwise is to avoid "the political question of how to establish just relations among different decentralised communities" while failing to understand "the basis for a specifically green politics of identity"—namely, a "recognition that one of the distinctive features of modern life is the interplay between . . . different communities of geography, interest and belief" (Kenny 1996: 29). Once this basis is understood, it becomes possible to grasp the prospect of "a more dialogic and differentiated public culture" at odds with what he calls "the closed, homogeneous and hierarchical implications of *gemeinschaft* communitarianism" (1996: 31). For green communities to promote such a prospect, they would need to be "fluid and dynamic" in a way that helps—rather than inhibits—"individuals to experience relations of difference on a continual and changing basis" (1996: 32).

The totalizing impulse of green communitarianism, if fully followed in undoing the fragmentation of modern society, leads back to the premodern embedded community. Not only is the economic embedded here; so too is the political. The political sphere as a space for debate—an open exchange of differing opinions—would at least tend to be obscured and constricted by the totalizing impulse. The effect would be to diminish the citizen as well as the possessive individual.

The identity of the citizen depends on a sphere of interaction suited to a type of actor willing and able to engage in critical debate, to take account of self and context, and to have the courage to stand apart and object to dominant opinions. The community Kenny wants, one that embraces political difference and debate, is the kind where there would be political space for citizenship. An echo of this prospect is not entirely absent among green thinkers who want to re-embed economic relations in community. Matthew Paterson, for example, argues that a green community would retain an irreducible political element: "ultimately there is no substitute for politics—even a 'Green utopia' will involve continual struggle over rights, justice, distribution questions, what forms of production are sustainable, and so on" (Paterson 2000: 161). To fully embrace the citizen, however, would mean treating political space not just as something necessary, but as something valuable in itself.

Beyond the level of the green community, André Gorz has called for consideration of the political character of "the possible links and mediations between the local, micro-social sphere of cooperative communities and the macro-society in which they remain immersed" (Gorz 1999: 109). In such potential linkages between community and society, we can glimpse another arena for citizenship, one that could promote—and simultaneously be reinforced by—citizen action in local communities.

The potential political connection between community and society can be viewed more concretely by focusing on an actual political possibility, and we can do this by turning again to the question of guaranteed basic income. Basic income is conceptually consistent with a rationalistic programme centred in the administrative sphere. A basic income policy could, in principle, be technocratically designed and implemented to operate in a virtually automatic manner (Schick 1971). However, to introduce basic income in this rationalistic way, as a kind of magic wand, would undermine political potentialities while likely reinforcing the quiescence—and perhaps pathologies (cf. Paehlke 1998)—of mass society. Even loosening the link between employment and livelihood might then not be enough to significantly challenge the place of the possessive individual as the action type central to the prevailing system.

Athough a guaranteed basic income is conceptually consistent with rationalistic design and implementation, we earlier saw that actual political differences—centring on persistent demands that income payments remain conditional—undermine the likelihood of a rationalistic scenario. Political complexities are not easily bypassed. If we accept such complexities and focus attention on them, concrete possibilities for a political approach to radical reform begin to appear. It is here, indeed, that efforts to promote a strong informal economy show a special promise.

The strengthening of local, informal institutions provides a political resource that could serve to block or subvert efforts from the administrative sphere to police the implementation of guaranteed income measures. With some creativity, such institutions could help individuals fulfil whatever work-related conditions might be imposed for the guaranteed income, doing so in a way that actually empowered individuals to determine their own life plans. The efforts of these institutions could, indeed, promote both individual self-determination and opportunities for individuals to join together in voluntary, collective activities. Because it is political, moreover, the process imagined here is not one that could be comprehended and controlled from a rationalistic standpoint.

Political potentialities become clear only when the basic income measure is placed in the context of a political process—oriented by public debate— that is open to learning through trial, error and discourse. This would be an open-ended process of experimentation—policy design, implementation, adaptation and evolution—that would not, in principle, ever come to an end because a need is anticipated for continuing adjustments in a changing context (cf. Majone and Wildavsky 1979; Weiss and Woodhouse 1992; Torgerson 1985, 1995, 1999). Advanced through such a process, basic income initiatives could connect with a broader cultural domain. The value of work could then be discussed without oppressive overtones, associating it with the type of activity that people often engage in not because they have to but because they want to: aesthetic, educational, recreational, athletic, domestic and— indeed—political.

A political orientation to radical reform clearly involves both functional and constitutive dimensions. A political process remains fragile, though, unless supported by the performative dimension. If politics is entirely restricted to instrumentality, to a concern only with getting results, to product at the exclusion of process, then it is altogether possible for politics to be sacrificed—indeed, for the sacrifice not even to be noticed. Politics as debate, an open exchange of opinions, is secure only in a context that values it for its own sake.

Valuing politics in this way is at odds with prevailing tendencies—if not the whole orientation of modernity—but is nonetheless often implicit in green political practices and much of contemporary activism. To value political action for its own sake is to resist the obliteration of politics—and the differences upon which political debate depends—by either community or society. It is, indeed, to put a particular value on the political actions of citizens. A citizen enacts an identity in which narrow interests and perspectives are pressed to the margins, rather than being left at the centre. Political debate becomes not simply a tool for possessive individuals to use in gaining their preferred outcomes. Debate, pursued instead as an interchange of considered opinions, has the capacity to foster an imaginative interplay of identities, interests and perspectives.

Evaluations and judgements from the enlarged viewpoint of the citizen become possible, in part, because outcomes are not everything: the political process itself becomes valuable for those involved (Arendt 1968: 219–21). To cultivate an intrinsically valuable politics is to promote an action type different from both the possessive individual and the cooperative member of a community. This different kind of action type—the citizen—can thus be recognized as potentially both a means and an end in the promotion of a green economy.

Notes

The author thanks Michael Cahill, Tony Fitzpatrick, John Barry and Michael Kenny for helpful advice.

1. See, e.g., Barry (1999: 161–72). The term "social economy" is often used to designate what is generally understood here as the informal economy (e.g. Young 1997; Williams 2000). For the purposes of the present discussion, the latter term is preferable because it helps to capture a key contrast in green economic thinking that is paralleled in social theory. The contrast between capitalism and socialism also remains important, but is no longer as sharply drawn as it once was. Both are typically understood as pertaining primarily to the formal economy; there is, moreover, a clear socializing tendency within capitalism that Marx emphasized and that remains central to the analysis of contemporary eco-Marxism (see O'Connor 1988).
2. All three of the action types identified in this essay—possessive individual, cooperative member, and citizen—can by Schutz's analysis (1967) be understood in a strict sense as abstract and anonymous. Something is distinctive about the possessive individual, however, because that action type is central to the operations of the formal economy—the source of its order and predictability—precisely as an abstract and anonymous actor. The informal economy possesses its own kind of order but one that, in contrast, cannot be realized in community relationships unless cooperative members enact particular identities at concrete and personal levels. Concrete and personal enactment becomes especially significant in the case of the citizen, an actor who both joins with others and stands apart in a context of meaningful and inventive conduct (see Arendt 1958: 176; 1968: 241, 268).
3. Young (1997) distinguishes among coops, mutuals and other types of association.
4. Efforts to reduce work time sometimes have a similar rationale and appear to be largely complementary.
5. Most notable here is Gorz, who long included work requirements in his proposals for reduced work time, though he has recently reversed himself and endorsed unconditionality (1999: 94–5).

References

Achterberg, W. (1999), From sustainability to basic income: a seamless web of justice. In M. Kenny and J. Meadowcroft (eds), *Planning Sustainability*, London: Routledge, pp. 128–47.

Arendt, H. (1958), *The Human Condition*, Chicago: University of Chicago Press.

Arendt, H. (1968), *Between Past and Future: Eight Exercises in Political Thought*, New York: Viking Press.

Atkinson, A. B. (1995), Beveridge, the national minimum and its future in the European context. In A. B. Atkinson, *Incomes and the Welfare State: Essays on Britain and Europe*, Cambridge: Cambridge University Press, pp. 290–304.

Atkinson, M. and Elliott, L. (2001), Labour imposes tough new rules on jobless, *Guardian*, 14 March: 1.

Barry, J. (1999), *Rethinking Green Politics*, London: Sage.

Booth, J. B. (1994), On the idea of the moral economy, *American Political Science Review*, 88, 3: 653–67.

Christoff, P. (1996), Ecological modernisation, ecological modernities, *Environmental Politics*, 5: 476–500.

Crozier, M. and Friedberg. E. (1980), *Actors and Systems: The Politics of Collective Action*, tr. A. Golhammer, Chicago: University of Chicago Press.

Dobson, A. (1991), Editorial comment. In A. Dobson (ed.), *The Green Reader*, San Francisco: Mercury House, p. 152.

Dobson, A. (1995), *Green Political Thought*, 2nd edn, London: Routledge.

Duchin, F. (1996), Ecological economics: the second stage. In R. Costanza, S. Olman and J. Martinez-Alier (eds), *Getting Down to Earth: Practical Applications of Ecological Economics*, Washington, DC: Island Press, pp. 285–99.

Eckersley, R. (1992), *Environmentalism and Political Theory*, Albany: State University of New York Press.

Faber, M., Reiner, M. and Proops, J. (1996), *Ecological Economics: Concepts and Methods*, Cheltenham: Edward Elgar.

Ferris, J. (1993), Introduction: political realism and green strategy. In H. Wiesenthal, *Realism in Green Politics: Social Movements and Ecological Reform in Germany*, Manchester: Manchester University Press, pp. 1–25.

Fitzpatrick, T. (1998), The implications of ecological thought for social welfare, *Critical Social Policy*, 18, 1: 5–26.

Fitzpatrick, T. (1999), *Freedom and Security: An Introduction to the Basic Income Debate*, London: Macmillan.

Foucault, M. (1980), *Discipline and Punish: The Birth of the Prison*, tr. Alain Sheridan, New York: Vintage Books.

Foucault, M. (1991), Governmentality. In G. Burchell *et al.* (eds), *The Foucault Effect: Studies in Governmentality*, Chicago: University of Chicago Press, pp. 87–104.

Freeman, A. M., Haveman, R. H. and Kneese, A. V. (1973), *The Economics of Environmental Policy*, New York: Wiley.

Gorz, A. (1999), *Reclaiming Work: Beyond the Wage-based Society*, tr. Chris Turner, Cambridge: Polity Press.

Gowdy, J. M. and Olsen, P. (1994), Further problems with neoclassical environmental economics, *Environmental Ethics*, 16: 161–71.

Grover, C. and Stewart, J. (2000), Modernizing social security? Labour and its welfare-to-work strategy, *Social Policy & Administration*, 34, 3: 235–52.

Habermas, J. (1984/1987), *The Theory of Communicative Action*, 2 vols, tr. T. McCarthy, Boston: Beacon Press.

Habermas, J. (1992), Further reflections on the public sphere. In C. Calhoun (ed.), *Habermas and the Public Sphere*, Cambridge, MA: MIT Press.

Halévy, E. (1955), *The Growth of Philosophic Radicalism*, Boston: Beacon Press.

Helleiner, E. (1996), International political economy and the greens, *New Political Economy*, 1, 1: 59–78.

Johnson, W. A. (1973), The guaranteed income as an environmental measure. In H. E. Daly (ed.), *Toward a Steady-state Economy*, San Francisco: W. H. Freeman, pp. 175–89.

Kenny, M. (1996), Paradoxes of community. In B. Doherty and M. de Geus (eds), *Democracy and Green Political Thought*, London: Routledge, pp. 175–89.

Latouche, S. (1993) *In the Wake of the Affluent Society: An Exploration of Post-Development*, tr. Martin O'Connor and Rosemary Arnoux, London: Zed Books.

Lindblom, C. E. (1959), The science of "muddling through", *Public Administration Review*, 19: 79–88.

Macpherson, C. B. (1964), *The Political Theory of Possessive Individualism: Hobbes to Locke*, Oxford: Oxford University Press.

Majone, G. and Wildavsky, A. (1979), Implementation as evolution. In J. Pressman and A. Wildavsky, *Implementation*, 2nd edn, Berkeley: University of California Press, pp. 177–94.

May, P. H. and Pastuk, M. (1996), Valuing social sustainability: environmental recuperation on favela hillsides in Rio de Janeiro. In R. Costanza, S. Olman and

19

J. Martinez-Alier (eds), *Getting Down to Earth: Practical Applications of Ecological Economics*, Washington, DC: Island Press, pp. 411–25.

Mellor, M. (1995), Materialist communal politics: getting from there to here. In J. Lovenduski and J. Stanyer (eds), *Contemporary Political Studies*, vol. 3, Belfast: Political Studies Association of the United Kingdom, pp. 1019–33.

Morgan, G. (1986), *Images of Organization*, Beverly Hills, CA: Sage.

O'Connor, J. (1988), Capitalism, nature, socialism: a theoretical introduction, *Capitalism, Nature, Socialism*, 1, 1: 11–38.

Offe, C. (1992), A non-productivist design for social policies. In P. Van Parijs (ed.), *Arguing for Basic Income: Ethical Foundations for a Radical Reform*, London: Verso, pp. 61–78.

Offe, C. and Heinze R. G (1992), *Beyond Employment: Time, Work and the Informal Economy*, Cambridge: Polity Press.

Offe, C., Mükenberger, U. and Ostner, I. (1996), A basic income guaranteed by the state: a need of the moment in social policy. In C. Offe, *Modernity and the State*, Cambridge, MA: MIT Press, pp. 201–21.

Paehlke, R. (1998), Work in a sustainable society. In D. V. Bell, L. Fawcett, R. Keil and P. Penz (eds), *Political Ecology: Local and Global*, London: Routledge, pp. 272–91.

Paterson, M. (2000), *Understanding Global Environmental Politics: Domination, Accumulation, Resistance*, London: Macmillan.

Polanyi, K. (1957), *The Great Transformation: The Political and Economic Origins of Our Time*, Boston: Beacon Press.

Sagoff, M. (1988), *The Economy of the Earth: Philosophy, Law, and the Environment*, Cambridge: Cambridge University Press.

Schick, A. (1971), Toward the cybernetic state. In D. Waldo (ed.), *Public Administration in a Time of Turbulence*, New York: Chandler Publishing, pp. 214–33.

Schutz, A. (1964), The problem of rationality in the social world. In A. Brodersen (ed.), *Collected Papers*, vol. 2, The Hague: Martinus Nijhoff, pp. 64–88.

Schutz, A. (1967), *The Phenomenology of the Social World*, tr. G. Walsh and F. Lehnert, Evanston, IL: Northwestern University Press.

Tönnies. F. (1957), *Community and Society (Gemeinschaft und Gesellschaft)*, tr. C. P. Loomis. East Lausing. Michigan State University Press.

Torgerson, D. (1985), Contextual orientation in policy analysis: the contribution of Harold D. Lasswell, *Policy Sciences*, 18: 241–61.

Torgerson, D. (1990a), Limits of the administrative mind: the problem of defining environmental problems. In R. Paehlke and D. Torgerson (eds), *Managing Leviathan: Environmental Politics and the Administrative State*, Peterborough, ON: Broadview Press, pp. 115–61.

Torgerson, D. (1990b), Obsolescent leviathan: problems of order in administrative thought. In R. Paehlke and D. Torgerson (eds), *Managing Leviathan: Environmental Politics and the Administrative State*, Peterborough, ON: Broadview Press, pp. 17–33.

Torgerson, D. (1995), Policy analysis and public life: the restoration of *phronesis*? In J. Farr, J. S. Dryzek and S. Leonard (eds), *Political Science in History: Research Programs and Political Traditions*, Cambridge: Cambridge University Press, pp. 225–52.

Torgerson, D. (1999), *The Promise of Green Politics: Environmentalism and the Public Sphere*, Durham, NC: Duke University Press.

Torgerson, D. (2000), Farewell to the green movement? Political action and the green public sphere, *Environmental Politics*, 9, 4: 1–19.

Van Parijs, P. (1992a), Competing justifications of basic income. In P. Van Parijs (ed.), *Arguing for Basic Income: Ethical Foundations for a Radical Reform*, London: Verso, pp. 3–43.

Van Parijs, P. (1992b), The second marriage of justice and efficiency. In P. Van Parijs (ed.), *Arguing for Basic Income: Ethical Foundations for a Radical Reform*, London: Verso, pp. 215–40.

Victor, P. (1979), Economics and the challenge of environmental issues. In W. Leiss (ed.), *Ecology versus Politics in Canada*, Toronto: University of Toronto Press, pp. 34–56.

Weber, M. (1978), *Economy and Society*, 2 vols, ed. G. Roth and C. Wittich, Berkeley: University of California Press.

Weiss, A. and Woodhouse, E. (1992), Reframing incrementalism: a constructive response to the critics, *Policy Sciences* 25, 2: 255–74.

Wiesenthal, H. (1993), *Realism in Green Politics: Social Movements and Ecological Reform in Germany*, ed. John Ferris, Manchester: Manchester University Press.

Williams, C. C. (2000), The social economy and local exchange trading systems (LETS). Paper presented at Greening the Welfare State, Social Policy Association Workshop, London, 14 September.

Young, S. (1997), Community-based partnerships and sustainable development: a third force in the social economy. In S. Baker, M. Kousis, D. Richardson and S. Young (eds), *The Politics of Sustainable Development: Theory, Policy and Practice within the European Union*, London and New York: Routledge, pp. 217–35.

CHAPTER 3

Green Citizenship

Hartley Dean

Abstract

This paper first describes the influence that environmentalism and ecologism have had upon thinking about citizenship before, second, moving on to discuss conventional models of citizenship and potential models of Green citizenship. The discussion focuses on the competing moral discourses that inform our understanding of citizenship and concludes by arguing in favour of an eco-socialist citizenship model that would embrace, on the one hand, an ethic of co-responsibility by which collectively to achieve the just distribution of scarce resources and, on the other, an ethic of care through which to negotiate the basis for human interdependency.

Keywords

Care; Citizenship; Ecologism; Environment; Humanity; Responsibility

There is something rather elusive about the idea of Green citizenship. Though references in the literature to environmental or ecological citizenship—which are not necessarily the same thing (cf. Dobson 1995)—crop up quite regularly, the concepts are never too clearly defined. In part, I would suggest, this is because Green thinking has impacted on thinking about citizenship in a number of rather disparate ways. In part it is because some strands of Green thinking are actually inimical to the concept of citizenship. In this article I shall attempt first to identify the different ways in which environmentalism and ecologism have influenced debates about citizenship, before moving on to develop a conceptual model that characterizes the ways in which competing moral discourses might construct a Green perspective on citizenship. Finally, I shall expand upon and advance the normative case for just one of those moral discourses, namely eco-socialism. If it is to become more than a discursive artefact or ideological fiction, "citizenship" must define substantive principles by which to defend social humanity against the dual threats of global capitalism and ecological crisis.

Address for correspondence: *Professor Hartley Dean, Department of Applied Social Studies, University of Luton, Park Square, Luton, LU1 3JU.*

The Greening of Citizenship

Citizenship is an ancient concept dating back some two and a half thousand years to the days of the Athenian city-state. Modern concepts of citizenship emerged from the seventeenth century onwards and evolved as the nation-state developed as the predominant unit of civil society and political administration. In the twentieth century the nations of the capitalist world became welfare states and so, according to T. H. Marshall (1950), consolidated the concept of citizenship by adding to it a *social* dimension.

However, political and popular understandings of citizenship are complex, multifaceted and often contradictory (Dean with Melrose 1999). While the evolution of modern citizenship has been closely associated with the development of capitalism, Bryan Turner has pointed out that the concept has also been fashioned by other influences—by war, migration and a variety of social movements (Turner 1986)—and it is a concept that is capable of being either imposed by rulers from above or seized by the people from below (Turner 1990). With this in mind it may be observed that, in recent times, Green thinking has impacted on our understandings of citizenship in at least three different ways. First, environmental concerns have entered our understanding of the rights we enjoy as citizens. Second, the enhanced level of global awareness associated with ecological thinking has helped to broaden our understanding of the potential scope of citizenship. Third, emergent ecological concerns have added fuel to a complex debate about the responsibilities that attach to citizenship.

Environmentalism

The rights-based conception of citizenship espoused by T. H. Marshall can quite readily be extended to accommodate the idea of environmental citizenship. Marshall's account of citizenship encompasses the development of civil rights (to civil liberties and legal protection), political rights (to democratic participation) and social rights (to basic welfare provision). It has been suggested that, with the coming of the contemporary environmental movement, Marshall himself would not have hesitated to add a fourth dimension to his concept of citizenship, namely environmental rights that provide for the protection of the individual against the effects of pollution and environmental degradation (e.g. Newby 1996; van Steenbergen 1994). In fact the environmental movement can be traced back beyond recent times to Victorian preoccupations with public health and, for example, the preservation of the nation's natural and cultural "heritage" (Newby 1996). What might be defined as environmental rights of citizenship were first realized in the British context with the enactment of the early Public Health Acts of the mid-nineteenth century and, later, such measures as the Town and Country Planning Act of 1946 (Thane 1982).

Preoccupation with arrangements for sanitation and water supply, the prevention of food contamination, the control of industrial effluent and public health hazards, and the regulation of building and land use have long been part and parcel of social and public policy and have given rise to a

23

range of enforceable rights (Dean 1996). The heightened level of environmental awareness that characterized the last decades of the twentieth century put new emphasis on such measures and was reflected, for example, in the discursive reframing of "Public Health" legislation as "Environmental Protection" legislation. In so far as social rights cater for such basic human needs as clean water, it is possible to reclassify certain social rights as environmental rights, especially in the context of the climatic and geophysical constraints experienced in some developing countries. The language of environmentalism has entered policy discourse in a variety of ways. A kind of environmentalism is also reflected in the developed world through increased public demands—of a somewhat parochial character—for enhanced protection of wildlife and the countryside and the "right" of citizens to access and enjoy such amenities. However, despite the prominence of wider concerns about environmental global sustainability (e.g. Brundtland 1987) and such scares as the Chernobyl disaster and the BSE crisis, demands for new kinds of substantive environmental rights—rather than for the extension and enforcement of existing kinds of civil liberties and social protection—have been virtually absent.

Academic commentators, including social policy academics like Twine (1994), have rightly focused on the link between environmental interdependence and the social rights of citizenship. If we accept that environmental considerations and the limitations of natural resources impose limits to economic growth (Meadows *et al.* 1974, 1992) this means, first, that we can no longer attempt to promote social justice by distributing the proceeds of economic growth: to the extent that a redistribution of resources is desirable or necessary—whether within or between the nations of the world—this can no longer be achieved other than at the expense of the privileged. Second, the social rights of future generations must now depend upon a reappraisal of the welfare entitlements of current generations. This means that we must rethink the nature of our social rights, but it need not of itself require us to define a distinctive set of environmental rights.

Global awareness

Broader ecological concerns with the sustainability of the planet have contributed or added salience to attempts both to widen and deepen our concept of citizenship. Falk (1994) has suggested that the "ecological imperative" is just one of several grounds upon which it is possible to conceive or advocate forms of global citizenship. The other grounds relate to: long-standing aspirational demands for global peace and justice; the consequences of economic globalization; and emergent modes of transnational political mobilization arising both from regional movements and new social movements. These grounds are intimately interconnected, and at least as pressing as any other is the argument that "[f]or the sake of human survival . . . some forms of effective global citizenship are required to redesign political choices on the basis of an ecological sense of natural viabilities, and thereby to transform established forms of political behaviour" (Falk 1994: 132).

Although such a vision of global citizenship is far from being realized, general thinking about citizenship has been changing at two distinct levels. It is necessary to recall that citizenship can be understood both as a status and as a practice (Lister 1997). It relates both to the way in which the individual is constructed in the context of the public sphere and to normative expectations as to her/his private as well as public conduct. The celebrated Green slogan or aphorism "think globally, act locally" implies a similar distinction between conceptualizing human individuals in their global context, on the one hand, but on the other endorsing or demanding particular kinds of individual behaviour at the everyday local level. The immanent logic that informs recent empirical and normative accounts of citizenship reflects this distinction. It also points to a tension that any form of Green citizenship would have to resolve.

First, at the level of global context, Soysal (1994) has demonstrated how the institution and meaning of citizenship is changing as the role of the nation-state is, in part at least, superseded (cf. Horsman and Marshall 1994). Soysal argues that two institutionalized principles of the global system—namely, national sovereignty and universal human rights—have collided (cf. Turner 1993). The concept of human rights is more global than that of citizenship in so far as it encompasses notions of entitlement that transcend considerations of nationality. Soysal illustrates how one consequence of this is to be observed in the rights that are begrudgingly afforded by developed nations to foreign guestworkers. None the less, to the extent that it is the developed nation-states that are accorded responsibility for maintaining human rights, paradoxically this can also fortify their authority and even justify humanitarian or military intervention in other parts of the world. Soysal implies that as our concepts of rights become globalized they become abstracted and detached from our sense of local belonging or identity—from our capacity to regulate our own lives.

Second, at the level of everyday experience and practice, writers like Clarke (1996) argue not for a widening, but for a deepening of citizenship. Clarke's notion of "deep citizenship" focuses on the citizen-self whose civic virtues cross the divide between the spheres of the public and the private and engage with a range of concerns about self, others and the world, including "environmental issues, economic issues and other issues that impact on the world" (1996: 119). Embracing the idea that the personal is political, Clarke argues that deep citizenship entails a sort of (re)negotiation or "discovery of the relation between the categories of citizen and human" (1996: 123). His argument is that "human" is no less a social and political construct than "citizen" and, he contends, is of more recent historical provenance. It is citizen rights that provide the model for human rights and not the other way round. States, whether they are city-states, nation-states or supranational states, are artificial entities, whereas deep citizenship entails a multiplicity of politicized identities and, potentially, an infinite variety of associations.

Dahrendorf (1994: 18) has archly concluded that "I am not sure whether one can stipulate an entitlement for all of us as world citizens to a liveable habitat, and thus to actions that sustain it, but something of this kind may well belong on the agenda of citizenship". Dahrendorf's diffidence would be justified if indeed the ecological imperative of which Falk speaks were to become stranded between a conception of global citizenship founded on abstract universal rights and a conception founded on a multiplicity of citizen-selves.

Discourses of responsibility

A possible, if ambiguous, resolution to this tension is provided by commentators who advocate a shift from an understanding of citizenship based on rights to an understanding of citizenship that is based on duties or responsibilities. Roche (1992), for example, has contended that since the crisis of the welfare state in the 1970s the "dominant paradigm" of social citizenship has come under attack from across the political spectrum as a "discourse of duty" as well as rights has emerged. This discourse has taken several forms, ranging from New Right and neo-conservative claims that welfare rights undermine the responsibilities of citizens to sustain themselves through work and provide for each other through the family, through to the challenges posed by new social movements, including the ecology movement. Roche credits the ecology movement with having forced on to the agenda the question of the responsibilities that human beings owe towards other species, the environment, the Earth itself, as well as to future human generations. Though Roche opposes the New Right's rejection of social rights, he accepts the case for rethinking the absolute priority that he believes has been given to social rights and urges a need "to reconsider the moral and ideological claims of personal responsibility, of parental and ecological obligations, of corporate and inter-generational obligations, and so on" (1992: 246).

To an extent, such arguments prefigured those that occurred within the British Labour Party in the mid-1990s and the principles eventually advanced by the New Labour government. The Labour Party went so far as to revise its constitution so as to declare itself in favour of a society in which "the rights we enjoy reflect the duties we owe" (Labour Party 1995) and nowhere has this been more clearly reflected than in the New Labour government's welfare reforms which have been built on the premise that those who can work and provide for themselves and their families have a responsibility to do so (DSS 1998). However, notions of responsibility have not extended very far in relation to environmental matters and, although New Labour's commitment to global sustainability is ostensibly less tokenistic than that of previous British governments, its initiatives on transport policy, for example, have not gone far enough to challenge the dominant consumerist ethos (Cahill 1999).

While ecological considerations may have percolated to political rhetoric and discourses of responsibility, ecologically informed notions of a "new politics of obligation" are largely confined to academic texts (e.g. Smith 1998). We noted above that an environmentalist approach to rights does not necessarily require a separate category of environmental rights, but an ecological approach to responsibility plainly does demand responsibilities on the part of the human subject to protect the natural environment: responsibilities for which there can be no directly correlative rights. Once again, aspects of Green thinking have influenced mainstream debates about the nature of citizenship, but without radically transforming them.

26

Figure 1

Taxonomy of conventional moral discourses

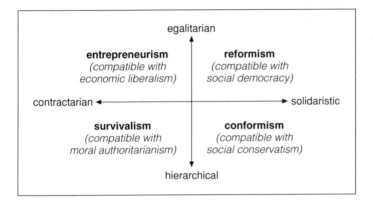

Modelling Citizenship

Citizenship remains a complex and contested idea and is conceptualized in several different ways. Similarly, Green thinking contains several disparate strands. In recent work (Dean with Melrose 1999; Dean 1998, 1999, 2001), I have sought to develop a heuristic model or taxonomy in order to delineate the discursive moral repertoires that underpin or make possible competing conceptions of citizenship. In this article, I shall model a similar account of Green moral repertoires, each with a competing perspective on citizenship.

Conventional moral discourses

First, therefore, I shall recount the basic elements of the model of those moral discourses that inform "conventional" ideas of citizenship. It is a model that can be made to resonate in quite complex ways with cultural theory, poststructuralist analyses and historical accounts of class formation. For the purposes of this article, however, I shall distinguish only the essential "moral repertoires" (cf. Offe 1993) that may be drawn upon to justify four distinctive conceptions of citizenship. The moral repertoires stem from classic Enlightenment ideals once encapsulated in the revolutionary slogan "*liberté, égalité, fraternité*", or liberty, equality and solidarity; ideals that in practice conflict. The model is schematically illustrated in figure 1, in which the two axes represent two normative conceptual continua.

The horizontal axis relates to the fundamental distinction between contractarian and solidaristic prescriptions for social order. These two prescriptions reflect what are commonly described as the liberal and the civic-republican traditions of citizenship, respectively (e.g. Oldfield 1990; Lister 1997). The contractarian prescription is informed by a commitment to liberty and the idea that to have *freedom* an individual must enter a contract with society and exchange some element of her/his sovereignty in return for a guarantee of social order. The solidaristic prescription is informed by a commitment to solidarity and the idea that to have *security* an individual must pool her/his sovereignty with the rest of the society to which s/he belongs, since social order depends on social cohesion. The vertical axis in figure 1 relates to the distinction between egalitarian and hierarchical prescriptions for the relationship between individuals within a society. The egalitarian prescription is informed by a commitment to equality—albeit that equality may be interpreted in different ways. The hierarchical prescription is informed by a commitment to established social traditions—albeit that the relations of power by which such traditions are established may be quite differently conceived. The intersection of the continua represented by the axes defines four distinctive moral discourses:

- The discourse of entrepreneurism is fundamentally contractarian since it envisages the contract as the moral basis for all human transactions. It denies or obscures the interdependency that is the basis of our social humanity. It is egalitarian in the formal sense: it embraces the ideas of equality before the law and of individual equality of opportunity, though it is tolerant of substantive inequality and regards unequal outcomes as inevitable or even necessary. It is a discourse that is compatible with economic liberalism. It implies a form of citizenship that is, in one sense, utilitarian, since it will admit a role for the state in underwriting an essentially economic calculus of harm and advantage; in regulating externalities and promoting efficiency.
- The discourse of survivalism is similarly contractarian, but fundamentally inegalitarian in so far as it does not necessarily accept that all competition within society is or ever can be fair: it does not question the unequal distribution of social power and resources. The imperative to which it subscribes is that of every person or family for itself. It is a discourse that is compatible with moral authoritarianism and support for "traditional" patriarchal family values. It implies a form of citizenship that is strictly Hobbesian or what some term "neo-conservative", since it will admit a role for the state in deterring certain forms of behaviour and enforcing others.
- The discourse of conformism is fundamentally solidaristic since it aspires to social integration and belonging. It is also hierarchical in that it acknowledges that the existing social order is premised on certain inequalities of social power and resources. It is a discourse that is compatible with social conservatism (characteristically, that is, with One Nation Toryism in the British context, and Christian Democracy in the continental European context). It implies a form of citizenship that is communitarian, since it will admit a role for the state in power-broking within a defined community while at the same time protecting its essential integrity.
- The discourse of reformism is similarly solidaristic, but egalitarian in a substantive sense. It embraces the idea that there should be a broad measure of equality in the distribution of social power and resources. It is a discourse that is compatible with Social Democracy. It implies a form of citizenship that is morally universalist, albeit perhaps more in the Kantian

Figure 2

Taxonomy of ecological moral discourses

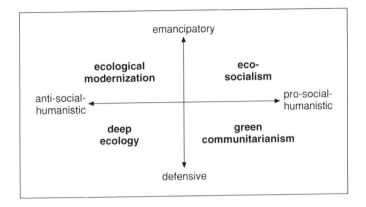

than the Marxist sense of moral universalism. It will admit a role for the state in promoting universal and inclusive rights.

The model therefore accounts for the discursive moral foundations of the principal conceptions of citizenship that are currently extant, at least within existing capitalist welfare states. The discursive repertoires it defines are ideal types. Actual political discourse may therefore combine or straddle potentially conflicting repertoires, without necessarily transcending them. For example, the liberalism of, say, Hobhouse (1974), Rawls (1972) or van Parijs (1995), I would argue, draws upon elements of both entrepreneurial and reformist discourse. In the context of this model, the social liberalism that has informed the development of welfare states, especially in the anglophone tradition, emerges as an ambiguous ideology that struggles to address competing moral repertoires. Additionally, the model relates only to "conventional" moral discourses and does not accommodate radical socialist, feminist or ecological moral discourse or the way in which they might engage with citizenship.

Ecological moral discourses

Previous attempts within Social Policy literature to classify the different moral bases on which Green thinking has developed have seldom moved very far from the distinction between "deep greenism" and "social ecology" (e.g. Ferris 1991). However, a somewhat more complex approach than this is required. To define the essential discursive moral repertoires that underpin different strands in Green thinking, it is possible to construct a model around a different (if related) set of conceptual continua or axes than those in the above analysis of conventional moral discourses. The model I propose is schematically presented in figure 2.

29

The horizontal axis in this figure relates to a fundamental distinction that I wish to draw between anti-social-humanistic and pro-social-humanistic strands of thinking;[1] between, on the one hand, prescriptive approaches that would subordinate the activities and the status of human beings to the needs of the global economy or capitalism *and/or* to the needs of the environment or the Earth, and, on the other, approaches that seek to protect the interests of humanity against the effects of capitalist exploitation and the consequences of socioeconomic polarization *and/or* the effects of environmental degradation and the consequences of ecological disaster. There is an important parallel between this continuum and the contractarian–solidaristic continuum. Both the anti-social-humanistic and the contractarian prescriptions presuppose that the human subject is quintessentially competitive, calculative and self-seeking. Both the pro-social-humanistic and the solidaristic prescriptions presuppose that the human subject is potentially cooperative, vulnerable and redeemable. The vertical axis in figure 2 relates to the distinction between emancipatory and defensive prescriptions for change, a distinction drawn directly from that made by Habermas (1987) between different kinds of social movement, but one that can also be applied within the Green movement. Once again, there is a parallel to be drawn—this time, between the emancipatory–defensive continuum and the egalitarian–hierarchical continuum. Both the emancipatory and the egalitarian prescriptions advocate changes that are seen as "progressive" and envision a transformation of the future. Both the defensive and the hierarchical prescriptions oppose changes that are seen as destructive of supposedly "natural" equilibria or else they seek to recapture or rehabilitate achievements of the past. The intersection of the continua represented by the axes defines four distinctive moral discourses:

- The discourse of ecological modernization (see Dryzek 1997; Christoff 1996; Hajer 1995),[2] though it is plainly anthropocentric, is also anti-social-humanistic in the sense that it places economic imperatives by implication above social ones. It is emancipatory in the sense that its objective is to save the capitalist order from capitalism's ecological consequences; to liberate economic actors from ecological constraints. It is a discourse that accommodates a notion of citizenship appropriate to the global capitalist (cf. van Steenbergen 1994: 148). By taking on the management of environmental concerns it is, strictly speaking, an environmentalist rather than an ecological discourse. It is premised on the imperative of continued economic growth, the necessity for a technological fix for all environmental obstacles to such growth, and indeed the possibility of an economic payback from such new environmentally friendly technologies. The discourse has its parallel in the entrepreneurial moral repertoire of conventional discourse.
- The discourse of deep ecology (e.g. Naess 1973; Fox 1984) is profoundly anti-social-humanistic in the sense that it subordinates the interests of the human species to those of other species, the environment and of the Earth itself. It is quintessentially defensive in the sense that its objective is to preserve the Earth. This discourse is inimical to any concept of citizenship since it rejects the anthropocentric ethic upon which citizenship

is based. Its alternative, an ecocentric ethic, is capable of sustaining anti-democratic and authoritarian "Earth First" tenets, extending to Malthusian beliefs regarding population control and punitive, even lethal, forms of direct action against human beings. The discourse has its parallel—albeit a partial one—in the survivalist moral repertoire of conventional discourse.

• The discourse of green communitarianism is pro-social-humanistic in the sense that it celebrates the place of the human species in Nature. It is defensive in the sense that its objective is to maintain ecologically sustainable human societies. This discourse accommodates a notion of citizenship that is close to that described by van Steenbergen (1994: 150) as that of the earth citizen: certainly it would accept that the natural self-regulating mechanisms of the ecosystem may provide a model by which humans might construct a form of citizenship. The discourse is capable of being inflected towards more romantic, mystical or spiritual ideas about "oneness with Nature" and the ascendancy of feeling over reason, but arguably it is also inherently conservative in the nature of its trans-generational perspective (which implies that future sustainability requires the replication of social relations from the past), its mistrust of individual human agency and its aversion to risk (see Gray 1993). The discourse has its clear parallel in the conformist repertoire of conventional discourse.

• The discourse of eco-socialism is profoundly pro-social-humanistic in the sense that it is epistemologically founded in the human project. It is quintessentially emancipatory in the sense that its objective is to realize the full potential of social humanity within an ecological context. This discourse accommodates a notion of citizenship appropriate to what van Steenbergen (1994: 149) has—too dismissively perhaps—defined as the global reformer. The discourse starts from the premise that human exploitation of the Earth has stemmed from humans' exploitation of other humans and that human emancipation is therefore a necessary condition for the emancipation of the Earth (Bookchin 1991). In particular, the discourse stresses the need for an anti-productivist ethic as the basis for any citizenship settlement (cf. Offe 1992; Fitzpatrick 1998) and it is therefore as much opposed to Stalinist forms of state socialism as to capitalism. The discourse has a parallel in the reformist repertoire of conventional discourse, though it is necessarily more radical: it is commensurate with democratic socialism rather than social democracy.

This outline amounts possibly to a somewhat controversial caricature of some complex philosophical and ideological discourses and it oversimplifies important tensions or differences within some of those discourses. As with the taxonomy of conventional moral discourses, however, the taxonomy is no more than a heuristic device. My argument is that the Green tent makes space for all these discourses, together on occasions with their related conventional discourses. It can be observed that individual exponents of Green thinking do not necessarily draw exclusively on one or other discourse but may draw upon several or even all of them, notwithstanding their mutually contradictory character. For example, a great deal of progressive Green thinking probably combines or straddles moderate versions of both eco-modernization and eco-socialism. Nor do I contend that ecologism is merely a "cross-cutting ideology" (Goodwin 1987: vii) that is best understood as a qualification to or variant of modernity's grand narratives: together with feminism it represents a major challenge to those narratives. The above taxonomy is intended merely to assist our understanding of what Green citizenship might mean.

The Normative Case for Eco-socialism

I do not here propose to develop this model, other than to make some speculative remarks about the potential scope for one of the ecological moral discourses defined above, namely eco-socialism. Nor shall I traverse the established debates between ecologism and socialism (see Weston 1986; Ryle 1988; Pepper 1993). Rather, I shall venture my own tentative view that an eco-socialist conception of citizenship should be founded upon two ethical premises; one relating to the distribution of scarce resources; the other to the provision of care.

Negotiating scarcity

Turner has argued that the "focal point of citizenship" (1997: 11) is the tension between the need to moderate scarcity on the one hand and to maintain solidarity on the other. Addressing that tension, I would argue, requires a macro-ethic that combines social justice with ecological sustainability; that can bind humanity together in a manner that enables it collectively to address its environmental predicament. The philosopher Apel (1980, 1991) has contended that this can be achieved by the ethical principle of "co-responsibility".[3] Apel argues that liberalism as the dominant ideological paradigm of modernity has effectively paralysed the possibility of a macro-ethic because it separates the public sphere of scientific rationality from the private sphere of preferences and values. However, a planetary principle of co-responsibility is possible, upon three conditions.

First, it must be rational and transcend tradition. Second, it requires a global communication community, something made possible by cultural, technological and economic globalization such that "we have become members of a real communication community or, if you will, members of the crew of one boat, for example, with regard to the ecological crisis" (Apel 1991: 269). This idea has obvious resonance with Habermas's (1987) counterfactual notion of the "ideal speech situation": a political objective through which it would be possible for human beings to engage in undistorted and uncoerced kinds of negotiation. Third, says Apel, a principle of co-responsibility requires that scientific and ethical claims to truth be taken equally seriously. This idea has an obvious resonance with Beck's (1992) demand for the demonopolization of science and a form of reflexivity based on negotiation between different epistemologies. The ethical fulcrum of such negotiation is human need:

the members of the communication community (and this implies all thinking beings) are also committed to considering all the potential claims of all the potential members—and this means all human "needs" in as much as they could be affected by norms and consequently make *claims* on their fellow human beings. As potential "claims" that can be communicated interpersonally, all human needs are ethically *relevant*. They must be *acknowledged* if they can be justified interpersonally through arguments. (Apel 1980: 277)

If this is what Apel means by "co-responsibility", it implies the universalizability of human needs through a form of global citizenship. It would seem to presuppose that there are certain basic human needs whose optimal satisfaction must precede the imposition of any social obligations (cf. Doyal and Gough 1991) and that it is possible to negotiate the empirical, ontological and normative consensus that is required to translate the particular demands of diverse social movements into universalizable human rights (cf. Hewitt 1993). The importance of this is that it implies a relationship between rights and responsibilities that goes far beyond the narrow contractarian calculus of New Labour's "Third Way" and Giddens's motto—"no rights without responsibilities" (1998: 65)—because responsibility is by nature cooperative and negotiated, not an inherent obligation or *a priori* doctrine. It takes us beyond Kantian moral universalism towards a socialist ethic and beyond environmentalist angst towards an ethic of ecological sustainability.

The argument is admittedly abstract, but citizenship itself is an abstract construct and co-responsibility as an ideal is no less abstract than an idealized social contract. If anything, the everyday human experiences of the kinds of obligations that are socially negotiated over time, within relationships and between the generations (cf. Finch and Mason 1993) are more concrete and immediate than those obligations that arise through the legal fiction of a contract. They provide a sounder basis for conceptualizing citizenship and for envisaging ways of achieving a just and sustainable distribution of resources.

The ethic of care

This leads to the second ethical premise, one that links the macro-ethics of rights and responsibility to quotidian reality. Drawing on philosophical anthropology, Turner has argued that "it is from a collectively held recognition of individual frailty that rights as a system of mutual protection gain their emotive force" (1993: 507). The human subject is endemically vulnerable and to survive requires collectively organized mechanisms for mutual cooperation and support: what matters, as Richard Rorty has put it, "is our loyalty to other human beings clinging together against the dark" (cited in Doyal and Gough 1991: 19). The corollary to a system of human rights founded on the ideal of the independent citizen is a system founded on the recognition of human interdependency.

Advocates of a deeper form of citizenship identify "care" as an essential civic virtue (e.g. Clarke 1996) and eco-feminists, like Valerie Plumwood, have articulated a form of ecological rationality that "recognises and accommodates the denied relationships of dependency and enables us to acknowledge our debt to the sustaining others of the Earth" (cited in Dobson 1995: 197). While some feminists remain sceptical of the essentialist claim that women are somehow closer to Nature and that caring feminine values are of an inherently higher moral order than dominating masculine ones, they none the less define an ethic of care that should become the property of men as well as women (e.g. Tronto 1993). In particular Sevenhuijsen (1998, 2000) has argued that "[a] democratic ethic of care starts from the idea that everybody needs care and is (in principle at least) capable of care giving" (2000: 15). Inclusive relationships are achieved in the context of specific social networks of care and responsibility and cannot be created by ascribing rights and responsibilities. The citizen must first be understood not as an abstract individual or "equal rights holder", but as a "self-in-relationship". On the one hand, Sevenhuijsen argues, "vulnerability is part and parcel of ordinary human subjectivity" (2000: 19), while on the other care is a daily practice. Drawing on Nancy Hirschmann, she contends that "we begin our understanding of human freedom from the perspective of interconnection and relatedness" (cited in Sevenhuijsen 2000: 22). This is redolent of a timeless aphorism attributed to the Xhosa people of South Africa: "a person is a person through other persons" (see du Boulay 1988: 114). It is also a simple but profound rebuttal of the commodity fetishism that characterizes the dehumanizing capitalist process of production and accumulation (Marx 1970). In the meantime, Third Way policy reforms are failing properly to recognize or to value care in the context of evolving patterns of family and household life (cf. Lewis 2000).

An ethic of care—whether it is defined as a feminist or an ecological ethic—provides the crucial link between an abstract principle of co-responsibility and the substantive practice by which we continually negotiate our rights and duties. These are the ethical components that furnish a moral discourse capable of sustaining an eco-socialist form of Green citizenship.

Conclusion

It is for others to elaborate alternative accounts of Green citizenship. My own unapologetically pro-social-humanistic perspective is based on two premises. First, while it is perfectly true that we cannot save humanity unless we save the Earth, there is no purpose in saving the Earth at humanity's expense. Second, while it is perfectly true that humanity has exhibited self-destructive tendencies, there is no reason to reject the possibility of human emancipation. I suspect we should remain sceptical of the Gaia Hypothesis (Lovelock 1979)—that the Earth itself is a self-sustaining living organism—but, if it were true, one interpretation of its meaning is that humanity's struggle is not to tame the Earth, but to ensure that the Earth does not extinguish humanity: provided of course that—through capitalism—humanity does not succeed in destroying itself. For this we require a form of Green citizenship that can equate global imperatives with our lived experiences.

Notes

1. I am grateful to John Ferris, Tony Fitzpatrick and Douglas Torgerson for challenging an earlier formulation of this model in which I failed explicitly to define my own conception of "humanism". It is important to differentiate Greek humanism (that sought to distinguish humanity from animals/nature), Renaissance humanism (that sought to establish autonomy for humanity from the interpreted ordinances of a divine creator) and Marxist humanism (that distinguished humanity with reference to its inherent social nature). The concept on which the model here presented is premised draws essentially upon Marxist humanism and to clarify this I have elected to use the somewhat inelegant terms: "pro-social-humanistic" and "anti-social-humanistic".
2. I am grateful to Caron Caldwell for guidance on the concept of ecological modernization. However, the potentially provocative interpretation that is offered here is strictly my own.
3. I am indebted to Shane Doheny for introducing me to Apel's concept of co-responsibility.

References

Apel, K. (1980), *Towards the Transformation of Philosophy*, London: Routledge.
Apel, K. (1991), A planetary macro-ethics for humankind. In E. Deutsch (ed.), *Culture and Modernity: East–West Philosophical Perspectives*, Honolulu: University of Hawaii Press.
Beck, U. (1992), *Risk Society: Towards a New Modernity*, London: Sage.
Bookchin, M. (1991), Where I stand now. In M. Bookchin and D. Foreman, *Defending the Earth*, Montreal and New York: Black Rose Books.
Brundtland, G. (1987), *Our Common Future*, Oxford: Oxford University Press.
Cahill, M. (1999), Sustainability: the twenty-first century challenge for social policy. In H. Dean and R. Woods (eds), *Social Policy Review 11*, Luton: Social Policy Association.
Christoff, P. (1996), Ecological citizens and ecologically guided democracy. In B. Doherty and M. de Geus (eds), *Democracy and Green Political Thought*, London: Routledge.
Clarke, P. B. (1996), *Deep Citizenship*, London: Pluto.
Dahrendorf, R. (1994), The changing quality of citizenship. In B. van Steenbergen (ed.), *The Condition of Citizenship*, London: Sage.
Dean, H. (1996), *Welfare, Law and Citizenship*, Hemel Hempstead: Prentice Hall/Harvester Wheatsheaf.
Dean, H. (1998), Popular paradigms and welfare values, *Critical Social Policy*, 18, 2.
Dean, H. (1999), Citizenship. In M. Powell (ed.), *New Labour, New Welfare State*, Bristol: Policy Press.
Dean, H. (2001), Poverty and citizenship: moral repertoires and welfare regimes. In F. Wilson, N. Kanji and E. Braathen (eds), *Poverty Reduction: What Role for the State in Today's Globalised Economy*, London: Zed Books.
Dean, H. with Melrose, M. (1999), *Poverty, Riches and Social Citizenship*, Basingstoke: Macmillan.
DSS (Department of Social Security) (1998), *New Ambitions for our Country: A New Contract for Welfare*, Cm 3805, London: Stationery Office.
Dobson, A. (1995), *Green Political Thought*, 2nd edn, London: Routledge.
Doyal, L. and Gough, I. (1991), *A Theory of Human Need*, Basingstoke: Macmillan.
Dryzek, J. (1997), *The Politics of the Earth*, Oxford: Oxford University Press.
du Boulay, S. (1988), *Tutu: Voice of the Voiceless*, London: Hodder and Stoughton.

Falk, R. (1994), The making of a global citizenship. In B. van Steenbergen (ed.), *The Condition of Citizenship*, London: Sage.

Ferris, J. (1991), Green politics and the future of welfare. In N. Manning (ed.), *Social Policy Review 1990–91*, Harlow: Longman.

Finch, J. and Mason, J. (1993), *Negotiating Family Responsibilities*, London: Routledge.

Fitzpatrick, T. (1998), The implications of ecological thought for social welfare, *Critical Social Policy*, 18, 1.

Fox, W. (1984), Deep ecology: a new philosophy of our time? *The Ecologist*, 14, 5/6.

Giddens, A. (1998), *The Third Way*, Cambridge: Polity Press.

Goodwin, B. (1987), *Using Political Ideas*, 2nd edn, Chichester: John Wiley.

Gray, J. (1993), *Beyond the New Right: Markets, Government and the Common Environment*, London: Routledge.

Habermas, J. (1987), *The Theory of Communicative Action. Vol. 2: Lifeworld and System*, Cambridge: Polity Press.

Hajer, C. (1995), *The Politics of Environmental Discourse*, Oxford: Clarendon Press.

Hewitt, M. (1993), Social movements and social need: problems with post-modern political theory, *Critical Social Policy*, 13, 1.

Hobhouse, L. (1974), *Liberalism* (first published 1911), New York: Galaxy Books.

Horsman, M. and Marshall, A. (1994), *After the Nation-State: Citizens, Tribalism and the New World Disorder*, London: HarperCollins.

Labour Party (1995), *Constitution*, London: Labour Party.

Lewis, J. (2000), Work and care. In H. Dean, R. Sykes and R. Woods (eds), *Social Policy Review 12*, Newcastle, Social Policy Association.

Lister, R. (1997), *Citizenship: Feminist Perspectives*, Basingstoke: Macmillan.

Lovelock, J. (1979), *Gaia*, Oxford: Oxford University Press.

Marshall, T. H. (1950), Citizenship and social class. In T. Marshall and T. Bottomore (1992), *Citizenship and Social Class*, London: Pluto.

Marx, K. (1970), *Capital, Vol. 1* (first published 1867), London: Lawrence and Wishart.

Meadows, D., Meadows, D. and Randers, J. (1992), *Beyond the Limits: Global Collapse or a Sustainable Future*, London: Earthscan.

Meadows, D., Meadows, D., Randers, J. and Behrens, W., III (1974), *The Limits to Growth*, London: Pan.

Naess, A. (1973), The shallow and the deep, long-range ecology movement. A summary, *Inquiry*, 16.

Newby, H. (1996), Citizenship in a green world: global commons and human stewardship. In M. Bulmer and A. Rees (eds), *Citizenship Today: The Contemporary Relevance of T. H. Marshall*, London: UCL Press.

Offe, C. (1992), A non-productivist design for social policies. In P. van Parijs (ed.), *Arguing for Basic Income*, London: Verso.

Offe, C. (1993), Interdependence, difference and limited state capacity. In G. Drover and P. Kerans (eds), *New Approaches to Welfare Theory*, Aldershot: Edward Elgar.

Oldfield, A. (1990), *Citizenship and Community: Civic Republicanism and the Modern World*, London: Routledge.

Pepper, D. (1993), *Eco-socialism: From Deep Ecology to Social Justice*, London: Routledge.

Rawls, J. (1972), *A Theory of Justice*, Oxford: Oxford University Press.

Roche, M. (1992), *Rethinking Citizenship: Welfare, Ideology and Change in Modern Society*, Cambridge: Polity Press.

Ryle, M. (1988), *Ecology and Socialism*, London: Rodins.

Sevenhuijsen, S. (1998), *Citizenship and the Ethics of Care*, London: Routledge.

Sevenhuijsen, S. (2000), Caring in the third way: the relation between obligation, responsibility and care in "Third Way" discourse, *Critical Social Policy*, 20, 1.

Smith, M. (1998), *Ecologism: Towards Ecological Citizenship*, Buckingham: Open University Press.

Soysal, Y. (1994), *Limits of Citizenship: Migrants and Postnational Membership in Europe*, Chicago: University of Chicago Press.

Thane, P. (1982), *Foundations of the Welfare State*, Harlow: Longman.

Tronto, J. (1993), *Moral Boundaries: A Political Argument for an Ethic of Care*, London: Routledge.

Turner, B. (1986), *Citizenship and Capitalism: The Debate over Reformism*, London: Allen and Unwin.

Turner, B. (1990), Outline of a theory of citizenship, *Sociology*, 24, 2.

Turner, B. (1993), Outline of a theory of human rights, *Sociology*, 27, 3.

Turner, B. (1997), Citizenship studies: a general theory, *Citizenship Studies*, 1, 1.

Twine, F. (1994), *Citizenship and Social Rights: The Interdependence of Self and Society*, London: Sage.

van Parijs, P. (1995), *Real Freedom for All: What (if Anything) can Justify Capitalism?* Oxford: Oxford University Press.

van Steenbergen, B. (1994), Towards a global ecological citizen. In B. van Steenbergen (ed.), *The Condition of Citizenship*, London: Sage.

Weston, J. (ed.) (1986), *Red and Green*, London: Pluto.

CHAPTER 4

Making Welfare for Future Generations

Tony Fitzpatrick

Abstract

This article attempts to construct a new temporal framework for social policy. It draws upon a theory of intergenerational justice that has been elaborated by the author elsewhere and uses that theory to elaborate upon the principles of "sustainable justice". The article addresses some of the difficult philosophical dilemmas that those principles generate and argues that reconciling the interests of present and future generations of the least well-off requires the design of a new property regime. An ecosocial regime is defined and discussed, especially in terms of substitutable goods. The article concludes by debating the prescriptive implications of the above for social policy and future welfare reform.

Keywords

Time; Justice; Sustainability; Collective ownership; Substitutable goods; Pensions

Introduction

As environmentalism gradually enters the consciousness of social policy, and vice versa, it is becoming clear that the time horizons of these two subjects need to converge. Environmentalists have tended to be the more flexible of the two, projecting the future consequences of present trends across a time span of several years to several centuries. Social policy makers have been less foresighted. Their time horizon usually stretches no more than two generations into the future, e.g. in estimations of demographic trends and of state pension levels. If the agendas of environmentalism and of social policy overlap in terms of a joint commitment to the well-being of society then the latter needs to re-equip itself with a new temporal frame of reference.

The consequences of not doing so may be severe. For instance, welfare debates are almost always framed in terms of GDP growth. Does high social expenditure damage competitiveness? How can full employment be created? What form of state/market mix is most conducive to productivity?

Address for correspondence: *Dr Tony Fitzpatrick, School of Sociology and Social Policy, University of Nottingham, Nottingham, NG7 2RD. Email: Tony.Fitzpatrick@nottingham.ac.uk.*

Obviously, such economic questions do not capture the full range of social policy's concerns, yet due to the radical Right onslaught of the 1970s and 1980s, as well as the more recent emphasis upon globalization, those committed to universal and generous state welfare systems have had to defend themselves in terms of received economic wisdom: GDP growth is good, full-time full employment is desirable, etc. (Bonoli *et al.* 2000; Sykes *et al.* 2001). What this does, at best, is to treat sustainability as a secondary issue that can be bracketed until the economic fundamentals have been worked out. When scientists call for carbon emissions to be cut by 60 to 80 per cent, in contrast to the modest objectives of governments for cuts of 5 to 10 per cent, then the implications of this for welfare reform do not work their way into mainstream social policy discussions. Unless we develop a concept of "sustainable welfare" we might awake in a world either where distributive justice today is bought at the expense of tomorrow or where existing inequalities ossify forever due to the recalcitrance of the affluent and the fragility of the ecosystem.

This is one of two papers that attempt to sketch a new temporal framework for social policy. Fitzpatrick (2001) develops a meta-generational theory which yields a principle of sustainable justice. These ideas are summarized below. We then proceed to explore two issues that Fitzpatrick (2001) had to set to one side: redistribution and the revaluation of the economic.

Contractualism and Dis/Counting

Fitzpatrick (2001) considers and then rejects Parfit's (1984) approach to intergenerational justice, arguing that it neglects the importance of social transition in its utilitarian focus upon population growth. It proceeds to defend Rawls's (1972: 284–93) contractualist alternative. Basically, the "just savings principle" is that to which the participants of the original position would agree if they did not know where in history they belonged and is meant to guide an appropriate level of savings and accumulation. In order to ensure that these intergenerational transfers would occur, Rawls initially characterized the original position participants as having emotional ties to their immediate descendants, though he later altered this stipulation (Rawls 1993: 274). However, Fitzpatrick (2001) also argues that Rawls is being both too ambitious and not ambitious enough. His theory is too ambitious in its insistence that the participants in the original position may be located *anywhere* in time. What this does is to impose upon any theory of intergenerational justice a zero discount rate, where the needs of the far future are as important as those of generations in the short to medium term. Yet it is also underambitious by populating the original position with members of the same generation. Fitzpatrick (2001) therefore proposes a slight modification to Rawlsian contractualism which yields a theory of meta-generational justice. According to this theory our time horizon should be longer than those we normally apply, but should certainly not be infinite, and should refer to the particular circumstances within which we find ourselves.

Armed with this theory Fitzpatrick (2001) then concludes that a "low-low" strategy is the most practicable option. This implies a low discount rate that increases our valuation of future generations, but also a low savings rate, for what is important is not so much the *level* of present savings and consumption as a transition towards economic, moral and ontological investment in non-material goods. So, a low-low approach allows a longer range of future generations to be valued but earlier generations are permitted to use and transform the world's resources so long as, in doing so, they improve both the condition of the ecosystem and humans' ability to appreciate non-monetary values. This suggests a principle of sustainable justice, which recognizes the long-term mutuality of intragenerational and intergenerational equity: the former without the latter is unsustainable; the latter without the former is undesirable. The problem is, how do we get from here to there?

Although a cultural revaluation of our economic priorities and activities might enable temporal conflicts to be avoided in the long term, that is, trade-offs between present benefits and burdens against future benefits and burdens, we are still left with some difficult distributional decisions in the short term. For instance, should we prioritize the needs of the present poor above those of the future poor? Might this hinder attempts to create a sustainable society by promoting short-termism? Then again, if we do not prioritize the present poor then we commit an additional injustice upon them given that the future poor may be better off in absolute terms anyway.[1] In short, it is easy to define sustainability as meeting the needs of the present without compromising the ability of future generations to meet their own needs (Brundtland Commission 1987) if needs are defined in simplistic terms. But if what we *need* is a radical redistribution of resources then full sustainability may have to be delayed until egalitarian social conditions are in place. Therefore, the principle of sustainable justice cannot just assume that distributional conflicts will automatically smooth themselves out over time as environmental crises worsen and people adjust their behaviour accordingly. We should not adopt an ecological determinism. As environmental hazards grow people may make the connections between social justice and environmental sustainability; then again, they may not.

So, in this paper we discuss the issues left over from Fitzpatrick (2001). The first concerns redistribution and how we weigh the needs of the present poor against those of the future; the second concerns substitutability and what an economic revaluation might imply. In addition, I want to indulge in some speculation and sketch what policies geared towards sustainable justice might actually resemble.

Sustainable Justice

The problem is this. Poverty, inequality and injustice currently exist at levels that few regard as desirable.[2] Poverty bears an environmental dimension, since the poorest are those most likely to suffer from ecological degradation. However, although many anti-poverty policies will be environmentally benign, and many pro-environment policies will reduce poverty, the conjunction between social justice and environmental sustainability is by no means total. Some anti-poverty policies may need to be environmentally damaging; for example, a dash for GDP growth, and some pro-environment policies may be detrimental to the poor, e.g. price rises on scarce resources. The question is, when are such trade-offs acceptable?

In this respect, therefore, I am agreeing with Dobson's (1998) thesis that justice and sustainability are contingently rather than necessarily related (cf. Langhelle 2000). Dobson's seminal treatment of the subject, *Justice and the Environment*, will therefore be a key source for what follows. Dobson, though, neglects the policy aspects of this subject. Although the relationship between justice and sustainability may always remain contingent in a philosophical sense it is also true that if we manage to design policies which strengthen that relationship then the non-conjunction of anti-poverty and pro-environment strategies may eventually fade to insignificance. However, in order to design such policies we first need to understand when poverty reduction might be allowed to trump sustainability and vice versa. Of course, much will ultimately depend upon the particular circumstances within which such judgements are made, yet Dobson is wrong to believe that this is always a matter of empirical determination.

In other words, we can devise general rules which allow such determinations to be made with greater assurance than otherwise. Let me state what I consider these to be:

The Non-futility Rule

Principle x should not be allowed to trump principle y when, under particular circumstances, doing so would be self-defeating.

Let us imagine ourselves making poverty reduction the priority. We might, for instance, make efforts to vastly increase global GDP in such a way that the developing world has access to the consumerist living standards that are still largely confined to developed nations.[3] The problem is that the environmental costs of an extra 2–3 billion cars, refrigerators, computers, etc. would be so great that the advantages of that strategy would be confined to several decades at best. Of course, we can also envisage technological innovations and some sustainability measures lengthening such a time horizon, yet only an economic/technological determinist could imagine ecological crises being forestalled forever. According to the Environmental Kuznets Curve (EKC) economic growth only produces environmental deterioration in its early stages, this being superseded by improvements in environmental quality later on (Panayotou 1995). However, even if the EKC applies to some pollutants in some geographical localities (Perrings and Ansuategi 2000), it is dangerous to generalize this hypothesis as it takes no account of the exponential deterioration of environmental quality on a global scale that can be expected to occur *before* the zenith of the EKC, e.g. the greenhouse effect. Of course, it is possible to envisage developed countries on the right side of the curve assisting those on the wrong side (Panayotou 1997), but developed nations have so far demonstrated little inclination to do so. This may be because they are not yet on the right side, obviously, but this only returns us to the dilemma of exponential degradation. In short, those who treat GDP growth as a panacea (e.g. Neumayer 1999) tend to assume that future environmental deterioration will not differ significantly from present deterioration.

Let us now imagine making sustainability the priority. The problem is that global inequality has doubled over the last 40 years (UNDP 1996) to a level that is damaging to sustainability (Stymne and Jackson 2000). This is, first, because those at the bottom overconsume resources as a means of trying to catch up with the affluent and follow environmentally damaging practices as a side effect of coping with their deprivation. Of course, many environmentally benign practices are carried out by those with scarce resources but it is clear that developing countries do not appreciate being told to develop sustainable economies by affluent nations who seem unwilling to take more than modest steps in the same direction. Second, therefore, inequality encourages those at the top to overconsume resources as a means of maintaining their relative position and so to pollute in greater proportions also. Consequently, sustainability that does not attend to the injustice of global inequalities will not be effective, remaining at the level of carbon sinks and tradable permits that, for the USA government in particular, are an excuse to maintain its environmentally damaging activities. None of this is to argue for absolute equality but, rather, for the kind of Rawlsian equality defended in Fitzpatrick (2001).

However, the Non-futility Rule does not disallow all attempts to permit one principle to trump the other:

The Deferred Enhancement Rule

Principle x is temporarily allowed to trump principle y when, under particular circumstances, doing so allows the objectives of principle y to be met more effectively in the medium term than would otherwise be the case.

There are two circumstances to which this rule might apply. First, when inequality is at levels so extreme that priority *must* be given to justice-enhancing policies. This is obviously so when we are faced with examples of severe deprivation, e.g. famine, but it also follows in cases falling short of such examples, e.g. when income inequality is so great that no moral consensus regarding sustainability can be expected to emerge (or, to put it bluntly, why should the poorest change their activities in order to save a planet ruined by the affluent?). Second, when environmental degradation is so acute that the ecological necessities of life are placed in jeopardy. We can think of these two circumstances in terms of a *Titanic* metaphor. If the ship is at risk of sinking because the steerage passengers are rebelling then this has to be the priority—no matter how many icebergs are around! If the ship is about to hit an iceberg then we had better manoeuvre out of the way and worry about the passengers later on.

However, in both instances we are not defending a principle (either equality or sustainability) for the sake of it but in order to augment and strengthen the other principle in the longer term. Where injustice is the problem then egalitarianism and justice-enhancement are appropriate responses only until the point where the Non-futility Rule begins to apply, i.e. the point at which further equality and justice without sustainability would be self-defeating. Under these circumstances it is an initial equal weighting of justice and sustainability which would be ineffective so that the latter is better served in the long run by being temporarily deferred. Where the problem is ecological crises, then strategies to enhance sustainability are the appropriate response only until the point where such strategies would be self-defeating without greater equality also. Here, again, an initial equal weighting would be ineffective so that justice and equality are better served by being temporarily deferred. Therefore, the Deferred Enhancement Rule is the means by which we create circumstances in which the Non-futility Rule begins to apply; or, to put it more simply, justice can only trump sustainability, or vice versa, if the objective is to allow the two principles to eventually converge.

(Remember that these rules are intended to guide the empirical judgements that Dobson emphasizes, but cannot substitute for the latter. Hence the incorporation within the rules themselves of "temporary", "under particular circumstances" and "medium-term". What these imply in practice is impossible to determine in advance. The real-world convergence of justice and sustainability will always be a matter of determination a posteriori.)

So, we can see that although there is no necessary relation between justice/equality and sustainability, such that we cannot realize one just by realizing the other, the contingent relationship is nevertheless very close. This suggests that distributive justice and environmental sustainability converge in the debate concerning future generations such that the debate is incomplete without reference to both. This supplies the rationale for the contractualist approach sketched in Fitzpatrick (2001) and the idea that we should not bequeath social and environmental conditions to future generations that we would not be willing to live in ourselves.

However, we are still left with the problem mentioned earlier: should we prioritize the needs of the present poor above those of the future poor? Are we any nearer to answering this question? Well, yes and no. The Non-futility and Deferred Enhancement rules both suggest that we cannot ultimately have greater justice/equality without greater sustainability, and vice versa. If so, then the policies which are most suitable for the present poor will closely resemble those most suitable for the future poor, i.e. policies that come under the heading of sustainable justice. As such, the real conflict may not be between present and future but, as always, between Left and Right. If we decide that we want a Leftist approach (as I am assuming in this essay we should) then decisions over the temporal distribution of benefits and burdens, whilst important, are of secondary consideration. In short, to characterize the debate in terms of irreconcilable interests between present and future is to reify it and overlook the fact that the main division remains ideological, whatever the precise time horizon involved. Indeed, to neglect the idea that the present and future poor are part of the same moral community might only hand the theoretical initiative to the Right by encouraging the Left to ignore the temporal dimension of social justice. By contrast, the Left must recognize that the road to intergenerational equity is through intragenerational equality (cf. Beckerman 1999; Barry 1999).

Ecosocial Property

Having brought ourselves to this point, then, we are obliged to say something about what the most appropriate policies might be and how present and future can be woven into a non-zero sum game. What kind of welfare policies synergistically serve the interests of both present and future poor? A useful entrance into this debate is provided by Dobson (1998, 1999). According to Dobson we can identify three main conceptions of environmental sustainability, each of which engenders its own unique account of social justice and the relationship between justice and sustainability.

Conception A (Dobson 1998: 41–7) is concerned with sustaining the most critical aspects of natural capital, i.e. those aspects which are essential for the perpetuation of human life—the ecosystem, for instance (cf. Benton 1999). Conception A incorporates an anthropocentric rationale, in that "critical natural capital" is to be preserved for the instrumentalist reasons of protecting human welfare. How might such preservation occur? First, through processes of renewal, e.g. reforestation; second, through the substitution of non-renewable critical natural capital, e.g. substitutes for oil; third, through the conservation of critical natural capital that is non-renewable and non-substitutable. Conception A states that the *needs* of future generations must override the *wants* of the present generation, a prioritization which allows the interests of the non-human to be accounted for also.

Conception B (Dobson 1998: 47–50) is concerned with sustaining those aspects of the natural world whose loss would be irreversible. In short, while conception B acknowledges the importance of human welfare it also wants to preserve those elements of non-human nature which risk disappearing forever, even when this loss might not impact upon human welfare at all. Therefore, conception B states that renewability is far less important than substitutability and conservation, since once a species is extinct it cannot, by definition, be renewed. However, there are also limits to the extent to which human-made capital can substitute for natural capital, e.g. an extinct species cannot be artificially recreated. Consequently, this conception gives priority to the needs of present generations of non-humans over the needs of future generations of humans, on the grounds that the loss of a non-human species cannot be justified in terms of the potential benefits of that loss to future generations.

Conception C (Dobson 1998: 50–4) identifies an intrinsic value to nature, the sustainability of which cannot therefore be measured in terms of human welfare. Of course, the former may enhance the latter but enhancing the latter cannot be the motivation for the former. Conception C abandons renewability and substitutability, since intrinsic natural value is lost in both instances, and concentrates upon conservation as the main instrument of sustainability. So although conception C does not necessarily want to abandon the prioritization of human needs it does want the profile of non-human needs to be raised within the calculus of policy making.

Each of these conceptions corresponds to a broad "menu" of ideas relating to social justice. These correspondences are too complex to summarize here, but we can outline the main features. Conception A (Dobson 1998:

87–164) seems to require the just distribution of critical natural capital, i.e. distribution according to universal needs. This means that critical natural capital cannot be sustained simply by attending to just social relations, as such justice might require the depletion of critical natural capital. Therefore, both the existing pattern of ownership and our ideas about property rights need to alter, perhaps around some notion of environmental space, the distribution of which would have to be global and egalitarian. Conception B (1998: 165–215) points in the direction of a Green communitarianism, such that justice must involve a broader interpretation of the moral community than that permitted by anthropocentrism and one, moreover, which is concerned with a single definition of the good (the sustainability of irreversible nature) rather than procedural neutrality between competing definitions. Conception B, though, is less clear than A regarding the just distribution of natural resources since distribution is functional for sustainability. With conception C (1998: 216–39), however, the link between environmental sustainability and social justice possibly breaks down altogether. At best, sustainability demands whatever pattern of distribution that is most likely to produce benign consequences for the environment and if this ever required social injustice then so be it. Intrinsic natural value cannot be interpreted as a distributive resource precisely because it is intrinsic. Dobson concludes (1998: 242–67) with a discussion of whether there can be a theory of social justice that incorporates notions of environmental sustainability from across the three conceptions. He accepts the argument of Norton (1991) that a "future generationalism" might be the means of producing consensus across the Green movement and between Greens and those non-Greens who are concerned with justice to others.

I am not convinced of the merits of this approach, however, due to a possible criticism that Dobson himself raises. The problem with future generationalism is that it focuses upon generalizable human interests and neglects distributional conflicts between rich and poor. Unless we operate some kind of discount rate we may leave present generations vulnerable, and unless we have some notion of distributional justice we leave the present poor especially vulnerable. For Dobson, then, future generationalism must give precedence to those generations closest to us in time. While agreeing with this prioritization, it seems to me that it fatally weakens future generationalism as conceived by Norton and revised by Dobson. For if we must possess some principle of social justice in order to resolve both intra- and intergenerational distributional conflicts over resources then conception C must be omitted due to its biocentric emphasis upon intrinsic value, since this emphasis seems to rule out a close link between justice and sustainability. We are therefore returned to the point made earlier (that the future generations debate is one between Left and Right long before it is a debate about present and future), contradicting the idea that focusing upon future horizons enables ideological conflicts to be resolved. This does not refute the proposition that nature has intrinsic value, but it does relocate that proposition so that it is internal to political contestation (Mouffe 2000). Nature may initially precede ideology but the natural world is also an ideological construct.

45

Sustainable justice as I have outlined it therefore maps on to conceptions A and B of Dobson's framework but that framework does not currently offer a way forward due to its neglect of political ideology. Can we therefore find a way of proceeding which is more profitable than future generationalism, i.e. one that enables us to answer the earlier question about serving the needs of both the present and future poor?

Neither conception A nor B seems to be entirely satisfactory (cf. Rogers 2000). The problem with conception A is its exclusive focus upon *critical* natural capital, for although this may cover a large part of the natural world it instrumentalizes the relationship between human and non-human. Now, to some extent an instrumentalism is appropriate, e.g. we need to repair the ozone layer for our benefit first and foremost, yet it would not seem appropriate to regard the natural world purely in such terms. Since the future well-being of humanity is in no way dependent upon the survival of the blue whale then the latter cannot be regarded as critical. Of course, it might be that we would lose the pleasure of co-inhabiting the earth with such a creature if it became extinct, but this, too, would hardly be a *critical* loss and so points beyond an instrumentalist ethic towards conception B.

On the other hand, the irreversibility thesis of conception B is too stringent. Although 20–50 species are made extinct every day (Weizsacker *et al.* 1998: 230–3), the disappearance of most of them probably does not affect our survival or sense of well-being at all. Obviously, there comes a point at which the loss of biodiversity is crucial, but biodiversity does not require us to maintain the existence of each and every species, even if this were possible! Therefore, we need to develop guidelines helping us to distinguish between those species whose irreversible loss would and would not be acceptable. This sends us back in the direction of conception A.

I am therefore going to leave open the question as to whether we should prefer A or B, or whether there is another theory of sustainability and justice which we could develop incorporating elements of both. For our purposes, it seems clear that for policies to be consistent with sustainable justice then the principle of substitutability (which both A and B embody) is crucial. The following argument may resemble a labyrinth in places but please bear with it as I think it leads us in the direction we need to travel.

Neither renewability nor conservation imply any major, direct impacts upon social redistribution, though they obviously have implications for the environmental conditions of future generations. Substitutables are different, however. Take fossil fuels. There is a very good case for using up the earth's supply of fossil fuels, albeit at a lower and less damaging rate than at present. First, because doing so helps to improve social welfare, at least as measured in a material sense. Second, because despite the aeons it took to create them fossil fuels have no intrinsic or aesthetic value: there is little point in just having them lie in the ground. Of course, pollution is an undesirable side effect of using fossil fuels but their conservation would have no value in itself. In short, a substitutable is a good whose utilization is acceptable, because the sum total of human welfare is raised as a result, but only if an environmentally benign replacement can be eventually found that does not reduce those levels of welfare.

However, the process of substitution is not only a technological question; it is also a question of who benefits, i.e. the distributive pattern of the welfare thereby created. Fossil fuels are subject to private ownership across a relatively limited range of countries. This means that the direct benefits of their depletion flow into the bank accounts of a lucky few. I would like to add the following principle to the above definition, therefore:

Substitutables should only be utilized if the welfare thereby created is subject to an egalitarian distribution.

The logic is simple: the depletion of a substitutable has implications for everyone, therefore everyone should be able to benefit from it on a scale that current property rights do not permit (Sathiendrakumar 1996: 159). This means initiating as wide a system of ownership as possible, but does this imply egalitarian private ownership or egalitarian collective ownership? The answer to this question depends largely upon the extent to which we can and should place a monetary value upon nature.

There are those who abhor any suggestion that nature can be commodified (Naess 1989) since it is the source of economic value and so cannot be measured in terms of a quantity of which it is the condition. In simpler terms, this means that a price tag cannot be placed on what is non-economic, as doing so is a category mistake. For others, commodifying nature, e.g. through a cost–benefit analysis, is the only way of ensuring that scarce resources are preserved (see O'Neill 1993: 44–82; Sagoff 1988) and a pricing mechanism is the best means for signalling when and where a resource is undersupplied. In practice, however, commodification and decommodification are not irreconcilable opposites but "economic ethics" that can be made to sit alongside one another: market societies do not commodify everything, nor would a profoundly ecological society be able to decommodify everything since conservation policies are unlikely to be efficacious without some notion of cost effectiveness. If the same principle is extended to this issue concerning the ownership of natural resources then the private/collective distinction begins to look rather crude.

Instead, it might be wise to prefer the kind of property regime envisaged by John Roemer (1993) and Roberto Unger (1987), i.e. a system of rights where a certain good is held in common—both intra- and intergenerationally —but each individual possesses a right to that dividend which is yielded by the utilization of the good. In what I shall call an "ecosocial" property regime, individuals are therefore not able to trade or sell the good itself, but they are entitled to a "rent", i.e. an equitable share of the value produced by the good translated into a monetary income, a share that reverts back to the commons on the death of the individual. What this would require, for reasons to become clear in a moment, is a sophisticated taxation system where destructive utilization is taxed at a higher rate than those activities which raise the level of sustainable welfare as measured on an appropriate index. Such taxes would need to be based upon an ethic of stewardship, for if natural resources are collectively owned then policies must recognize our role as being that of trustees who have a duty to bequeath to the future a level of critical natural capital not less than that we ourselves inherited. In effect, this means internalizing that which is currently externalized, so whereas GDP growth takes no account of hidden environmental costs—nor, for that matter, of hidden benefits—a sustainable welfare index would ensure that these are made fully visible. What this implies is that a shift in the onus of taxation from the poor to the rich can be more effectively accomplished through Green taxes that fully quantify environmental costs and benefits than through an income tax system that takes little account of externalities. Obviously, the principle of Green taxes has been long established (Robertson 2002) but in a system of private accumulation they are widely seen as little more than another expenditure-raising exercise by the state, i.e. as a public measure that invades the private. Where the aim is both to protect resources as they are held in common and to boost individual incomes then Green taxes may be altogether more acceptable since public necessity and private interests would be much more inclusive. Green taxes and an ecosocial property regime are therefore dependent upon one another: without the latter, the former simply encourage taxpayer revolts; without the former, the latter would not necessarily be any more conducive to sustainability than a system of private capital accumulation.

To illustrate this second point we might identify similarities between an ecosocial regime and what Blackburn (1999, 2001) calls the "new collectivism" (Aglietta 1998; Self 2000). Blackburn, like Drucker (1994, 1996) before him, spies a radical potential in the shift to pension-fund capitalism, with pension funds now totalling some $13,000 billion. If such funds were democratically controlled by the policyholders themselves and invested in equities and bonds then substantial portions of the economy could be brought under some form of social control. What this represents, of course, is an alternative version of the Meidner plan for wage-earner funds against which the Swedish bourgeois parties mobilized so effectively in the late 1970s. Indeed, the idea that capitalism contains the seeds of its own socialization has a long history and Blackburn (1999: 40) notes Milton Friedman as fearing that this could still happen! However, pension fund reform is a necessary but not sufficient condition of socialization and a new fiscal and legal framework for the political economy, e.g. global capital controls, would also be required in order to prevent financial globalization from undermining the trend towards socialized accumulation. Similarly, all citizens would need to be covered by such funds, requiring pension reforms much more far-reaching than those introduced by, for instance, New Labour (Ward 2000).[4] If this were to occur, of course, then "pension fund" might become a misnomer with "endowment fund" being a preferable alternative (cf. Unger 1998: 205). Nevertheless, with such reorganizations in place Blackburn envisages that a proper system of stakeholder welfare would emerge, one less vulnerable than the welfare state to capital flight and taxpayer revolts. Echoing the point made above about commodification and decommodification, Blackburn (1999: 63) represents this as a synthesis of private and collective property rights.

So, in answer to the obvious and legitimate question "How do we wrestle control of substitutables from private hands?", the most obvious solution is through the investment and gradual takeover of the companies and trusts who presently control such assets by democratically controlled endowment funds. However, unless the new political economy that Blackburn mentions also incorporates Green taxes then there is no incentive for the fundholders to be any more environmental than existing pension fund managers. The ideal to work towards would be something like the following. Field X has been earmarked for the development of a Conservation Park that would charge for research into natural habitats; field Y has been earmarked for the construction of a car park. In the absence of Green taxes the investment decision will flow in the direction of whichever plan promises the greatest returns. But with Green taxes that take full account of all externalities then the taxes on field Y's development will have to be high enough to subsidize the lower taxes on field X's development, making the former less attractive to investors. So, an ecosocial regime (i.e. the shift towards socialized capital through pension fund reform) requires Green taxes if it is to be sustainable— otherwise, there is little point in initiating such reform at all according to the Non-futility Rule—and Green taxes require an ecosocial regime in order to secure their legitimacy and ensure that they are not interpreted as statist intrusions into the sphere of private accumulation.

Of course, the system of taxation is likely to alter depending upon the nature of the substitutable in question. In the case of fossil fuels, for instance, taxation could fall most heavily on those activities which, while being dependent upon fossil fuels, are in no way concerned with their eventual substitution. This is what would distinguish an ecosocial property regime from, say, the dividend scheme operating in Alaska where oil from Prudhoe Bay is distributed to all Alaskan residents on an annual and egalitarian basis (Fitzpatrick 1999: 147–9). Although the Alaskan scheme combines some of the benefits of both collective and private ownership it is not based upon a sustainable welfare index and so has few ecological credentials. Nevertheless, the same principle could be made to serve more sustainable objectives if the political will were in place.

Conclusion

An ecosocial property regime, then, is concerned with (a) collective owner-ship of natural resources; (b) private ownership, in the form of an ecosocial dividend; (c) sustainability, as steered through Green taxes, so that overall capital stock does not decline and the future inherits a level of well-being at least equivalent to our own; and (d) a new political economy which subdues financial globalization. The point of this long and winding argument has been to present prima-facie evidence that appropriate social and economic reforms can weave present and future interests and needs into a non-zero sum game. To repeat the basic thesis of this paper, the real conflict is between Left and Right; once this is acknowledged and once an ideological stance has been adopted then it is relatively easy to imagine policies that reconcile present and future. In the reforms sketched here the present poor benefit from the democratization of pension funds and an equal distribution of the wealth derived from substitutables; the future poor benefit likewise, in addition to inheriting a cleaner environment than the one we are currently creating for ourselves. Of course, none of this is to pretend that present and future needs and interests dovetail completely. As Dobson observes, our task is to link sustainability and social justice rather than assume that the link is already there, awaiting discovery; and in an ecosocial regime hard decisions would need to be made regarding taxation and dividend levels. As Fitzpatrick (2001) argues, we have got ourselves into such a social and ecological mess that today's problems must take precedence over those which may appear tomorrow, so long as the Deferred Enhancement Rule is observed, however. In short, the principle of sustainable justice merely establishes the point that a temporal balancing act is *possible* but, as always, the devil is in the detail and whether that balance will or will not actually be maintained depends upon many thousands of policy decisions that have yet to be made.

(It is also worth adding that an ecosocial regime would imply far more than has been covered here, e.g. basic income, working-time reductions, associational reform, extensive informal economies. Such ideas are reviewed elsewhere, however [Fitzpatrick 1998; Fitzpatrick with Caldwell 2001; Fitzpatrick and Cahill 2002].)

We also now have a clearer idea of what the "revaluation of the economic" implies. Currently, ours is a strongly anthropocentric culture that has barely begun to incorporate environmental imperatives into its social and economic structures. Relocating ourselves somewhere between conceptions A and B requires that we regard natural resources as commonly owned (an idea presently restricted to Antarctica) and acknowledge the extent to which our fabulous economic wealth is dependent upon a natural base. Although we still face the problem of private affluence and public squalor we must recognize how this overlaps with a second problem of economic wealth and environmental degradation. To my mind, this requires us to utilize the benefits of both collective and private ownership, of both commodification and decommodification; and it is here, in the overcoming of the either/or logic which dominates at present, that the seeds of a new cultural economy may lie. Of course, some insist that these dilemmas can be addressed from within the existing political paradigm (Jacobs 1999) and, in a way, I almost hope that they are correct. But if they are not then social policies will have even more of a crucial role to play. The wheel has turned full circle. For just as Fitzpatrick (2001) began by using pensions to illustrate our temporal myopia, the irony is that radical pension reform might be the key to a door that continues to remain firmly locked.

Notes

1. Though whether they would also be better off in relative terms is precisely what we are trying to determine. If we get it right, obviously, then there may be no need to talk of the "future poor" at all!
2. In treating these three terms as synonymous I am adopting an egalitarian perspective which defines each term relative to the others. This is not to neglect the importance of absolute poverty to this discussion, but because eliminating absolute poverty requires a relatively modest transfer of resources (UNDP 1997)— though the political will to effect even this transfer still appears to be lacking

—then it can be set to one side for our purposes. Organizations such as the UNDP (e.g. 1996) casually regard poverty reduction and sustainability as compatible precisely because, like the Brundtland Commission, they are using a simplistic definition of need. Their analysis is correct so far as it goes, of course, but would still leave a massive amount of inequality between the global rich and poor.
3. This seems to be the path down which we are headed, which is why it is being considered here in preference to alternative approaches.
4. Though Blackburn is certainly not suggesting that these could ever substitute for an adequately financed basic state pension.

References

Aglietta, M. (1998), Capitalism at the turn of the century: regulation theory and the challenge of social change, *New Left Review*, 232: 41–90.
Barry, B. (1999), Sustainability and intergenerational justice. In A. Dobson (ed.), *Fairness and Futurity*, Oxford: Oxford University Press.
Beckerman, W. (1999), Sustainable development and our obligations to future generations. In A. Dobson (ed.), *Fairness and Futurity*, Oxford: Oxford University Press.
Benton, T. (1999), Sustainable development and accumulation of capital: reconciling the irreconcilable? In A. Dobson (ed.), *Fairness and Futurity*, Oxford: Oxford University Press.
Blackburn, R. (1999), The new collectivism: pension reform, grey capitalism and complex socialism, *New Left Review*, 233: 3–65.
Blackburn, R. (2001), *Pension Power*, London: Verso.
Bonoli, G., George, V. and Taylor-Gooby, P. (2000), *European Welfare Futures*, Cambridge: Polity Press.
Brundtland Commission (1987), *Our Common Future*, Cambridge: Cambridge University Press.
Dobson, A. (1998), *Justice and the Environment*, Oxford: Oxford University Press.
Dobson, A. (ed.) (1999), *Fairness and Futurity*, Oxford: Oxford University Press.
Drucker, P. (1994), *Post-Capitalist Society*, Oxford: Butterworth-Heinemann.
Drucker, P. (1996), *The Pension Fund Revolution*, New Brunswick, NJ: Transaction Books.
Fitzpatrick, T. (1998), The implications of ecological thought for social welfare, *Critical Social Policy*, 18, 1: 5–26.
Fitzpatrick, T. (1999), *Freedom and Security*, London: Macmillan.
Fitzpatrick, T. (2001), Dis/Counting the future. In R. Sykes, N. Ellison and C. Bochel (eds), *Social Policy Review 13*, Bristol: Policy Press.
Fitzpatrick, T. with Caldwell, C. (2001), Towards a theory of ecosocial welfare: modelling the convergence of social policy and environmental politics, *Environmental Politics*, 10, 2: 43–67.
Fitzpatrick, T. and Cahill, M. (eds) (2002), *Greening the Welfare State*, London: Palgrave.
Jacobs, M. (1999), *Environmental Modernisation*, London: Fabian Society.
Langhelle, O. (2000), Sustainable development and social justice: expanding the Rawlsian framework of global justice, *Environmental Values*, 9: 295–323.
Mouffe, C. (2000), *The Democratic Paradox*, London: Verso.
Naess, A. (1989), *Ecology, Community and Lifestyle*, Cambridge: Cambridge University Press.
Neumayer, E. (1999), Global warming: discounting is not the issue but substitutability is, *Energy Policy*, 27: 33–43.
Norton, B. (1991), *Toward Unity Among Environmentalists*, Oxford: Oxford University Press.

O'Neill, J. (1993), *Ecology, Policy and Politics*, London: Routledge.
Panayotou, T. (1995), Environmental degradation at different stages of economic development. In I. Ahmed and J. Doelman (eds), *Beyond Rio*, London: Macmillan.
Panayotou, T. (1997), Demystifying the environmental Kusnets curve: turning a black box into a policy tool, *Environmental and Development Economics*, 2, 4: 465–84.
Parfit, D. (1984), *Reasons and Persons*, Oxford: Oxford University Press.
Perrings, C. and Ansuategi, A. (2000), Sustainability, growth and development, *Journal of Economic Studies*, 27, 1/2: 19–37.
Rawls, J. (1972), *A Theory of Justice*, Oxford: Oxford University Press.
Rawls, J. (1993), *Political Liberalism*, New York: Columbia University Press.
Robertson, J. (2002), Sharing the value of resources in a Green society. In T. Fitzpatrick and M. Cahill (eds), *Greening the Welfare State*, London: Palgrave.
Roemer, J. (1993), *A Future for Socialism*, London: Verso.
Rogers, B. (2000), The nature of value and the value of nature: a philosophical overview, *International Affairs*, 76, 2: 315–23.
Sagoff, M. (1988), *The Economy of the Earth*, Cambridge: Cambridge University Press.
Sathiendrakumar, R. (1996), Sustainable development: passing fad or potential reality? *International Journal of Social Economics*, 23, 4/5/6: 151–63.
Self, P. (2000), *Rolling Back the Market*, London: Palgrave.
Stymne, S. and Jackson, T. (2000) Intra-generational equity and sustainable welfare: a time series analysis for the UK and Sweden, *Ecological Economics*, 33: 219–36.
Sykes, R., Palier, B. and Prior, P. (2001), *Globalisation and European Welfare States*, London: Palgrave.
UNDP (1996), *Human Development Report—1996*, Oxford: Oxford University Press.
UNDP (1997), *Human Development Report—1997*, Oxford: Oxford University Press.
Unger, R. (1987), *False Necessity*, Cambridge: Cambridge University Press.
Unger, R. (1998), *Democracy Realised*, London: Verso.
Ward, S. (2000), New Labour's pension reforms. In H. Dean, R. Sykes and R. Woods (eds), *Social Policy Review 12*, London: Social Policy Association.
Weizsacker, E., Lovins, A. and Lovins, L. H. (1998), *Factor Four*, London: Earthscan.

CHAPTER 5

The Sustainable Use of Resources on a Global Scale
Meg Huby

Abstract

The need to reconcile social and environmental goals for sustainable development still poses problems for policy makers in the richer parts of the world. Using the examples of domestic water and energy, this paper argues that the problems are reflected, and often magnified, in developing countries. They arise largely from conflicts between the short-term need to alleviate poverty and longer-term objectives for environmental sustainability. The dual nature of water and energy as both social and economic goods raises questions about the most appropriate forms of provision and allocation of the utilities. It is in no one's long-term interest for developing countries to repeat the environmentally damaging mistakes of the industrialized world. But an equitable distribution of the short-term costs attached to a more environmentally responsible use of resources demands new ways of thinking about global social justice.

Keywords

Domestic energy; Water; Social and environmental sustainability; Equity; Social development; Public and private provision

Introduction

The pressures placed on natural resources to meet people's demands for domestic energy and water, even in the richer industrialized parts of the world, present a dilemma for policy makers concerned with sustainable development. On the one hand, sustainable social welfare goals require increased access to the utilities so that vulnerable households are able to obtain the water and energy they need to improve and maintain their living standards. On the other, overall reductions in water and energy use are necessary to meet long-term goals for environmental sustainability. The problem is that, used alone, policies to promote social welfare carry long-term costs to both society and the environment, while policies for long-term

Address for correspondence: *Dr Meg Huby, Department of Social Policy and Social Work, University of York, Heslington, York, YO10 5DD. Email: meh1@york.ac.uk.*

environmental protection tend to produce distributional effects that work to the detriment of vulnerable groups of people in the shorter term.

However, social and environmental objectives are closely linked. Protecting the environment can enhance social welfare, for example by improving air quality, reducing the incidence of respiratory problems in children, and by reducing the potential for climate change to affect the prevalence of disease, disrupt food supplies and increase risks of hardship caused by extreme weather events. Conversely, higher levels of social welfare can benefit the environment. People who do not have to confront immediate day-to-day difficulties in meeting their basic needs are more likely to show concern for and take action to protect the natural environment.

Developing policies to address both social and environmental problems together is not easy. The difficulties revolve around three key themes. First, there is the issue of how to reconcile long- and short-term goals for sustainability. Second, many problems arise because of the dual nature of domestic energy and water as both social goods and commodities. Third, political conditions, turning upon issues of ownership and the participation of stakeholders—often with conflicting interests—in the policy-making process, can operate to promote or to hinder progress.

The problem of reconciling social and environmental goals for domestic energy and water use is essentially the same in low-income countries and in the industrialized world, even though the scale of the problem is often very different.\Whereas, in richer parts of the world, inadequate access to the utilities results in hardship and discomfort, in the poorest regions it is often a matter of life or death. Social policy analysis traditionally confines itself to countries where government policies already exist to deal with problems of social welfare, and strong arguments for taking into account environmental factors in analysing such policies are increasingly being recognized (Huby 1998; George and Wilding 1999; Cahill 2001). Addressing the causes of these problems requires that we take a global perspective.

Inequalities Between and Within Countries

Income inequalities between countries have been rising for nearly two centuries (United Nations Development Programme 1999). While the richest 20 per cent of countries account for over 82 per cent of world income, the poorest 20 per cent receive only just over 1 per cent (Redclift 1996). Table 1 shows how the gross national product (GNP) per capita for high-income economies in 1998 was more than five times that of low-income economies. It also shows how income differences between groups of economies are accompanied by differentials in other indicators of social development.

These global figures, however, mask huge inequalities between people within the countries of each group. Table 2 illustrates cases for three countries with high- and three with low-income economies and shows that, in each example, the percentage share of income for the poorest 20 per cent of the population is disproportionately low. The Gini index provides a measure of this inequality and is often higher for poorer countries. These income

Table 1

Indicators of income and social development in low-, middle- and high-income economies

Economies with populations of >30,000	n	GNP per capita ($) 1998	Life expectancy at birth (years) 1997		Adult female illiteracy rate (%) 1997	Under-5 mortality rate (per 1,000) 1997
			Male	Female		
Low income (≤US$760)	63	520	62	64	42	97
Middle income (US$761–9,360)	94	2,950	66	72	16	42
High income (≥US$9,361)	54	25,510	74	81	—	7

Source: Adapted from World Bank (2000a), tables 1 and 2.

Table 2

Income inequalities within six selected countries

Country	Survey year	Ranked GNP per capita 1998 (of 210)	% share of income or consumption		Gini index
			Lowest 20%	Highest 20%	
Denmark	1992	6	9.6[a]	34.5[a]	24.7[a]
USA	1997	10	5.2[a]	46.4[a]	30.5[a]
United Kingdom	1991	22	6.6[a]	43.0[a]	36.1[a]
Niger	1995	204	2.6	53.3	50.5
Ethiopia	1995	210	7.1	47.7	62.9
Tanzania	1993	210	6.8	45.5	38.2

Source: Adapted from World Bank (2000a), table 5; and (2000b), table 2.8.

inequalities are reflected in the kinds of access which people have to water and domestic energy to meet their most basic needs.

The Availability of Water and Domestic Energy Sources

During the past 100 years the population of the world has tripled. Over the same period fresh water extracted for human use has increased sixfold (Cosgrove and Rijsberman 2000) and the rate of worldwide energy use has increased ninefold (Royal Commission on Environmental Pollution 2000).

Yet in poorer countries with subsistence economies based largely on biomass production "households typically do not have the easy access to household energy and water that are standard for households in industrialized countries" (Hanna and Munasinghe 1995: 23).

Problems in finding access to sources of water and domestic energy are compounded by their uneven distribution, both in space and time. Water availability varies spatially on a global and a national scale. Most of the world's readily accessible supplies of fresh water are concentrated in the industrialized countries which account for only about a fifth of the global population. Currently, 166 million people are living in 18 countries estimated to be suffering from water scarcity, defined as less than 1,000 cubic metres of water available per person each year. There are 270 million more people living in an additional 11 countries experiencing water stress, with less than 1,700 cubic metres per person per year. The worst-off areas tend to be arid or semi-arid regions, rapidly growing coastal zones and the huge megacities of the developing world (World Bank 2000a).

The types of energy source available in different geographical areas depend upon both natural and economic factors. In 1995, 90 per cent of primary energy supply came from fossil fuels, 40 per cent oil, 28 per cent solid fuels and 22 per cent gas. The remaining 10 per cent came from nuclear, hydropower and other renewable sources. Between 1971 and 1995 the global final demand for electricity increased by 147 per cent and electricity now accounts for 25 per cent of energy consumption. But the provision of electricity infrastructure to bring supplies to rural areas requires a level of capital investment beyond the reach of many developing countries. Despite the increasing amount of electricity generated, some 2 billion people worldwide have no access to electricity in their homes and are consequently without means for refrigeration and electric lighting (Royal Commission on Environmental Pollution 2000). Poorer households, particularly in rural areas, have to rely on fuel-wood, dung, agricultural residues or charcoal for burning to produce the energy they need. In 1996 these "traditional" fuels accounted for 19.5 per cent of total energy use in low-income economies. In high-income economies the figure was only 2.4 per cent (World Bank 2000b).

Access to Domestic Water and Energy Supplies

In the United States and Europe, where potable water is used for flushing lavatories, watering gardens and washing dishes, clothes and cars, residents use an average of 400 litres and 200 litres per person per day respectively. In contrast, in parts of sub-Saharan Africa residential use rates are around 10 to 20 litres a day (Cosgrove and Rijsberman 2000). But even where water is in short supply, richer residents are able to pay the increased costs of meeting their needs.

On a local scale, disparities in access to utilities between rich and poor are sharpened by their high visibility. "Poor people not only note that their communities are worse off, but that the politics surrounding the provision of infrastructure and public services frequently reinforce these inequalities.

Table 3

Some comparative prices for water from different sources

Location	US$ per cubic metre	Source
USA	0.40–0.80	pipes
Lima, Peru	0.15	pipes in central city
	3.00	vendors on city margins
Jakarta, Indonesia	0.09–0.50	pipes supplying <25% population
	1.80	tanker trucks
	1.50–2.50	private vendors
Port-au-Prince, Haiti	1.00	pipes
	5.50–16.50	mobile vendors

Source: Adapted from Cosgrove and Rijsberman (2000).

They often express a sense of having been abandoned or forsaken by their governments" (Narayan *et al.* 2000: 81). Visibility is especially marked in urban areas where poorer households often have to pay more for access to any utilities that do exist. Narayan *et al.* quote a respondent from Ho Chi Minh City in Vietnam: "Water and electricity connection charges depend on how far houses are from the main lines, which are situated on the thoroughfares. As a result, most poor families, who live on small alleyways far from the street, have to pay more" (Narayan *et al.* 2000: 83).

Water and sanitation in urban areas

In a total population of around 5 billion, 3 billion people live in low-income countries with high rates of urban growth (Kinnersley 1994). In 1994, at least 220 million urban dwellers lacked access to clean drinking water. While 80 per cent of high-income urban residents in less developed countries have piped water supplies, only 18 per cent of low-income households are connected and their supplies are often shared (World Bank 2000a).

Even in major cities, public supplies of piped water may be absent or of poor quality, needing treatment before use. In such cases people rely on other sources of drinking water, ranging from luxury bottled mineral water to filtered ground water supplied by mobile vendors using bottles or trucks. The latter can be of very poor quality but, as shown in table 3, water quality is not necessarily reflected in price (Cosgrove and Rijsberman 2000).

More than half of the population has no sanitation and over the past ten years, provision has failed to keep up with population growth. In 1990, 2.6 billion people lacked adequate sanitation and this figure had risen to 3.3 billion in the year 2000 (Cosgrove and Rijsberman 2000). Even in densely populated urban areas in 1994, over 400 million people lacked access to "even the simplest latrines" (World Bank 2000a: 140). "About a third of the people in Manila, Kuala Lumpur, Bangkok, Jakarta and Dacca are estimated

Table 4

Water withdrawals by sector

	Domestic (%)	Industrial (%)	Agricultural (%)
Low-income countries	4	5	91
High-income countries	14	47	39

Source: Kinnersley (1994): 181.

to occupy informal settlements with little or no access to sewerage systems or, in many cases, even clean water" (Kinnersley 1994: 190).

Water and sanitation in rural areas

Some 70 per cent of the poorest people in developing countries live in rural areas and even where village wells exist shortages can still occur during the dry season. Hardly any part of India has a reliable 24-hour water supply (Kinnersley 1994). The problem is compounded by the fact that, for households dependent on subsistence crop and livestock production, domestic use of water has to compete with the need to use water for irrigation and stock watering. Table 4 shows that while 14 per cent of water abstracted in high-income countries is used for domestic purposes, the figure is only 4 per cent for low-income countries.

Domestic energy in urban areas

In developing countries the main consumers of commercially produced energy are a minority of the population, those living in cities and those with high personal incomes. Access to energy supplies in colder or temperate countries is usually related to the need for heating but in warmer climates energy is still needed for cooking and lighting. Electricity in towns and cities is seen as a priority both for home use and for lighting local streets to improve personal safety and security (Narayan *et al.* 2000). Electricity and other fuels are generally available in urban areas but access depends very much on the ability of households to pay. Ironically, the poorest households are likely to place least demand on urban electricity supplies as they have few electrical appliances to run.

Domestic energy in rural areas

In rural areas, and in the "informal" sectors in cities, the poorest people in developing countries are largely dependent on local biomass for their survival (Redclift 1996). Domestic energy is generated from firewood but this resource is becoming increasingly scarce in many regions. The reasons for scarcity vary enormously. In some villages in Sri Lanka, for example,

58

deforestation has reduced the natural supply of domestic fuel (Narayan *et al.* 2000). In Tanzania, access to firewood by local populations has been limited by changes in land use and ownership, designed to protect and preserve natural forest reserves and game parks. In Western Kenya the problem is complicated by social, economic and cultural traditions and practices which deny women the right to grow their own firewood or to collect wood from the trees on family farms. Where no other fuel is available women must rely on less energy-efficient brushwood collected from hedgerows and small shrubs (Bradley and Huby 1993). Alternatively, in many rural and some urban situations money must be found to purchase firewood, or other more expensive fuels such as kerosene. Electricity in many rural areas is not perceived as a realistic concept. Even if it was available, its price would put it out of the reach of most poor rural dwellers (Narayan *et al.* 2000).

Social Problems Caused by Lack of Domestic Water and Energy

Inadequate access to water for drinking, cooking, bathing and cleaning, and to energy for heating, cooking and lighting gives rise to a number of social problems associated with poverty. Indeed, the lack of these vital utilities must be regarded as an acute form of deprivation by any standards. Not only does it threaten health and physical well-being but it affects gender relations and population patterns. The financial hardship that it both reflects and reinforces has severe repercussions on household livelihoods and family relationships.

Effects on health are perhaps the most starkly obvious. It has been estimated that 13 million children under five die each year from poor sanitation and diseases linked to poverty (Redclift 1996). "Dirty water and dirty air are major causes of diarrhea and respiratory infections, the two biggest killers of poor children" (World Bank 2000b: 111).

Millions of people die each year from contaminated drinking water, mostly in low- and middle-income countries. Water-related diseases were responsible for 3–4 million deaths in 1998, more than half of these among children (World Health Organization 1999). Access to clean drinking water and sanitation are closely linked. Where water is in short supply, pollution by human waste is more likely to occur. The consequent health hazards are due not only to diseases such as malaria and dengue fever, spread by water-related vectors, but also other water-borne diseases transmitted in sewage. The World Bank estimates that at any given time almost half the urban population in developing countries may be suffering from one or more of these diseases and makes very clear the links with poverty. "In Jakarta, a poor resident typically pays 10 times more than a rich resident does for a litre of clean water and suffers 2 to 4 times more gastroenteritis, typhoid and malaria" (World Bank 2000a: 141).

Health impacts of inadequate access to safe and efficient forms of domestic energy are borne most heavily by women. The time they spend in the kitchen makes them vulnerable to the effects of indoor air pollution from smoky biomass fuel, burned in chimney-less kitchens. In many developing cities,

59

conditions can be worse than in rural areas. "Poor urban dwellers are likely to be exposed to additional air pollution from inadequate, badly ventilated cooking facilities and to further outdoor pollution from industrial sites" (World Bank 2000a: 142). But shortage of fuel for cooking has an impact on other family members. A study of poor rural households in Western Kenya found that at times of acute shortage, women were forced to change their cooking practices. They provided fewer cooked meals, chose foodstuffs with shorter cooking times, or cooked in bulk on the morning fire so that meals only required briefly heating up later in the day (Huby 1990).

Personal physical safety is often an issue for women and children who are responsible for fuel and water collection in rural areas. As supplies dwindle, the need to travel further from home increases risks from injury due to rough terrain, falling boulders or even from wild animals. Piped supplies in urban areas can pose problems caused by inadequate infrastructure and lack of maintenance. "In Ulugbek, Uzbekistan discussion groups say that when there is no water pressure in their pipes, people have to go to slippery and polluted drainage ditches" (Narayan et al. 2000). In poor areas, it is not uncommon to find electricity supplies obtained through illegal "hookups", often involving unsafe connections and tangles of bare wires.

The daily hardships resulting from the time and energy needed for water and wood collection place burdens on women who already have many other household responsibilities. Several hours a day are needed depending on levels of availability of water and fuel that vary, often unpredictably, with weather patterns and competition from other uses. In some areas, such as rural Ecuador, the growing migration of men to towns to find work adds further to women's responsibilities (Narayan et al. 2000). Although there is a paucity of data on the effort intensity of fuel and water collection and other tasks carried out by women, Jackson and Palmer-Jones (1999) suggest that the pressures are likely to be reflected in longer-term health outcomes. It is possible that in some cases, these may be complicated by increased repro-ductive effort. "As the community's natural resources are depleted, more hands are needed to gather fuel and water for daily use. More children are then produced, further damaging the local resource base and in turn providing the 'household' with an incentive to enlarge. When this happens, poverty, fertility and environmental degradation reinforce one another in an escalating spiral" (Dasgupta 1995: 156).

The time taken to carry water and fuel competes with time needed for other productive activities and can have economic consequences for rural households. Especially in times of shortage, water for household use com-petes with water needed for the crops and animals on which subsistence and livelihoods depend. Financial hardship and lack of access to utilities have a reflexive relationship. It is low-income households and families who have the biggest problems in obtaining water and domestic energy, and it is these people who often have to pay more for supplies. As shown in table 3, poorer households without access to piped water supplies can pay up to 20 times more for a litre of water than better-off households. Even when supplies do not actually cost more, pressures on household budgets can render adequate water and energy inaccessible, especially to the most vulnerable.

Environmental Impacts

Today's problems, under current patterns of energy and water use are likely to get worse, not better. Not only are inequalities in access likely to persist, but the environmental impacts of increased consumption will hit the poorest people hardest.

Burning coal and other fuels for domestic energy causes air pollution harmful to health, especially that of women and children. But it is also the carbon dioxide emitted during the combustion of fossil fuels that makes the greatest contribution to the enhanced greenhouse effect, largely responsible for global warming and climate change. The major adverse effects of climate change on the natural world and human society are well documented (Department of the Environment, Transport and the Regions 1998; Royal Commission on Environmental Pollution 2000). If no preventative action is taken, temperature increases of 1–3.5°C are predicted to occur by the year 2100. Sea levels will rise by 15–95 cm, flooding low-lying areas, increasing erosion of soft rocks, destroying many protective coral reefs and mangroves, and threatening island economies such as the Maldives. Especially at risk are deltas like the Nile and the Ganges. These regions are highly populated and the number of people affected by flooding is predicted to increase from 13 million to 94 million a year by 2080, leading to needs for large-scale migration and resettlement (Royal Commission on Environmental Pollution 2000).

Changes in climatic conditions will affect the range and dispersion of many non-human organisms, including disease vectors such as mosquitoes. They will also alter the kinds of plant species able to thrive in different areas, in some cases jeopardizing forestry and agricultural production. The inherent variability in weather systems makes it difficult to predict exact effects in particular regions. Nevertheless, assuming some global improvement in energy efficiency and some shift away from fossil fuel use, the Intergovernmental Panel for Climate Change predicts large-scale die-back of tropical forests in South America and southern Africa with additional forest growth in parts of North America, northern Asia and China. While cereal crop yields are likely to increase at these high to middle latitudes, they will be reduced in Africa, the Middle East and India (Royal Commission on Environmental Pollution 2000).

Deforestation and changing patterns of rainfall and heat evaporation caused by climate change affect the hydrological cycle and water table levels so that environmental impacts of human energy use combine with the effects of increasing levels of freshwater abstraction. Over-abstraction of water is already a problem in many areas. In Mexico City, for example, ground water is pumped out at rates 40 per cent faster than the natural recharge rate. Over-pumping of ground water in Bangkok is leading to problems of building subsidence (Kinnersley 1994). Many rivers are drying up and over half of the world's wetlands were destroyed during the twentieth century. Further linkages between energy and water use are vividly illustrated by the argument of Cosgrove and Rijsberman (2000) that it is the unregulated access of people using affordable small pumps, powered by subsidized electricity and diesel, that is to blame for the lowering of the water table in some areas.

Abstraction affects watersheds, aquifers, wetlands, rivers and lakes in terms of water quantity but flooding, salination, siltation and pollution also affect water quality. Seasonal flooding increases the risks of contamination of fresh water by sewage and other pollutants, especially in densely populated urban areas. As well as causing problems for human health, ecosystems are damaged to such an extent that many streams and rivers running through major cities are dead or dying. Biodiversity losses are widespread and, worldwide, 20 per cent of freshwater fish species are classified as vulnerable, endangered or extinct (Cosgrove and Rijsberman 2000). Additional effects on food production include rising costs as agricultural demand for water, currently responsible for 70–80 per cent of abstractions, competes increasingly with water for industrial and domestic use.

The potential for political conflict to occur where neighbouring countries compete for water supplies is noted by the World Bank (2000a). Almost 47 per cent of the earth's land area, excluding Antarctica, covers water basins shared by two or more countries. In the Middle East, growing populations are already putting pressure on limited supplies of fresh water, described as "more valuable than oil" (Hinrichsen 1990: 42).

It is clear that the adverse environmental impacts of energy and water consumption are not evenly distributed. In the tropics, for example, the regional effects of climate change are likely to be more severe for the farmers, pastoralists and fishermen who rely directly on natural resources for subsistence. Many of the world's poorest people live in areas with fragile ecosystems, susceptible to the worst effects of environmental degradation—on flood plains, swampy land, steep hillsides, in drought-prone areas or near to industrial sites. These are the very people least likely to have the income or capacity to enable them to make adequate adaptive responses to the effects of environmental change.

> Poor people are often more vulnerable to environmental changes because they use natural resources directly and because they have fewer alternative ways to earn income, fewer places to live, and fewer mechanisms for coping with shocks. And the rural poor are vulnerable because they often live on marginal land and in unstable housing—places most susceptible to natural disasters and extreme weather. (World Bank 2000b)

On a larger scale, poorer parts of the world are affected more than richer regions. The predicted effects of climate change include a reduction in gross domestic product of 2–9 per cent for less developed countries, compared to only 1.0–1.5 per cent for industrialized countries. Most of the world's biodiversity is concentrated in developing countries so its loss will also be felt there hardest (World Bank 2000a). These countries, then, have a strong interest in protecting the environment, but they are the least able to pay the price, especially if this means slower economic progress. Environmental change is likely to require drastic alterations in land use and the way of life of their citizens, hardship, economic disruption and a growth in numbers of environmental refugees. Economic, social and political stability is at risk, and environmental protection must necessarily be linked to the elimination of poverty and changes in the international economic system.

The Environment, Poverty and Economic Growth

The need for shifts in thinking, analysis and policy making to deal with problems of sustainable resource use on a global scale can be justified for reasons of self-interest or because of wider concern for people and the environment. On the one hand, we might be concerned about social and environmental progress in the developing world because of the global effects it is likely to have on our own. Sustainable energy policies are of crucial importance for mitigating the impact of climate change. Increasing numbers of people mean more demand for energy and higher living standards mean more consumption. In addition, deforestation in the Amazon alone is estimated at 10,000 square kilometres a year, destroying a significant "sink" for carbon sequestration. "The Amazon . . . contains one-fifth of the globe's fresh water resources and half of the tropical forest. The population of the Brazilian Amazon, currently 17 million, is increasing at over a million a year. Because of the scale and global importance of the Amazon region, the decisions made by one country, Brazil, carry implications for the rest of humanity" (Redclift 1996: 100). On the other hand, it is the developed nations with less than a fifth of the world's population, that are responsible for three-fifths of current carbon emissions. "Patterns of consumption are driven by effective demand in the North; but the outcome of increased consumption, in the form of changes in climate and loss of biodiversity, is felt throughout the globe" (Redclift and Benton 1994: 15).

The nature of environmental problems demands global action. But global redistributive justice requires that the urgent and immediate social needs of poorer nations are recognized and taken into account. Current international agreements for reducing carbon emissions under the Kyoto Protocol place no commitments on developing countries. The rationale is that their industrial and developmental processes should not be constrained, especially energy production and consumption (Galeotti and Lanzo 1999). But if these countries are not included in internationally binding agreements on emissions, there is a danger that total greenhouse gas outputs will increase significantly over the next 20 years. "Developing countries will need to be more closely involved in these international efforts to cut emissions, in a way that recognises the common and differentiated responsibilities of all countries to act, the principle of equity and the need of developing countries to grow" (Department of Environment, Transport and the Regions 1998). Deciding exactly *how* responsibilities should be differentiated to reflect different levels of need for economic growth is currently exercising the minds of the policy makers involved in international negotiations.

Short-term alleviation of poverty could doubtless be promoted by the improved provision of water and sanitation and expansions in labour-saving technologies using fossil fuels. Some authors might consider the environmental costs of such development as worth paying. "We can see in such arguments the possibility that exploiting the environment in the short term may be a necessary evil in the transformations of poverty reduction" (Jackson and Palmer-Jones 1999: 577). Others, however, recognize the long-term benefits of balancing social demands for growth in the use of natural resources with their environmental impacts and see this as achievable through innovation in the ways that utilities are provided. "Sustainable electricity must be available to all, reliably, at an affordable cost. It must not impose an unacceptable burden on the environment, either locally, regionally or globally. It must be compatible with politically tolerable processes of control" (Patterson 1999: 170). Others see the problem also as one of management. "There is a water crisis today. But the crisis is not about having too little water to satisfy our needs. It is a crisis of managing water so badly that billions of people—and the environment—suffer badly" (Cosgrove and Rijsberman 2000: xix).

The extent of poverty and need for basic utilities is so extreme in many low-income countries, there is little wonder that their overriding priorities are to achieve economic development and alleviate poverty. We have a situation where economic stagnation is reinforcing social inequalities in the ability of people to meet their basic needs for energy and water. But, ironically, economic growth may actually serve to exacerbate problems of availability by increasing pressures on natural resources, as higher living standards in some sectors of the population lead to higher levels of consumption.

Economic growth is associated with increased use of domestic water, but the global average availability of renewable water supply per person is projected to fall from 6,600 cubic metres in the year 2000 to 4,800 in 2025. The patchy distribution of this decline in water availability means that 3 billion people will be living in countries having less than 1,700 cubic metres per capita per year, the level defined as constituting "water stress". The impact of water stress is likely to be felt most in urban areas where human use of water is intensive, and in rural areas during dry seasons when limited sources must be used (Cosgrove and Rijsberman 2000).

Economic growth is also strongly associated with increased energy demand. Increasing affluence and the extension of electricity supplies leads to increasing household demand as people use more, and more varied, electrical appliances. By 1992, 67 per cent of households in China were connected to mains electricity. Since 1978, the number of electric fans in the country has increased 20-fold and the number of washing machines has risen from almost none to 97 million (Redclift 1996). Carbon emissions from energy use in developing countries are forecast to grow on average by 3.2 per cent a year between 2000 and 2020, compared with growth of only 1.3 per cent for industrialized countries. Galeotti and Lanzo (1999) show that developing countries with high populations and low GDP per capita are most likely to show steep increases in emissions. By 2050, energy consumption in the less developed countries is projected to be more than twice that of OECD countries, even though per capita consumption will remain much lower (World Bank 2000a). Is it possible to reduce global consumption of energy and water while ensuring that the poor have sufficient to meet their needs?

Markets and State Welfare

The World Bank (2000a) argues that there are benefits in treating utilities as economic goods and setting prices to reflect the economic and environmental costs of provision. Such a strategy can be an efficient way to reduce consumption. As difficulties in fetching fuel and water, or paying others to perform this service, get greater, people have an incentive to use less. This is good for the environment but carries short-term costs borne disproportionately by the poor.

In industrialized countries market-based instruments to protect the environment can, to some degree, be socially sustainable if welfare systems are used to compensate poorer households for high fuel and water charges. This is not easy to achieve in practice and is especially problematic in countries where state welfare is less extensive or non-existent. The slowing of economic and social progress in the developing world in general has been accompanied by a decline in effectively operating social assistance. The poorest countries are in the grip of foreign debt, and their situations have not been helped by the structural adjustment programmes imposed by the International Monetary Fund. Civil strife, border conflicts, climatic adversity and the increasing incidence of HIV and Aids can all act to limit economic progress and aggravate the deterioration of social conditions. Even in countries where gains have been achieved, their uneven distribution has led to "distorted development" (Midgley 1997). State welfare programmes that do exist are often limited to people in regular waged employment and exclude people living in rural areas or in the "informal" urban sector.

If we accept that, at least at low levels of use, water and energy should be regarded as social goods, then market mechanisms are not the best way of allocating them. This is particularly true when it is difficult or impossible to provide social assistance to offset the effects of full cost pricing on the poor. This is not to say that market-based instruments should not have a role to play in providing incentives to reduce consumption of energy and water. Some existing energy subsidies are highly regressive and bring neither social nor environmental benefits, but carbon taxation could pay huge environmental dividends and provide revenue for improving social assistance schemes (Royal Commission on Environmental Pollution 2000).

Forms of Utility Provision

Meeting the social objective of improving access of poor households to energy and water supplies is hindered not only by a lack of funds and resources for extended welfare programmes but also by inadequate availability and distribution infrastructure. Dasgupta (1995) argues the need for public policies to provide cheap fuel and infrastructures to supply potable water.

Centralized networked services offer economies of scale in areas of high population density but the high capital investment required and the high up-front costs of delivery and collection make their introduction problematic. In the case of sewerage, for example, "the high-cost, centralized sewerage systems used throughout industrialized countries are not feasible in developing

65

cities that have no sewerage service at all" (World Bank 2000a: 148). Patterson presents a similar argument against the expansion of large-scale, centrally controlled electricity generating plants. "The traditional configuration . . . has left two billion people without electricity. Extending it to reach them is impossible on grounds of cost and logistics alone, to say nothing of the implications for the environment or politically tolerable control. Traditional electricity is not and cannot be sustainable" (1999: 170).

The World Bank (2000a) notes the poor performance to date of the public sector in providing essential services in less developed countries. The public sector is often the monopoly provider of water, sewerage, electricity and gas, but if it falls short private companies and individuals offer utility services on "an ad hoc basis, outside the reach of formal rules—a situation that creates many dilemmas and inefficiencies" (World Bank 2000a: 144). The World Development Report 2000 argues that public provision of services in urban areas of industrialized countries succeeded initially because it served the interests of wealthier residents who could not otherwise escape the effects of unhealthy living conditions. Now, however, advances in medicine and technology allow wealthy citizens of developing countries to do just that. The development of portable generators and water pumps, water filters and bottled water, vacuum trucks and septic tanks allow them to take individual action to mitigate the shortcomings of public service provision. The investment of richer households in their own private systems, with modern showers, flush lavatories, washing machines, refrigerators and air conditioning, constitutes a form of unregulated privatization. Not only is this economically inefficient, but it also weakens any impetus to improve the public systems for the benefit of the wider community.

One of the strengths of developing countries is that they often have well-established informal systems for social welfare. These operate through social networks and can be highly organized and closely regulated by traditional culture and practice (Midgley 1997). The existence of such systems forms a good base for community development at a local level. Community initiatives can incorporate methods of providing and managing utilities which differ from the conventional forms of provision and management dominating the western industrialized world. The idea that empowered communities could work together to obtain secure and equitable access to utilities, and ensure that the costs and benefits are fairly distributed, is an attractive one. "Improving poor people's control over the environment usually gives them a strong motivation to protect it . . . win-win solutions start with the assumption that the poor are part of the solution, not the source of the problem" (United Nations Development Programme 2000: 99).

However, there are problems confronting community development and resource-management initiatives revolving around participation and power. There is, for example, no guarantee that the short-term interests of a particular user group will not conflict with the interests of long-term environmental resource stewardship (Hanna 1995). Or that any improved earning potential accruing to some participants will be used to benefit the whole community.

A study of the Australian Government's initiative for a water reform package found that fair decision-making processes are of paramount importance to community acceptance of water allocation decisions and that water markets alone are not considered fair or acceptable processes for allocating or re-allocating water (Syme *et al.* 1999). The notion of "fairness" does need to be culturally agreed but it does not seem unreasonable to suggest that these conclusions might be extrapolated to other countries and to energy as well as water. In the context of poorly developed infrastructure for state utility provision, failure of the market to deal with distribution inequities, and lack of formal social welfare schemes, an alternative way forward is needed in which the utilities are managed fairly for the public good and for the environment and future generations.

Future Prospects

Notwithstanding the criticisms levelled at market mechanisms for allocating water and domestic energy services, private provision is increasing rapidly. The International Forum for Utility Regulation (2000) refers to "the wave of infrastructure privatization that has been sweeping the world over the past decade or so". Even the self-provision of utility services by a community, often with help from a non-governmental organization (NGO), can be construed as a form of privatization in which property rights are shared by a group of individuals.

For social and environmental protection to be ensured, attention must be paid to the accountability of these institutions. Just as regulation is crucial for the socially just and environmentally sustainable management of privatized utility services in the UK (Hills *et al.* 1997), it is essential that the government sector in developing countries takes on an enhanced regulatory role. Some current water and energy projects are proving successful in helping some households out of poverty, but they are often ignored by municipal authority planners. Nevertheless, "around the world, governments are transforming their roles from the exclusive financiers and providers of infrastructure services to the facilitators and regulators of services provided by private firms" (World Bank 2000c). There is a real need for more strategic partnerships to be developed between the public, private and community sectors, recognizing and adding legitimacy to local cooperative ventures (World Bank 2000a).

The World Bank position is predicated on the notion that lower-income countries can learn from the experiences of wealthier nations in adopting policies and technologies to alleviate poverty while avoiding risks to the environment. The process is aided by greater access to information and markets and new ways of doing business. Together with policies for liberalization, deregulation and privatization these are seen as aspects of globalization that have "stimulated growth and prosperity and expanded possibilities for millions of people all over the world" (United Nations General Assembly 2000: 2). But, as the United Nations report points out, benefits accruing from globalization are far from evenly distributed. Many groups of people and countries are finding themselves even further marginalized. The danger of following development paths advocated by the World Bank is that they will lead to deeper social inequalities (Kaivo-oja 1999).

A further criticism of the Bank's position is that it relies on the, far from certain, notion that economic growth is positively correlated with poverty reduction, ignoring the lessons to be drawn from industrialized nations. ÿyen (2000) points to the example of the United States with its many poor and homeless people. It is all very well to argue that the governments of developing countries should be doing more to address social and environmental problems related to water and domestic energy. But adequate policy mechanisms to resolve social and environmental concerns in utility provision in richer industrialized countries have not yet been developed successfully.

The scale of the problem is greater in the low-income countries with the fewest resources to deal with it. Many developing nations are locked into particular relationships with other forms of global organization—financial debt arrangements, international markets and trade agreements, and mass production processes—that combine with internal economic and political constraints to limit their options for sustainable development. They may also face opposition from powerful groups whose interests are not served by putting social and environmental issues at the top of the political agenda. The real questions to be addressed go beyond economics and concern current imbalances of power on a global scale. It is unlikely that real change can come about without some potentially uncomfortable shifts in ideas about the environment, global responsibility and redistributive justice.

References

Bradley, P. N. and Huby, M. (eds) (1993), *Woodfuel, Women and Woodlots Volume 2: The Kenya Woodfuel Development Programme*, London: Macmillan.

Cahill, M. (2001), *The Environment and Social Policy*, London: Routledge.

Cosgrove, W. J. and Rijsberman, F. R. (2000), *World Water Vision: Making Water Everybody's Business*, Report for the World Water Council, London: Earthscan.

Dasgupta, P. (1995), Poverty, population and the environment. In S. Hanna and M. Munasinghe (eds), *Property Rights and the Environment: Social and Ecological Issues*, Stockholm: Beijer Institute/Washington: World Bank, pp. 141–64.

Department of Environment, Transport and the Regions (1998), *UK Climate Change Programme*, London: Stationery Office.

Galeotti, M. and Lanzo, A. (1999), Richer and cleaner? A study on carbon dioxide emissions in developing countries, *Energy Policy*, 27: 565–73.

George, V. and Wilding, P. (1999), *British Society and Social Welfare: Towards a Sustainable Society*, Basingstoke: Macmillan.

Hanna, S. (1995), Efficiencies of user participation in natural resource management. In S. Hanna and M. Munasinghe (eds), *Property Rights and the Environment: Social and Ecological Issues*, Stockholm: Beijer Institute/Washington: World Bank, pp. 59–68.

Hanna, S. and Munasinghe, M. (eds) (1995), *Property Rights and the Environment: Social and Ecological Issues*, Stockholm: Beijer Institute/Washington: World Bank.

Hills, B., Huby, M. and Kenway, P. (1997), *Fair and Sustainable: Paying for Water*, London: New Policy Institute.

Hinrichsen, D. (1990), *Our Common Seas*, London: Earthscan.

Huby, M. (1990), *Where You Can't See the Wood for the Trees*, Stockholm: Beijer Institute/Stockholm Environment Institute.

Huby, M. (1998), *Social Policy and the Environment*, Buckingham: Open University Press.

International Forum for Utility Regulation (2000), www.worldbank.org/html/fdp/psd/ifur/index.html (accessed 13 January 2001).

Jackson, C. and Palmer-Jones, R. (1999), Rethinking gendered poverty and work, *Development and Change*, 30: 557–83.

Kaivo-oja, J. (1999), Alternative scenarios of social development, *Sustainable Development*, 7: 140–50.

Kinnersley, D. (1994), *Coming Clean: The Politics of Water and the Environment*, Bungay, Suffolk: Penguin.

McKean, M. A. (2000), Common property: what is it? what is it good for, and what makes it work? In C. C. Gibson, M. A. McKean and E. Ostrom (eds), *People and Forests*, London: MIT Press, pp. 27–55.

Midgley, J. (1997), *Social Welfare in Global Context*, London: Sage.

Narayan, D., Chambers, R., Shah, M. K. and Petesch, P. (2000), *Voices of the Poor: Crying Out for Change*, World Bank, New York: Oxford University Press.

Patterson, W. (1999), *Transforming Electricity*, London: Earthscan.

Redclift, M. (1996), *Wasted: Counting the Costs of Global Consumption*, London: Earthscan.

Redclift, M. and Benton, T. (eds) (1994), *Social Theory and the Global Environment*, London: Routledge.

Royal Commission on Environmental Pollution (2000), *Twenty-second Report: Energy— the Changing Climate*, Cm 4749, London: Stationery Office.

Syme, G. J., Nancarrow, B. E. and McCreddin, J. A. (1999), Defining the components of fairness in the allocation of water to environmental and human uses, *Journal of Environmental Management*, 57: 51–70.

United Nations Development Programme (1999), *Human Development Report 1999*, New York: Oxford University Press.

United Nations Development Programme (2000), *Overcoming Human Poverty: UNDP Poverty Report 2000*, New York: Oxford University Press.

United Nations General Assembly (2000), *Impact of Globalization on Social Development*, Report of the Secretary-General A/AC.253/25.

World Bank (2000a), *Entering the 21st Century: World Development Report 1999/2000*, New York: Oxford University Press.

World Bank (2000b), *World Development Indicators 2000*, Washington: Oxford University Press.

World Bank (2000c), *Private Participation in Infrastructure*, www.worldbank.org/html/fpd/privatesector/ppi.htm (accessed 13 January 2001).

World Health Organization (1999), *World Health Report 1999*, Geneva: World Health Organization.

ÿyen, E. (2000), *Six Questions to the World Bank on the World Bank Development Report 2000/2001: Attacking Poverty*, Comparative Research Programme on Poverty (CROP) www.crop.org/wdrcom.htm (accessed 13 January 2001).

CHAPTER 6

Food, Social Policy and the Environment: Towards a New Model

Tim Lang, David Barling and Martin Caraher

Abstract

Food policy is high on the public policy agenda, but still suffers from a lack of overview and integration. The paper reviews examples of policy limitations where tighter and more explicit links could usefully be made between environmental, social and public health considerations. The paper proposes a new ecological health approach to public policy. This offers marked advantages over the present "productionist" approach to food policy. With this old policy regime in crisis, the paper reviews current moves towards adoption of the ecological health model in Britain, Europe and globally.

Keywords

Food policy; Food system; Food poverty; Food safety; Public health; Ecology; Governance

Introduction: Food Crises and the Pressure for a New Food Policy

By the turn of the new millennium, the fact that UK food and agriculture policy was in some difficulties had become increasingly apparent. For the two previous decades, a series of health scandals and problems had questioned the seeming impregnability of the postwar food and agricultural framework. A catalogue of food scandals or "scares" dented the productionist food and agricultural policy put in place by the Attlee Labour government in the 1947 Agriculture Act (Lang 1999a).

The list of crises since the 1980s is long: additives, pesticide residues, nitrate residues, BST (bovine somatotrophin), Alar (a plant growth inhibitor used on apples), food irradiation, patulin in apple juice, BSE, *Salmonella* in eggs (not to mention rising *Campylobacter*, *E coli 0157* and other food poisoning), the introduction of genetically modified (GM) foods, variant Creutzfeld-Jakob

Address for correspondence: *Professor Tim Lang, Centre for Food Policy, Thames Valley University, St Mary's Road, Ealing, London, W5 5RF. Email: tim.lang@tvu.ac.uk.*

Disease (CJD), swine vesicular disease, and in 2001 foot and mouth disease (FMD). The last is an exception to the more general rule that such crises have centred on possible direct effects on human safety. FMD may have engendered a crisis but it was not primarily for human health.

This litany of safety concerns has dominated the public agenda and helped frame the public policy debate but it tended to shroud other equally or arguably more serious food-related problems. For the purpose of this paper, such issues can be grouped as stemming from four policy areas: health, environment, social and economic policy.

With regard to health, evidence mounted from the 1950s, with the work of pioneers such as Ancel Keys (Keys 1970), of the link between diet and the rise of degenerative diseases. These include coronary heart disease, some cancers (breast, colon, etc.), diabetes and dental decay. Despite hostility from the powerful food industry—particularly the fats and sugar trades—this evidence was almost impossible to refute (Cannon 1992). By the 1990s, the UK was emulating the USA's pattern of obesity (which is itself a risk factor for heart disease). If the evidence suggested poor or inappropriate diets, the policy choice was to stop promoting them or accept the consequences.

In the realm of environmental policy, evidence also mounted of damage to soil structure, biodiversity, water systems and wildlife, as well as of environmental implications associated with changed lifestyle and shopping patterns. With the food revolution of the post-World War II period, the distance food travels between primary producer and end consumer rises, the so-called "food miles" problem. The bill for these environmental costs is externalized, i.e. not included in the price the consumer pays at the checkout. These costs are borne either by the taxpayer (the consumer with another hat) or, in the case of global climate change, by no one, a legacy for which future generations might not be grateful.

In social policy, evidence mounted again from the 1970s that problems of food poverty—assumed to have been abolished by post-World War II prosperity—had not departed but merely altered (Leather 1996). Research showed that access to shops was not just a matter of income but also of geospatial restructuring of the retail sector (Lang 1997; Marsden et al. 2000). What the Department of Health's Low Income Project Team, in a much quoted phrase, called "food deserts", was alleged to be associated with, if not due to, the collapse of local shops and the rise of supermarkets (DoH 1996).

In economic policy, even as the New Right celebrated the triumph of neo-liberalism and the renewed emphasis on trade-oriented deregulation in the 1980s and 1990s, concerns were re-emerging about remarkable levels of market concentration in the food sector (e.g. Feder 1977; Wrigley 1998). Studies of the impact of transnational corporations (TNCs) and of their control of supply chains suggested that while the nation state was being used to promote a new freedom for business, those most likely to benefit were the larger and better capitalized companies. The global reach of TNCs created a new geospatial politics in which the face of the earth could literally be shrunk (Barnet and Cavanagh 1994).

How has this situation developed? How can a situation where from diverse sources, outside the main citadels of food and agricultural policy, a consensus has emerged that public policy is delivering huge quantities of food (for some) without meeting other public policy goods? In this paper, we argue that a proper understanding of the relationship between social and environmental policy has to centre on the complexity which the post-World War II food revolution has unleashed. From the 1940s it was clear to enough people within the British state that the previous century's experiment with mercantilism—preferential "free" trade within the Empire—was over. First, there was no longer an Empire which could feed the UK, but second, and more importantly, the experience of two world wars had shown that food security could not be guaranteed under blockade conditions. Third, there was, as today, mounting political pressure to end the indignity of food poverty—the hungry 1930s (e.g. Boyd Orr 1936).

From the 1940s on, a food revolution unfolded which within half a century had transformed not just what primary food is grown and how, but how it is processed, distributed and even cooked (Goodman and Redclift 1991). Public policy nurtured and supported this transformation, yet now this revolution is seen to pose a huge challenge. Corporate concentration, at the manufacturing and retail ends, is facilitating private systems of regulation along the food supply chain (Marsden *et al.* 2000). Agrochemical and food manufacturing interests are introducing new technologies into the food system, as for example with biotechnology and the new wave of functional foods. Such developments have stimulated further unrest from consumers, engendering business and regulatory concern about consumer confidence and societal responses to food issues. A new architecture of food governance is emerging with the creation of new national food agencies and new trade bodies changing world food trade rules. In short, the context in which food policy has to be formed is rapidly changing.

Food is an illustration of how and where social policy and environmental policy meet. Our argument is that current public policy lacks any adequate holistic perspective with which to analyse this complex relationship. The analysis of the dynamics of the food system has tended to be partial, narrowly confined to particular policy areas (agriculture or health, environment or industry, trade or development), or specific disciplines (agricultural economics, nutrition, environmental science, medicine, geography, etc.).

In this article we contend that in order to address food policy adequately it is necessary to produce an integrated, long-term strategy that links both the social and the environmental dimensions. Such a strategy needs a fresh conceptual framework for food policy, rooted in what we have termed a new model of ecological public health (Lang and Caraher 2001). Table 1 gives some comparisons of the current production-oriented food policy with that outlined for the new ecological health model. We follow this with a discussion of different levels of governance at which public policy is manifest. The article then explores some key features of food in both social and environmental policy.

Table 1

Some features of the old productionist and new ecological health models of food policy

Key policy feature, by area	"Old" productionist model	"New" ecological health model
Economic policy	Increase production and supply by application of science and capital. Consumers have right to choose.	Reducing inequality by state action provides health safety net. Citizenship requires both skills and protection.
Health policy	Health stems from prosperity, availability and some equity of distribution; rising prosperity makes health services affordable.	Population approach; ill health stems from entire supply chain; degenerative diseases suggest how food is grown and delivered is important.
Environment policy	Should not dislocate market forces; long supply chain; global reach for affluent consumers.	Has to be built into food practices; short supply chains where possible; bioregionalism for all?
Social policy	Family responsibility; plus welfare safety net.	Population approach; the state applies correctives to imbalances between individual and social forces.
Morality	Individuals should be responsible for food within market rules.	Societal responsibility should be based on citizenship.
Price policy	Cheapness of food may externalize costs.	It is false accounting if costs are externalized to other budget headings; costs should be internalized where possible.
Policy coordination	Primacy of economics; fragmented specialist decision making.	Social goals as significant as other policy goals; new mechanisms for integration.

Towards a New Model of Food and Public Policy

Although food policy is in crisis in the UK, there have been two levels of response: national and regional.

At the national level, many European countries began to set up food agencies from the late 1990s. These included the UK, France, Finland and Greece, with the Netherlands debating whether to do so (Lang *et al.* 1997). Agencies were presented as the way both to win consumer confidence in food governance and to take food safety standards out of political influence. The UK Food Standards Agency (FSA) began work in April 2000 and was

73

committed to ensuring a 20 per cent drop in food poisoning within five years, an ambitious target (FSA 2001).

At the European regional level, there were positive moves to reform food policy from two sources: the EU itself and the World Health Organization European Region, a much larger area of 51 member states (including the EU). In the late 1990s, a number of initiatives at the European level came to fruition that might balance Europe's currently warped food and agricultural policies, which are heavily oriented to promote the agricultural sector. The first was through the World Health Organization European Region whose 51 member states conducted a four-year consultation process, culminating in a Food and Nutrition Action Plan (WHO-E 2000a) endorsed by all member states at the Regional Committee in September 2000 (WHO-E 2000b). This proposed a five-year process of upgrading food policies to give equal weight to nutrition, food safety and sustainable food supply. The latter is to include social policy objectives such as reducing health inequalities. This process is to be reviewed politically at a ministerial meeting to be held in 2005.

These moves were paralleled within the European Union. In order to address a loss of public confidence in the public process after BSE, on 12 January 2000 the European Commission produced a White Paper on Food Safety which announced a process for introducing a new General Food Law or regulation, a new European Food Authority (EFA), and 84 proposals (including one on nutrition) mostly targeted at improving food safety within the EU (CEC 2000a; Trichopoulou *et al.* 2000). The proposed EFA is intended to start work in 2002 with a budget of 44.4 million euros. Under the French Presidency of the EU (July–December 2000), an 18-month process for modernizing EU policy on food and health produced a new audit of elements for European action (SFSP 2000). The new health and consumer protection Directorate General, DG SANCO, was asked to prepare new initiatives to strengthen and broaden EU food policy. This was agreed on 8 December by social and employment ministers (CEC 2000b). At the same time, a three-year process of setting new pan-EU nutrition guidelines was completed at Crete in May 2000. This Eurodiet Project produced a consensus from specialists from every member state on the need for new EU data-gathering, health-promotion and public policy initiatives (Kafartos and Codrington 2001).

These moves are significant, because within EU circles they represent a shift away from the Common Agricultural Policy's pre-eminence in Brussels and because they represent a willingness to accept that the older productionist policies are inappropriate. The possibility of a broader, more integrated policy is at least on the agenda. The WHO European Region now represents this conceptually in figure 1. This shows health as a roof, under which we all can shelter, as having to stand on three pillars: nutrition, food safety, sustainable food supply. Informally, WHO Geneva HQ is already adding a fourth pillar to this list: healthy lifestyles. We might prefer this to be called something like culture. In a sense, the rather vague notion of "sustainable food supply" ought to include the notion of lifestyle and culture. But if we take supply as distinct from consumption, there is an argument for having a

Figure 1

World Health Organization European Region Policy Model, 2000

Source: WHO-E (2000a).

fourth pillar. Perhaps "sustainable consumption" would be better. Waltner-Toews and Lang (2000) have argued that in fact, if the pillars approach is to be adopted, it ought to acknowledge that there are many more than three pillars. They argue that many factors sustain health. They have argued that the pedestal on which the pillars rest is also very important for health. Figure 2—the impact of food on health in the twenty-first century— represents this. While this may be more complex and accurate, it loses the simplicity and elegance of the WHO-E's three-pillars approach.

Multi-level Food Governance

Part of the complexity of the modern food system is that no one level of governance can even pretend to have control over food supply. Initiatives such as those at the European level are reminders that although crises create huge political and policy challenges for national politicians, they are in fact increasingly matters for international negotiation. Conceptually, the new food

Figure 2

A more complex model of food policy

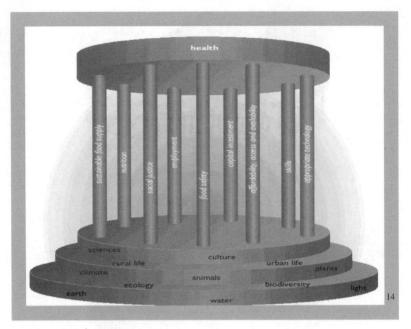

Source: Waltner-Toews and Lang (2000).

policy has to address public policy challenges at four interacting levels: the global, regional, national and subnational or local levels. Some features of these are given in table 2.

One of the advantages of conceiving food policy in terms of these levels is that it helps explicate tensions within public policy, over and above tensions over policy direction. These structural features are central to any appreciation of whether food policy is capable of yielding outcomes that are more or less integrated. The concept of multi-level governance recognizes, also, the interconnectedness of the different levels, as policy outcomes at each level are impacted by, and part of, the dynamics at the other levels. Hence, policy making in the EU is a confluence of national, subnational, intergovernmental, European polity, and wider international institutional and policy network dynamics (Marks *et al.* 1996).

Inequalities and Food Poverty: the Pressure from Social Policy

Traditionally public health concern has rightly focused upon *absolute* underconsumption as a source of malnutrition. More recently, evidence has

76

Table 2

Some features of multi-level food governance

Level	Institution	Rationale	Comment
Global—trade	World Trade Organization (formerly General Agreement on Tariffs and Trade)	GATT (1948 ff.); Agreement on Agriculture (1994; review 2000 ff.)	Trade liberalization focus; food and agriculture under GATT rules post-1994
Global—economic	World Bank; International Monetary Fund, etc.	Bretton Woods (1942)	Increasingly powerful in food, social and now environment; tensions with UN system
Global—food regulation	Codex Alimentarius Commission	GATT (1994) Sanitary and Phytosanitary Measures Agreement	Joint WHO-FAO secretariat (1950s ff.); new influence and powers with 1994 GATT; criticized for high TNC input
Global—United Nations (UN)	Food and Agriculture Organization; World Health Organization; UNICEF; UN Development Programme; UN Environment Programme	UN Declaration of Human Rights (1948)	Set up in 1950s as part of new UN; operates regionally, through member states. Programmes such as UNDP, UNEP, etc. bolted on.
Regional—UN system	United Nations Regional bodies, e.g. for WHO, FAO	Managerial; closer links with governments	European Region now taking lead in new WHO food thinking 2000 ff.
Regional—European Union (EU)	European Council; EU Presidency; Council of Ministers; European Commission, e.g. DG SANCO, DG Agriculture, DG Environment, etc.; European Parliament	Treaty of Rome (1958); Single European Act (1986); Agenda 2000 reform and mid-term review	Common Agricultural Policy is powerhouse of EU food practice; market harmonization of food standards has been contentious but successful; new thinking in 2000s?

Table 2

(cont'd)

Level	Institution	Rationale	Comment
Regional—new EU initiatives	European Food Authority	Commission proposal (COM (2000) 716 final)	Safety focus; some acknowledgement of nutrition but little of social or environmental integration
National—UK	Food Standards Agency	Food Standards Act (1999)	Began in April 2000; safety focus but has some nutrition responsibilities e.g. surveys
	Government Depts: MAFF, DoH, DETR, DiFID	Various—production and food supply, environmental protection, rural life, health	Departmentalism until crisis periods
Subnational—UK	Wales, Scotland and N Ireland Assemblies/Parliaments and Food Standards Agency Committees	Devolution Act (1998; Food Standards Act (1999)	Relationship with national bodies, e.g. Parliament, FSA is evolving
Local—UK	Two main involvements: Local Authorities (LAs), District Health Authorities (DHAs)	*LAs*: Environmental Health and Trading Standards officers; *DHAs*: Public Health, Public Health Laboratories, etc.	Enforcement is centuries-old; note also the new parallel private sector regulation via supply chain contracts

grown of the importance of *relative* poor consumption as well as of food insufficiency (Acheson 1999; James *et al.* 1997; Leather 1996). The less income people have, the narrower the range of foods they consume, the higher the proportion of their household expenditure is on food, and the worse their diet-related ill health is. This is not a natural but a human-created state of affairs. At its most extreme, poverty locks people into a cycle of hunger and premature death, a cycle that is known to be preventable. An equitable food supply would have major public health benefits. History shows us that food poverty is not inevitable. In both war and peace, equitable public policy can decrease infant mortality and increase overall human health. This applies to affluent countries as much as lower-income countries. For example, when the UK introduced a system of food rationing in World War II, health improved because poorer social groups at least ate better and the health inequality gap was reduced (Boyd Orr 1953).

The global picture on food and poverty is sobering. UNICEF and UNDP calculate 800 million children globally are undernourished, and 2 billion people exhibit effects of poor diet (UNICEF 1998). This is the result both of macronutrient—protein, carbohydrates and fats—and micronutrient deficiencies. One key issue is the policy choice between a strategy giving more priority to local produce for otherwise marginalized populations and one giving priority to providing food security by earning enough currency to import food sufficient for nutritional needs. The latter is currently in the policy ascendancy with neo-liberal trade policies favouring reduction of subsidies and import-substitution strategies. Like all models, this has certain assumptions. The food import–export approach to food security can work well in nutrition terms as long as the national currency is strong, but this is rarely the case for less developed countries (LDCs).

Food trade policy impacts upon and shapes the room for policy manoeuvre in tackling the links between public health and food poverty. G77 critics argue that current trade rules have been unnecessarily biased against the poor, particularly in LDCs. Under trade liberalization the LDCs have not been able to trade out of poverty (Watkins 1997). A World Bank report found that greater openness to trade has had a negative impact on the income growth of the poorest 40 per cent of people in developing countries (Lundberg and Milanovic 2000). The UN's Food and Agriculture Organization found that the impact of the Agreement on Agriculture (AoA) on 16 developing countries had been a surge of food imports, not an increase in food exports (FAO 1999). The Seattle meeting of the World Trade Organization (WTO) put the concerns of the LDCs back on the world trade agenda. These countries have proposed the introduction of a development/food security box, under the current review of the AoA, within which selective domestic trade barriers would be permitted for LDCs to foster domestic food production (WTO 2000a). Food security for populations in the developing world remains a policy battleground between advocates of free trade and the self-reliance standpoint (Madeley 2000).

In Europe, it should be recognized that poverty is not confined to less affluent countries; in situations where absolute poverty is rare, relative deprivation becomes more important (Halsted *et al.* 1985). Women, children and older people are at greatest risk of poverty (Beaglehole and Bonita 1998). There is strong evidence that more unequal societies have worse indices of health (Wilkinson 1995). There are considerable disparities of income within the EU. The top 10 per cent of households shared over a quarter of disposable income in 1993, while the bottom 10 per cent shared 2 per cent. Some 57 million individuals in the EU live in 23 million poor households (Eurostat 1997).

Food inequalities in developed countries suggest that food poverty is not just financial but social and emotional (Koehler *et al.* 1997). Within the EU, which has an explicit commitment to tackle "social exclusion", there is no food poverty database, although a methodology to enable intra-EU analysis has been developed under the DAFNE programme (Trichopoulou *et al.* 1999). The European Commission's Communication on Public Health proposed improving information on "inequalities in health, covering variations between population groups of the determinants of health, morbidity and mortality and assessment of interventions to reduce them" (CEC 1998).

The picture in the UK also illustrates the fact that food poverty can have a marked health impact. Food poverty in the 1990s was higher in the UK than other EU countries (Lang 1999b). Inequalities in income and health widened from 1979 to 1997 and the proportion of people with less than half the average income grew. The economic and social costs of this concerned the 1992–7 Conservative government and it set targets for tackling what it called "variations in health". One initiative it set up was a Low Income Project Team under the Department of Health, which reported in 1996 (DoH 1996). In 1997, the new Labour government set up an independent Inquiry into Inequalities in Health chaired by a former Chief Medical Officer. When this reported, it showed that the lowest income decile had experienced a real, not just relative decline in income (Acheson 1999). In effect, both reports showed that the health costs of economic policy had thus been "externalized" on to worsening food-related ill health of people on (relatively) low incomes. One issue which has been raised by the government's Social Exclusion Unit (SEU) is the issue of improving access to shops (DoH 1999), an issue that has received some considerable social policy analysis (Ellaway and Macintyre 2000). From the 1970s the decline in local (small) food shops had accelerated, as supermarkets grew in both sales and power in the food supply chain. The SEU's Policy Action Team 13 (PAT 13) concluded that to improve access to shops in general, a complex set of initiatives was needed, ranging from planning to credit and new community shopping. The PAT 13 report has not been followed up at the time of writing.

The Acheson Inquiry into Inequalities in Health 1999 found that lower socioeconomic groups have a greater incidence of premature and low birthweight babies, heart disease, stroke, and some cancers in adults (Acheson 1999). Other studies have shown that risk factors including lack of breast-feeding, smoking, physical inactivity, obesity, hypertension, and poor diet are clustered in the lower socioeconomic groups (James *et al.* 1997). The diet of lower socioeconomic groups in the UK provides cheap energy derived from foods such as meat products, full cream milk, fats, sugars, preserves, potatoes, and cereals but has poor variety and little intake of vegetables, fruit, and wholemeal bread. This type of diet is lower in essential nutrients such as calcium, iron, magnesium, folate and vitamin C than that of the higher socioeconomic groups. The importance of fruit and vegetables and their link with degenerative diseases is one such simple message both policy makers and consumers can appreciate.

Environmental and Health Impacts of Agricultural Production and the Food Supply Chain

The new ecological public health has to give equal policy focus to *what* people eat, *how* their diet is produced and distributed, and *who* eats what. The environmental impacts of the food system can be linked to the adverse health and social impacts. These problems occur from agricultural production right along the food supply chain. Initiatives are coming forward to address these aspects of the impacts, and some are attempting more holistic solutions, but they fall short of the degree of integration and reach sought by the ecological model of public health.

The dominant model for agriculture in Western Europe, notably in the United Kingdom, after the end of World War II became one driven by the priorities of the state for economic self-sufficiency in food production. The further industrialization of agriculture, increasingly capital- and chemical-intensive, led to increase of: farm size, external technological inputs, and yield and food output. The adverse effects of this process were realized from the 1970s onwards with increasing concern over the environmental, animal welfare, food safety, health and social impacts. The sustainability of the land and the conservation of the landscape, as well as public health, were affected by: pollution of soil and water media with chemical inputs; biodiversity loss and ecological impacts of large monoculture production (as opposed to mixed farming and rotations); and restricted numbers of technologically enhanced cultivars (Conway and Pretty 1991; Pretty 1998: 49–71).

Intensive rearing and "factory" farming of animal livestock supplemented by chemically enhanced and industrialized feed, and the subsequent increased and often cross-border travel from farm to abattoir, heightened concerns over both animal welfare and food safety. The success of this state support, in terms of increased production, resulted in overproduction of certain food-stuffs, adding budgetary pressures to a potential reform agenda. The drive to greater production also led to rationalization within farming, with technical inputs replacing labour and concentration of farm holdings leading to the subsequent reduction of numbers of farmers and farm workers and so to the dislocation of rural communities and of social sustainability.

Social theorists of agriculture have conceptualized such developments as part of an industrial model of agriculture (Goodman *et al.* 1987) or, as a variation, the "productivist" model (Clunies-Ross and Cox 1994). Certainly, policy makers have come to regard this intensive model as the pre-eminent or conventional model of agriculture (House of Commons 2001). The state of European agriculture and rural life is heavily influenced by the CAP regime, which has provided a macro policy framework, in a somewhat contradictory and imperfect manner. The CAP has found itself under pressure to reform for the past decade. The key pressures have emanated more recently from the proposed enlargement of the EU to central and eastern European countries and the need to prepare for, and subsequently conform to, the rules agreed under the GATT Uruguay round in 1994 and administered through the World Trade Organization, including the Agreement on Agriculture.

In response to concerns about the adverse impacts of the conventional model, a variety of different approaches to farming have emerged. On the one hand conventional agriculture has adopted management strategies to mitigate specific problems. Strategies to reduce pesticide use at the farm level, for example, have led to the introduction of integrated crop management and pest control techniques. On the other hand, a range of more alternative agricultural systems has been developed, under a variety of terms, advocating more ecological and post-productionist strategies (Beus and Dunlap 1990). The most developed amongst these alternative approaches is organic farming which sees "the farm as an organism . . . a coherent, self-regulating and stable whole" rather than seeing farming in terms of external inputs (Lampkin *et al.* 1999: 1). A related theme within both of these differing approaches (conventional and alternative) is an attempt to make agriculture more sustainable. Sustainability has proven to be a universally embraced and often appropriated concept, and consequently its meaning is highly contested.

Jules Pretty (1998: 81–2) has identified the key components of sustainable agriculture, as needing to draw upon, and in turn sustain, both natural capital and social capital. Natural capital (including soil, water, air, plants, animals and ecosystems) has to be integrated in agricultural systems in the form of regenerative technologies such as: use of nitrogen-fixing plants for soil conservation, use of natural predators for pest control, integration of animals into cropped systems. Social capital entails utilizing farmer and community labour, knowledge and experience, and underpinning community cohesion. The aim is to achieve enhancement of both the quality and quantity of wildlife, water, landscape and other public goods of the countryside. The importance of greater reliance upon natural organic inputs, farmer participation and reduction of external and non-renewable inputs, is also reflected in the development of agroecology as a model for poor farmers in developing world agriculture (Altieri 1995; Pinstrup-Andersen *et al.* 1999).

There are signs that some of the aspects of sustainable agriculture are finding their way into EU thinking on agricultural policy, but in a piecemeal fashion. The EU's position as put forward to the WTO's Committee on Agriculture is that further liberalization of trade in agricultural products must be underpinned by public support, which can only be garnered if the multifunctional role of agriculture is met. The multifunctional role "covers the protection of the environment, and the sustained vitality of rural communities, food safety and other consumer concerns" (WTO 2000b). Notwithstanding suspicions in the trade policy communities that the model is a screen for protectionism, the multifunctional model of agriculture is endorsed by more progressive environmental interests and will help shape the next stage of CAP reform, with the mid-term review of the Agenda 2000 reforms in 2003. The multifunctional model shows some complement to sustainable agriculture, but lacks the latter's emphasis on alternative production methods. The model also fails to provide a comprehensive enough reach to fulfil the goals of ecological public health, but may provide a useful platform for the advocacy of environmental benefits.

Environmental impacts occur not only on the farm but along the whole food supply chain. The notion of "food miles/kilometres" refers to the distance that food travels between primary producer and end consumer. Between 1975 and 1991/3, while the tonnage of food consumed remained constant, the amount of food transported on UK roads increased by 30 per cent and the distance it travelled increased by nearly 60 per cent (Paxton 1994). If the food travelled further, so do consumers getting to the shops. In the UK, over the same period, the distance travelled for shopping in general rose by 60 per cent and the number of shopping trips taken by car more than doubled (Raven and Lang 1995). Changes in the food retail sector meant that smaller, local shops fell in numbers while larger supermarkets grew considerably. Environmentally, it would make better policy to encourage people to shop locally. The distance taken by shopping trips to town-centre food stores is less than half that of trips taken to edge-of-town stores (Whitelegg 1994). In policy terms, the question is: why should a rich growing country like the UK be fed by others when it could feed itself and others could feed their own or local populations? The net import of "hidden" land, i.e. land used elsewhere to feed the British, was 4.1 million hectares in 1995 (MacLaren et al. 1998). Much of this hidden importation was produce fed to animals.

Managerially, there have been astonishing efficiency improvements in the food supply in recent years, but some food "efficiency" also creates unnecessary pollution. The UK food, drink and tobacco sector, for instance, emits 4.5 million tonnes of carbon annually, compared to the chemical industry's 7 million and the iron and steel industry's 10 million. It also creates nearly 6 million tonnes of waste, most of which is dumped in landfill sites (DETR 1998). This is not efficient.

Energy is a key concept linking nutrition and environmental policy. In 1993, for instance, 685,000 giga joules of energy (equivalent to 14 million litres of fuel) were consumed in transporting 417,207 tonnes of dessert apples imported into Britain (Garnett 1999), yet such apples can grow in the UK. Four out of five pears consumed in the UK are now imported, and two-thirds of its apples (Hoskins and Lobstein 1998a, 1998b). Fruit farmers were "encouraged" out of business by CAP subsidies to destroy trees. The role of the CAP upon food supply in the EU is considerable. There is a deficiency in understanding CAP's impact on health within the EU (Lang 1999b; Lobstein and Longfield 1999). The budget for the CAP in 1998 was approximately €38,748 million, yet even after the recent Agenda 2000 reforms, the subsidy levels for different produce pay no attention to food-related health needs. Hence 52 per cent of CAP support goes to meat, 14 per cent to dairy and just 7 per cent to fruit and vegetables (Lobstein 1999).

The link between poor production conditions, the supply chain and diet-related human health has featured in many recent public policy crises and concerns. Although crises may start in one state, their impact has spread far partly due to trade liberalization between countries, as "we all swim in the same microbial sea" (Brundtland 2001). Since the early 1980s there has been a marked increase in the reports of food-borne diseases, resulting from chemical or pathogenic contamination (Brundtland 2001). The concentration, lengthening and changing nature of the food supply chain has given rise to increases in food-borne pathogens, notably: *Salmonella* (73 reported cases per 100,000 in the EU in 1997), *Campylobacter* (30 per 100,000), and *E coli 0157* (lower incidence but high mortality) (Trichopoulou *et al.* 2000). The incidence is higher as food-borne illness is seriously under-reported, possibly only 1 in 10, or even 1 in 100. The economic costs can be immense. Between 1991 and 1994 it has been estimated that food poisoning cost the UK National Health Service £83,139,685 for inpatient care alone (Djuretic *et al.* 1996). In 1994 Roberts estimated the costs of food poisoning to the UK economy were of the order of £0.5–1 billion/year (Roberts 1996). The BSE crisis has already cost UK taxpayers £4 billion (*c.* €6 billion) in direct costs (Lang 1998).

There are also considerable political costs. Governments and institutions can be seriously damaged or fall, as happened in 1999 with the dioxin scandal in Belgium (McKee 1999). There can also be serious intergovernmental tensions, as was shown by the 1999 UK–French problems following discovery that animals were being fed recycled sewage in animal feed. The incidence of food-borne illness can be seen as a breakdown in the food system, that demands a holistic, not a reactive response. Incidence of zoonoses in livestock has also raised fresh public concern about the nature of the food supply chain, as with the foot and mouth outbreak in the UK and on continental Europe in 2001. The political reaction to the food safety crises has seen the ushering in of a new range of food safety agencies at national and now at regional (EU) level. The new European Food Authority, for instance, will begin work by the end of 2002. At the national level, a majority of member states also have their own agencies. This is probably set to become a source of future tension between the levels of governance.

The costing of the externalities of the food supply chain is slowly being addressed. An estimate of the total external costs of UK agriculture was £2.343 billion for 1996. This assessment included costs of contamination of drinking water with: pesticides (£120 m/year), nitrate (£16 m), *Cryptosporidium* (£23 m), and phosphate and soil (£55 m). Costs also included: damage to wildlife, habitats, hedgerows and drystone walls (£125 m), from emissions of gases (£1113 m), from soil erosion and organic carbon losses (£106 m), from food poisoning (£169 m), and from BSE (£607 m) (Pretty *et al.* 2000).

While the analysis of Pretty *et al.* represents a significant attempt to unravel the false costs surrounding the cheap food policy that has dominated the UK food system, from an ecological public health model it does not include the full externalities of consumption and diet-related health costs. Cardiovascular diseases (basically coronary heart disease and stroke) are the main cause of death in the UK, accounting for over 250,000 deaths, and 80,000 deaths before the age of 75. About a third of deaths from cardiovascular disease before the age of 75 (i.e. about 30,000) are due to poor nutrition—i.e. diets which are too high in fat, saturated fat and salt and too low in fruit, vegetables and cereal-based products. About the same number of premature deaths from cancer are also due to poor nutrition. Coronary heart disease alone costs the NHS about £1.6 billion and costs the economy a further £8.5 billion in lost production due to death and illness in those of working age.

This means that coronary heart disease costs the country about £10 billion a year, £3.3 billion of which could be saved if diets were improved (BHF 2001).

There is a clear need for a more integrated approach to health and environmental impact assessments (British Medical Association 1998). There is also need for food and nutrition policy to develop new methodologies such as Life Cycle Analysis to assess the impact of food production and distribution both on nutrition and on the environment. Sweden is one country that is pioneering integrated policy experimentation. Both the Agriculture and Environment Ministries are developing reorientation programmes to reduce fossil fuel/ energy use and to meet health targets. This is based on the Factor Four approach of the Wuppertal Institute (von Weizacher *et al.* 1997) trying to increase efficiency fourfold by increasing technological sophistication. Sweden intends to halve resource use by 2021 (Swedish Environmental Protection Agency 1999). Sweden is also exploring how to achieve tough targets on reducing greenhouse gases from food consumption (Carlsson-Kanyama 1998). This was one of the public health recommendations of the joint WHO, World Meteorological Organization and UN Environment Programme report on climate change and public health (McMichael *et al.* 1996). On current evidence, Sweden reports that it is not close to meeting those targets. One comprehensive audit of the consequences of eating and travelling in Sweden has shown that far more energy is used than fits the proposed, self-imposed energy quotas. The situation appears to suggest the need for "substantial lifestyle changes" (Carlsson-Kanyama 1999). To ensure that policy is both comprehensive and accurate, new methodologies are required to improve energy auditing in food systems.

Conclusions

After a period of some considerable turbulence, food policy has emerged as an area of public policy with both peculiar and common themes. Its importance centres on the fact that food is a basic human need and that humanity's capacity to produce enough health-enhancing food requires a sensitivity to ecology that has recently been somewhat lacking. As the first industrial nation, the UK experience is particularly rich and worthy of scrutiny. The last two decades of the twentieth century brought the UK productionist experiment with a combination of intensive and industrialized food production and highly concentrated distribution and logistics systems under particular scrutiny. The critique of this post-World War II food revolution has moved food policy from the periphery of public policy to its heartlands.

At the core of the twenty-first century policy challenge also lie some old goals: social justice, food for all, a decent quality of diet, full democratic accountability in governance, a desire to ensure that there is not just enough food but also well-produced food and fair access to food. These are policy goals that food thinkers and campaigners from public health or popular movements in the eighteenth, nineteenth and twentieth centuries would recognize as theirs too (Paulus 1974; Birchall 1994).

This paper has suggested that a central challenge for future public policy is the need to link policy areas too often dealt with in a disparate manner. Failures of governance make harder humanity's capacity to harvest rather than weaken the earth's capacities to generate food. We have suggested that the immense challenges of the future—e.g. population, sustainability, social justice—require better links between environmental and public health. It is easier to raise questions about whether human health can be achieved without compromising ecological health than it is to produce solutions. Yet sustainable agriculture and food networks now have a rich tradition of experimentation with growing and distributing food in ways which at least recognize the enormity of the ecological challenge.

If in the past, food policy has been a national concern, today public policy requires coordinated action at all levels. We are encouraged by initiatives at the European level; these are long overdue. We argue, too, that governments should promote a view that what matters is not just *what* people eat but also *how* food is produced and how equitably it is distributed and consumed. This requires the exploration of new configurations. If, for instance, consumers are to increase their fruit and vegetable consumption to reduce cardiovascular disease, it surely matters if that fruit generates more long-distance food distribution rather than encouraging more local production. Similarly, the goal of improving and protecting biodiversity should mean biodiversity not just on supermarket shelves but also back in the fields whence the produce came. In our ecological health model, the goal would be to get biodiversity from the field to the stomach as locally as feasible and with minimal energy use. The currently dominant productionist model, however, is unconcerned about where food comes from, only its traceability (to meet due diligence legal requirements and protect brand value).

On a positive note, after years of denial, governments are reforming their role and relationship with food. Setting up a food agency could enable the state to put distance between it and political blame for food crises. Governments still have not taken on board the need to espouse what we call the ecological health model; sustainable farming is still a "niche". Policy is still too focused on food safety and not enough on the social and wider ecological concerns raised in this article. The UK has now abolished the Ministry of Agriculture, Fisheries and Food, and replaced it by a Department of the Environment, Food and Rural Affairs. The Blair government was re-elected in 2001 committed to setting up an Independent Commission into food and farming. The challenge faced by these bodies is to create a genuinely appropriate food supply chain for the twenty-first century that fits the ecological health model outlined here.

There are, in short, critical policy choices ahead. If, as is predicted, over 90 per cent of Europeans will be living in cities by the year 2015, it is important for food and health policy planners to ask who will produce this food and how. The ecological consequences of increasing urbanization suggest new need to rebuild local food systems and policies. But such policies are in conflict with the dominant neo-liberal, trade-oriented approach of macro-economic theory. This tension, too, would have been recognizable to our policy ancestors.

References

Acheson, D. (1999), *Independent Inquiry into Inequalities in Health: Report*, London: Stationery Office.

Altieri, M. (1995), *Agroecology: The Science of Sustainable Agriculture*, 2nd edn, Boulder, CO: Westview Press.

Barnet, R. and Cavanagh, J. (1994), *Global Dreams: Imperial Corporations and the New World Order*, New York: Simon and Schuster.

Beaglehole, R. and Bonita, R. (1998), Public health at the crossroads: which way forward? *The Lancet*, 351, 21 February: 590–2.

Beus, C. and Dunlap, R. (1990), Conventional versus alternative agriculture: the paradigmatic roots of the debate, *Rural Sociology*, 55: 590–616.

BHF (2001), *European Coronary Heart Disease Statistics*, Oxford: British Heart Foundation Health Promotion Research Group, Oxford University.

Birchall, J. (1994), *Co-op: The People's Business*, Manchester: Manchester University Press.

Boyd Orr, J. (1936), *Food, Health and Income*, London: Macmillan.

Boyd Orr, J. with Lubbock, D. (1953), *White Man's Dilemma: Food and the Future*, London: George Allen and Unwin.

British Medical Association (1998), *Health and Environmental Impact Assessment: An Integrated Approach*, London: Earthscan/BMA.

Brundtland, G. H. (2001), Food Safety—a World Wide Challenge. Speech to Food Chain 2001 Conference, 14 March, Uppsala, Sweden.

Cannon, G. (1992), *Food and Health: The Experts Agree*, London: Consumers' Association.

Carlsson-Kanyama, A. (1998), Climate change and dietary choices: how can emissions of greenhouse gases from food consumption be reduced? *Food Policy*, 23, 3/4: 277–93.

Carlsson-Kanyama, A. (1999), *Consumption Patterns and Climate Change: Consequences of Eating and Travelling in Sweden*, Doctoral thesis, Stockholm: University of Stockholm Department of Systems Ecology.

CEC (1998), *Communication from the Commission on the Development of Public Health Policy in the European Community*, COM (98)230 final, Brussels: Commission of the European Communities.

CEC (2000a), *White Paper on Food Safety in the European Union*, COM (99)719, Brussels: Commission of the European Communities.

CEC (2000b), *Council Resolution on Health and Nutrition*, 8 December, Brussels, 14274/00.

Clunies-Ross, T. and Cox, G. (1994), Challenging the productivist paradigm: organic farming and the politics of agricultural change. In P. Lowe, T. Marsden and S. Whatmore (eds), *Regulating Agriculture*, London: David Fulton.

Commission on Environmental Health (1996), *Environment for Sustainable Health Development: An Action Plan for Sweden*, Stockholm: Ministry of Health and Social Affairs, Swedish Official Reports Series 1996, 124.

Conway, G. and Pretty, J. (1991), *Unwelcome Harvest: Agriculture and Pollution*, London: Earthscan.

DETR (1998), *Sustainable Business: Consultation Paper on Sustainable Development and Business in the UK*, London: Department of the Environment, Transport and the Regions.

Djuretic, T., Ryan, M. J. and Wall, P. G. (1996), The cost of inpatient care for acute infectious intestinal disease in England from 1991 to 1994, *Communicable Disease Reports and Reviews*, 6: R78–R80.

DoH (1996), *Low Income, Food, Nutrition and Health: Strategies for Improvement*, Report by the Low Income Project Team for the Nutrition Taskforce, London: Department of Health.

DoH (1999), *Improving Shopping Access for People Living in Deprived Neighbourhoods: A Paper for Discussion. Policy Action Team: 13*, London: Department of Health for the Cabinet Office Social Exclusion Unit.

Ellaway, A. and Macintyre, S. (2000), Shopping for food in socially contrasting localities, *British Food Journal*, 102, 1: 52–9.

Eurostat (1997), Income distribution and poverty in EU12—1993, *Statistics in Focus: Population and Social Conditions*, no. 6, Luxembourg: Eurostat.

FAO (1999), *FAO Symposium on Agriculture, Trade and Food Security, Geneva, 23–24 September 1999, Synthesis of Case Studies, X3065/E*, Rome: Food and Agriculture Organization.

Feder, E. (1977), *Strawberry Imperialism*, The Hague: Institute of Social Studies.

FSA (2001), *Annual Report*, London: Food Standards Agency.

Garnett, T. (1999), *City Harvest: The Feasibility of Growing More Food in London*, London: Sustain.

Goodman, D. and Redclift, M. (1991), *Refashioning Nature: Food, Ecology and Culture*, London: Routledge.

Goodman, D., Sorj, B. and Wilkinson, J. (1987), *From Farming to Biotechnology: A Theory of Agro-Industrial Development*, Oxford: Blackwell.

Halsted, S. B., Walsh, J. A. and Warren, K. S. (eds) (1985), *Good Health at Low Cost*, New York: Rockefeller Foundation.

Hoskins, R. and Lobstein, T. (1998a), *The Pear Essentials*, Food Facts (3), London: Sustainable Agriculture, Food and Environment Alliance.

Hoskins, R. and Lobstein, T. (1998b), *How Green are our Apples?* Food Facts (4), London: Sustainable Agriculture, Food and Environment Alliance.

House of Commons (2001), *Organic Farming: House of Commons Agriculture Committee Second Report*, vol. 1, HC 149-I, London: Stationery Office.

James, W. P. T., Nelson, M., Ralph, A. and Leather, S. (1997), Socioeconomic determinants of health: the contribution of nutrition to inequalities in health, *British Medical Journal*, 314, 7093: 1545–9.

Kafartos, K. and Codrington, C. A. (2001), Eurodiet Project Proceedings, *Public Health Nutrition*, 4, 1(A), February, special issue.

Keys, A. (ed.) (1970), Coronary heart disease in seven countries, *Circulation*, 41 (suppl. 1): 1–211.

Koehler, B. M., Feichtinger, E., Barloesius, E. and Dowler, E. (eds) (1997), *Poverty and Food in Welfare Societies*, Berlin: Wissenschaftzentrum für Sozialforschung.

Lampkin, N., Foster, C., Padel, S. and Midmore, P. (1999), *The Policy and Regulatory Environment for Organic Farming in Europe: Synthesis of Results. Organic Farming in Europe: Economics and Policy Volume 1*, Stuttgart: Universität Hohenheim.

Lang, T. (1997), Dividing up the cake: food as social exclusion. In A. Walker and C. Walker (eds), *Britain Divided: The Growth of Social Exclusion in the 1980s and 1990s*, London: Child Poverty Action Group, pp. 213–28.

Lang, T. (1998), BSE and CJD: recent developments. In S. Ratzan (ed.), *The Mad Cow Crisis: Health and the Public Good*, London: UCL Press, pp. 67–85.

Lang, T. (1999a), The complexities of globalization: the UK as a case study of tensions within the food system and the challenge to food policy, *Agriculture and Human Values*, 16: 169–85.

Lang, T. (1999b), Food and nutrition. In O. Weil, M. McKee, M. Brodin and D. Oberlé (eds), *Priorities for Public Health Action in the European Union*, Vandoeuvre-les-Nancy: Société Française de Santé Publique, pp. 138–56.

Lang, T. and Caraher, M. (2001), International public health. In D. Pencheon and D. Melzer (eds), *Oxford Textbook of Public Health*, Oxford: Oxford University Press, forthcoming.

Lang, T., Millstone, E. and Rayner, M. (1997), *Food Standards and the State*, London: Centre for Food Policy, Thames Valley University.

Leather, S. (1996), *The Making of Modern Malnutrition*, London: Caroline Walker Trust.

Lobstein, T. (1999), Agenda 2000 hits the rocks, *Food Magazine*, 45, April/June: 14–15.

Lobstein, T. and Longfield, J. (1999), *Improving Diet and Health through European Union Food Policies*, London: Health Education Authority.

Lundberg, M. and Milanovic, B. (2000), The truth about global inequality, *Financial Times*, 25 February.

MacLaren, D., Bullock, S. and Yousuf, N. (1998), *Tomorrow's World: Britain's Share in a Sustainable Future*, London: Earthscan.

Madeley, J. (2000), *Hungry for Trade: How the Poor Pay for Trade*, London: Zed Books.

Marks, G., Hooghe, L. and Blank, K. (1996), European integration from the 1980s: state-centric v. multi-level governance, *Journal of Common Market Studies*, 34, 3: 341–78.

Marsden, T., Flynn, A. and Harrison, M. (2000), *Consuming Interests*, London: UCL Press.

McKee, M. (1999), Trust me, I'm an expert, *European Journal of Public Health*, 9, 3: 161–2.

McMichael, A. J. (1999), From hazard to habitat: rethinking environment and health, *Epidemiology*, 10, 4: 1–5.

McMichael, A. J., Bolin, B., Costanza, R., Daily, G. C., Folke, C., Lindahl-Kiessling, K., Lindgren, E. and Niklasson, B. (1999), Globalization and the sustainability of human health, *BioScience*, 49, 3: 205–10.

McMichael, A. J., Haines, A., Slooff, R. and Kovats, R. S. (eds) (1996), *Climate Change and Human Health*, Geneva: World Health Organization, UN Environment Programme, World Meteorological Organization.

Paulus, I. (1974), *The Search for Pure Food*, Oxford: Martin Robertson.

Paxton, A. (1994), *The Food Miles Report*, London: Sustainable Agriculture, Food and Environment Alliance.

Pinstrup-Andersen, P., Pandya-Lorch, R. and Rosegrant, M. (1999), *World Food Prospects: Critical Issues for the Early Twenty-first Century*, Washington, DC: International Food Policy Research Institute.

Pretty, J. (1998), *The Living Land*, London: Earthscan.

Pretty, J. N., Brett, C., Gee, D., Hine, R. E., Mason, C. F., Morison, J. I. L., Raven, H., Rayment, M. D. and van der Bijl, G. (2000), An assessment of the total external costs of UK agriculture, *Agricultural Systems*, 65: 113–36.

Raven, H. and Lang, T. (1995), *Off our Trolleys? Food Retailing and the Hypermarket Economy*, London: Institute for Public Policy Research.

Roberts, J. (1996), *Economic Evaluation of Surveillance: Report on Economic Aspects of Surveillance Systems for the Public Health Laboratory Service*, London: London School of Hygiene and Tropical Medicine, August.

SFSP (2000), *Health and Human Nutrition: Elements for European Action—French Presidency 24 August*, Paris: Société Française de Santé Publique.

Swedish Environmental Protection Agency (1999), *A Sustainable Food Supply Chain: A Swedish Case Study*, Report 4966, Stockholm: SEPA.

Trichopoulou, A., Lagiou, P., Nelson, M., Remaut-De Winter, A.-M., Kelleher, C., Leonhauser, L., Moreiras, O., Shmitt, A., Sekula, W., Trygg, K. and Sajkas, G. (1999), Food disparities in 10 European countries: their detection using household budget survey data—the Data Food Networking (DAFNE) initiative, *Nutrition Today*, 34, 3: 129–39.

Trichopoulou, A., Millstone, E., Lang, T., Eames, M., Barling, D., Naska, A. and van Zwanenberg, P. (2000), *European Policy on Food Safety*, Report to Science and Technology Options Assessment (STOA), Luxembourg: European Parliament.

UNICEF (1998), *State of the World's Children 1998*, New York: UN Children's Fund/ Oxford University Press.
von Weizacher, E., Lovins, A. B. and Lovins, L. H. (1997), *Factor Four: Doubling Wealth, Halving Resource Use*, London: Earthscan.
Waltner-Toews, D. and Lang, T. (2000), A new conceptual base for food and agriculture: the emerging model of links between agriculture, food, health, environment and society, *Global Change and Human Health*, 1, 2: 116–30.
Watkins, K. (1997), *Globalization and Liberalization: Implications for Poverty, Distribution and Inequality*, Occasional Papers, 32, New York: UNDP Human Development Report Office.
Whitelegg, J. (1994), *Driven to Shop*, London: Eco-logica/Sustainable Agriculture, Food and Environmental Alliance.
WHO-E (2000a), *The Impact of Food and Nutrition on Public Health: The Case for a Food and Nutrition Policy and Action Plan for the European Region of WHO 2000–2005*, 24 August, Copenhagen: World Health Organization Regional Office for Europe Food and Nutrition Policy Unit.
WHO-E (2000b), *The Impact of Food and Nutrition on Public Health: The Case for a Food and Nutrition Policy and an Action Plan for the European Region of the WHO 2000–2005*, Resolution of the Regional Committee for Europe, 50th Session, Copenhagen: World Health Organization European Region.
Wilkinson, R. G. (1995), *Unhealthy Societies*, London: Routledge.
Wrigley, N. (1998), How British retailers have shaped food choice. In A. Murcott (ed.), *The Nation's Diet: The Social Science of Food Choice*, London: Longman, pp. 112–28.
WTO (1999), *Trade and Environment Bulletin*, PRESS/TE/029, 30 July: 7–11.
WTO (2000a), *Agreement on Agriculture: Special and Differential Treatment and a Development Box. Proposal to the June 2000 Special Session of the Committee on Agriculture by Cuba, Dominican Republic, Honduras, Pakistan, Haiti, Nicaragua, Kenya, Uganda, Zimbabwe, Sri Lanka and El Salvador*, Committee on Agriculture Special Session, World Trade Organization, G/AG/NG/W/13, 23 June.
WTO (2000b), *EC Comprehensive Negotiating Proposal*, Committee on Agriculture Special Session, World Trade Organization, G/AG/NG/W/90, 14 December.

CHAPTER 7

People, Land and Sustainability: Community Gardens and the Social Dimension of Sustainable Development

John Ferris, Carol Norman and Joe Sempik

Abstract

Community gardens vary enormously in what they offer, according to local needs and circumstance. This article reports on research and experience from the USA. The context in which these findings are discussed is the implementation of Local Agenda 21 and sustainable development policies. In particular, emphasis is given to exploring the social dimension of sustainable development policies by linking issues of health, education, community development and food security with the use of green space in towns and cities. The article concludes that the use of urban open spaces for parks and gardens is closely associated with environmental justice and equity.

Keywords

People; Land; Community gardens; Sustainability; Green space; Poverty; Food security

Introduction

This article is dedicated to the memory of Maylie Scott, who died of cancer on 10 May 2001. Maylie Scott was an outstanding exemplar of a new generation of Zen Buddhist women priests. Her courage and qualities of leadership were outstanding and renowned among social activists in the San Francisco Bay area. Maylie's life and actions have inspired whatever merit this article about the role of community gardens, and we must say the role of women, may have in helping to make our cities environmentally and socially more civilized places in which to live and work. Maylie's life, as a Buddhist, was dedicated to helping all living things. There was no distinction between natural and human interests. At the centre of this vision is an image of all life forms being deeply interconnected.

Address for correspondence: *John Ferris, c/o PLS, Humanities Research Unit, Old Engineering Building, University of Nottingham, University Park, Nottingham, NG9 1DQ.*

Research Aims and Objectives

The research that underlies this article was carried out in the USA at various times during the 1990s: first in Pennsylvania and then in the San Francisco Bay area. The research in the United States was exploratory and aimed at identifying the possible relevance of US experience to urban regeneration and community development policies in the UK. The first step was to survey the range of community gardens and develop a loose typology of the forms and types of garden and, by means of interviews, to establish the range of purposes intended by those involved. The research was policy-orientated in that we sought to gather information that might be useful to local community groups and municipalities as part of Local Agenda 21 and efforts to promote sustainability in urban areas. Would it be possible to replicate initiatives developed in a North American context in Britain, with different governmental, legal and cultural values? As one of the researchers was an occupational therapist with a strong interest in healing and therapy gardens, this became an important dimension in the research.

People, Land and Sustainability Conference, Nottingham, 2000

An important part of this exploratory research process was the organization of an international conference in Nottingham in September 2000. Although the primary purpose of the conference was aimed at raising the profile of community gardening and its contribution towards global sustainability, a secondary aim was to gather more information about community gardening. Thus the conference report was both promotional and an interim product of an ongoing research process. An informational and promotional video film was another outcome of the conference. An interactive website will be set up before the end of 2001 (see Ferris *et al.* 2001).

What Is a Community Garden?

What distinguishes a community garden from a private garden is the fact that it is in some sense a public garden in terms of ownership, access, and degree of democratic control. Community gardens exist in many nations and in both urban and rural areas. They vary in what they offer according to local needs. Some provide open space and greenery. Sometimes they provide cheap vegetables for a local community. With the spread of cities and consequent land scarcity, the demand for communal gardens seems to be increasing. Community gardens are now recognized to be an international phenomenon, and urban gardening is widely seen to be a way of improving local food supplies as well as leisure and recreational activity. This was publicized very widely by the UN Urban Habitat Conference held in Instanbul in 1996.

At the Nottingham conference a wide range of perspectives on community gardening was gathered together in a way that was intended to promote a very broad and inclusive vision of community gardening. It is not very useful to offer a precise definition of community gardens as this would impose arbitrary limits on creative communal responses to local need. The contributions to the conference were organized under five main headings:

- Gardening in the Community
- Gardening and Health
- Children and Gardening
- Food Security
- Reclaiming the Land

The idea underlying this way of organizing the contributions was that the conference would seek to highlight the social dimension of sustainability. The themes were community, health, children, food security and poverty. We also wanted to make the case for recognizing the need for public green spaces in our urban settlements. We contend that the concept of community gardens should be very broadly conceived to include many kinds of civic intervention with local governments and other public agencies acting in partnership with citizen groups of various kinds. What is now very evident is that the environmental issues discussed at the UN conference held in Rio de Janeiro in 1992 (see *Environmental Politics* 1993) are demanding common responses from local communities globally. Food security and access to open green space for recreation are by no means the least of these. Community is a protean concept and can take many forms and serve diverse interests. We should expect community gardens to reflect this pluralism and diversity. All the types of garden referred to here serve, in our view, to contribute to the objective of promoting environmental justice by reconciling people, land and sustainability. This is what the Nottingham conference in September 2000 was about (Ferris *et al.* 2001).

Community Gardens in the San Francisco Bay Area

In this section we consider the question of what a community garden is by reporting on research carried out in the summer of 1997 in the San Francisco Bay area. A loose classification and characterization of community gardens emerged from our research. We were satisfied that most of the forms of gardening activity that we were able to see could be found in other North American cities and, indeed, in other nations worldwide. The list that emerged is not definitive but does, we feel, cover most of the kinds of garden we were able to visit in the San Francisco Bay area:

- Leisure gardens
- Child and school gardens
- Entrepreneurial gardens
- Crime diversion gardens/Work and training gardens
- Healing and therapy gardens/Quiet gardens
- Neighbourhood pocket parks

- Ecological restoration gardens/parks
- Demonstration gardens

These labels are not mutually exclusive and gardens can often combine more than one of these functions. What all of these gardens have in common is the fact that specific communities actively support them. Frequently, but not invariably, they are supported by charitable or municipal grant aid. They all reflect in some way mutual aid and forms of communal reciprocity. It is also quite likely that there will have been a fair degree of altruism in getting them started. It is this complex of motivations that makes it appropriate to call them community gardens. Although community gardens do have a long history there is no doubt that they have been given a fresh impetus by the emergence of international concern with the environment and sustainability. Local Agenda 21, agreed at the UN Conference on the Environment held in Rio de Janeiro in June 1992, placed great emphasis on sustainable development at the local level (see Roddick and Dodds 1993).

Urban regeneration policies increasingly tend to include some provision for community involvement in green space planning. Advocacy for more sustainable cities includes advocacy for access to land for local community purposes, especially recreational space and for food growing.

Leisure gardens

Perhaps the most common type of garden to be found in the Bay area and in most other cities is the recreational or leisure garden. In the San Francisco area these are usually organized for a neighbourhood with a relatively high proportion of apartment-dwellers and people without gardens. These gardens typically contain between 20 and 50 small plots where gardeners grow flowers and vegetables by intensive deep-bed methods. There is also likely to be a picnic/barbecue space and a communal tool shed. The plots are about 10 × 20 feet. The whole area would be enclosed by a chain link fence and secured gate. Such gardens are tended very zealously and reflect great cultural diversity in terms of plants and vegetables that are grown. Residents have often taken over neglected urban sites that were occupied by teenage gangs and drug dealers. For example, many of the New York gardens were built on vacant lots that were left empty and derelict by the New York City Council. They were in effect squatted by local community activists so as to create additional green space and to create gardens for flower and vegetable growing (see Ferris *et al.* 2001).

Child and school gardens

In California school gardens are very popular and are actively promoted by the State Education Department with slogans like "*a garden in every school*". The Le Conte Elementary School on Russell Street, Berkeley, is a very good example. This is a multicultural school with pupils from very diverse backgrounds. The garden, which has flowers and vegetables, also has livestock such as goats, sheep and chickens. It offers many activities, which involve children and parents. The science curriculum is integrated with a wide range of garden activities like propagation, transplanting, harvesting, composting and soil preparation. This garden project has been fully supported by the head teacher and developed by a technician, Ms Jackie Omania, who has a degree in environmental science.

Another example of a lively school garden is the *Edible Schoolyard* at Martin Luther King Junior High School in Berkeley (Ferris *et al.* 2001: 35). Like Le Conte this school aimed to integrate the activities of the garden with elements of the curriculum. The most innovatory aspect of the Edible Schoolyard is that it sought to implement a vision of a garden growing food for the kitchen. The students at the School built and maintained the garden. One acre of derelict land was transformed into a beautiful and productive garden. The founder of the Edible Schoolyard was Alice Waters, the widely celebrated chef who is the founder of the home of *California cuisine*, the restaurant Chez Panisse in Berkeley. Alice Waters is a passionate advocate of both organic food production and good cooking of fresh vegetables (see Waters 1996; Ferris *et al.* 2001).

Perhaps the most impoverished community in the Bay area is North Richmond, an area with a mostly non-white population. The Verde Elementary School, which is 100 per cent non-white and in the midst of an impoverished community, was clearly living on the margins in 1997. A garden was created and maintained at the school by Mien hill people who were refugees from Laos in the mid-1970s. This garden was one of the most productive we saw in California. The Mien women simply recreated the kind of garden they would have grown at home using iron-age methods and tools. Supporting the teachers was a volunteer master gardener and a volunteer child psychologist, Cassie Scott, who worked closely with preschool children who came along with their mothers to the garden as well as older children experiencing difficulties in class. The garden was the platform for a wide range of educational activity as well as vegetable production.

There were numerous other school garden projects in the San Francisco Bay area and this was clearly a growing area of community garden activity. It should be stressed here that the garden activity reached out into the community through parental involvement in these gardens.

Entrepreneurial gardens

Another type of garden that we visited in California can best be described as *entrepreneurial*. The purpose of these gardens is diverse, but is clearly driven by the need to alleviate poverty and social exclusion in some of the more disadvantaged neighbourhoods in the Bay area. For example, the *Berkeley Youth Alternatives Garden* aims to create leisure opportunities for children with a special children's garden, as well as earning opportunities for young people from low-income homes. Organic produce is sold to local retailers and in the Berkeley Farmers' Market. This activity has a dual purpose in offering job training as well as generating income for the participants.

In cities all over the world drugs, crime, and poverty interact with devastating effects on the lives of young people. This is especially so in California where the crime and drugs problems are exacerbated by easy access to guns. The biggest gun shop in California is in Leandro, just south of Oakland with its high percentage of disadvantaged residents. Maylie Scott, with other women from the Buddhist Peace Fellowship, picketed this shop. To protest in this way is neither utopian nor idealistic. It is a way of reminding those who choose to forget, especially the lawmakers and state officials, that the privilege of citizenship comes with responsibilities for what happens in our communities.

The effect of guns and drugs on poor neighbourhoods in American cities has been devastating. Although the Bay area must be among the richest communities in the world social polarization is also very high, with "people of colour" suffering the greatest deprivation. Community gardens are now being used to develop alternatives for young people exposed to the drugs and crime economy. The *Strong Roots Gardens* in Oakland and Berkeley are examples of this. Melody Ermachild Chavis founded these gardens with neighbours from her East Bay neighbourhood. Melody is also an activist in the Buddhist Peace Fellowship. Strong Roots Gardens are gardens which offer job training, and earning opportunities to African-American and other socially excluded young people.

In San Francisco a very ambitious project of this type is the *St Mary's Youth Farm*. The farm is being created on about six acres of land and features bio-intensive food production along with habitat restoration and environmental education. The farm and garden now supply cheap organic vegetables to the residents of a nearby housing project and with the support of the Mayor's Office has been able to offer wages that are nearly double the minimum wage to young people after school hours and during school vacations. It also offers work and training opportunities to local young people who mostly come from the nearby housing project. The need to counter the local drug economy and its impact on teenagers of high-school age is very much part of the rationale for this project. The involvement of the local community in the Youth Farm is seen as essential for its success.

Another outstanding success story in the Bay area is that provided by the *Garden Project* founded by Cathrine Sneed, an African-American who started her first garden in San Mateo County Jail while she was a legal counsellor there. Cathrine Sneed's work with offenders is now internationally recognized (see Ferris *et al.* 2001). The Garden Project, in partnership with the Mayor's office in San Francisco, now maintains a garden in one of the poorest neighbourhoods in San Francisco. Ex-prisoners were also planting ten thousand trees in San Francisco. The success rate of this project, measured by non-return to jail within three years, is 75 per cent. The rate of pay is twice minimum wage. Part of the secret of this success resides in the fact that a living wage is only part of the story for African-Americans discharged from prison. The Garden Project also addresses issues of self-esteem that are equally important in overcoming a criminal record and the stigma of jail, especially for those exposed to virulent racism in the criminal justice system (Ladipo 2001).

Healing and therapy gardens

A growing, and not always recognized, dimension of the community gardening movement is the healing and therapy gardens. There were a number of these in San Francisco. This can be seen very clearly in San Francisco City in the *AIDS Memorial Grove* which was created in the famous Golden Gate Park. The AIDS Memorial Grove is a fifteen-acre wooded dell that has been especially landscaped so as to provide a place for those who have been touched in some way by AIDS and also as a memorial garden for those who have died of the disease since the 1980s. It has been maintained with voluntary donations and labour. The President of the USA and Congress conferred national public landscape status on the garden in 1996. The effort to provide for and maintain this garden has contributed to overcoming the stigma that is still attached to the disease. Like the AIDS hospice movement, largely financed by voluntary contributions, it is a public expression of compassion.

Less high-profile, but in many ways just as effective, has been the creation of the *Comfort Garden* at the San Francisco General Hospital. The original aim of the garden was to pay tribute to the staff of the hospital who had died. The garden was offered as a memorial to their work over the years. The San Francisco General Hospital is a striking building. The garden was designed and planted by Alain Kinet, one of two gardeners employed at the hospital. This garden is now used by patients and staff, who can retreat there for peace and quiet. It can clearly be seen as making a substantial contribution to the healing role of an important city hospital in one of the poorest areas of the city. Alain Kinet and his colleague also had a vegetable garden, which supports a scheme for providing food at home to AIDS and other patients. Alain Kinet was an employee of the City Parks and Recreation Department. It seems to us that the way in which civic values are embodied in this garden and in how the garden is used make it very much a community garden, the community being the hospital itself. This is an example created from the 'bottom up'. Hospital managers can now be proud of this garden because of the initiative of members of the gardening staff (see Cooper-Marcus and Barnes 1995).

Healing and therapy gardens are becoming very much an important element in community care provision following the closure of large mental hospitals and the perceived need to treat many more people in the community. These gardens also offer rehabilitation programmes to people who have suffered barriers to full social inclusion. A good example of this is the *Rubicon Centre* in Richmond, California. Many, if not all, of those who benefit from the horticultural services offered by Rubicon suffer from mental illness or learning disabilities. An important dimension of healing gardens is that of restorative and quiet gardens, often provided by religious foundations, such as the Quiet Garden Movement (see Ferris *et al.* 2001; Spriggs *et al.* 1998).

97

Neighbourhood pocket parks

A new kind of civic park is emerging in cities where finance and resources for conventional parks and open spaces have been cut back in recent years. This is the neighbourhood pocket park. A good example can be found in Berkeley. The *Halcyon Commons* is in the South Berkeley neighbourhood. It is a striking example of a residential neighbourhood reclaiming land from the great twentieth-century 'encloser', the automobile. Halcyon is in a residential area that had become a favoured parking place for nearby businesses and shops. The residents, in collaboration with the City Planning Department, raised the money and contributed voluntary labour to create a small park where cars used to park. It is rather like a residential London Square but without a fence or gate. There is a children's playground, trees, shrubs and attractive flower beds, along with a Japanese Peace Gate. It is now a very attractive and accessible pocket park, open to public and residents alike. It is a genuine public space that exists as a result of civic initiative. The City of Berkeley now has a number of these parks.

Ecological restoration

Ecological restoration has combined with social objectives to provide another form of community garden. There are many urban areas where long-established waterways have been enclosed in concrete culverts. Many of these are now being restored to something resembling their natural state. The *Strawberry Creek Gardens and Park* in Berkeley are an example. The creek itself has been partially restored to its natural state with voluntary labour and scientific expertise from the East Bay Conservation Corps. This creek flows from the famous botanical gardens above the University at Berkeley down to the Bay itself. It is in many ways a good example of creek (or river) restoration that could be copied elsewhere.

Demonstration gardens

A good example of a garden devoted to public education is the *Garden for the Environment* in San Francisco. This garden, like the St Mary's Youth Farm mentioned above, is managed by SLUG, the San Francisco League of Urban Gardeners. The function of this garden is to teach city residents about composting, organic gardening and water conservation. Another garden of this type is the *Gill Tract Urban Farm* on land owned by the University of California at Berkeley. While the primary purpose of this farm is to provide a site for research into sustainable agriculture it is also an organic farm that is used for adult education and youth employment. At the time of our visit in 1997 the future of this farm was in doubt as there were proposals to build on some or all of the land. The campaigning organization "Food First" based in Oakland was hoping that it would be possible to find funds to acquire the land and take over and develop the educational project from the University of California.

Conclusion

The research in the USA on community gardens was concerned with two broad questions. First, what policies would be effective in giving persuasive meaning to the social dimension of sustainability within the framework of Local Agenda 21? Second, in what ways might community gardens and green space policies in urban areas contribute to greater environmental justice?

In many cities in the USA, although by no means all, community gardening can be seen as the outcome of civil rights struggles of the 1960s and 1970s. This is especially so inasmuch as they generated local and participative forms of neighbourhood-level politics. The community gardens have grown up in the wake of the abandonment of inner-city areas by the white majority and especially the major employers (see Bass Warner 1987). The middle classes have vacated the inner city to the so-called *Edge City* (Garreau 1991). At the same time service-sector enterprises and jobs have also migrated there. African-Americans and Hispanic people along with other "people of colour" have found themselves trapped in economically and environmentally damaged neighbourhoods (Bullard 1994; Gottlieb 1993). Around the San Francisco bay are the *flatlands*, the areas located near the old naval bases, docks, petrochemical refineries and former heavy manufacturing districts. These are the *rustbelt* places that were poisoned by toxic chemicals and illegal dumping of waste. Many of the community gardens are in these places and it is the poor and people of colour who are exposed to the greatest environmental risks. The community garden movement in the USA is, in part, one of the positive responses in the struggle to restore these damaged neighbourhoods to ecological and social health.

The information presented here is mainly concerned with the USA and, in particular, focused on California. Nevertheless, the Nottingham Garden Conference in 2000 demonstrated that these are global issues. There are many themes and issues that emerged in the USA that have become apparent in the *Future of Allotments* debate in the UK (HC 1998). The government has made it clear in their town planning policies that they expect 60 per cent of all new housing will be built on brownfield and inner-city sites. With the scarcity of urban land for new building there will be intense pressure on local government to develop on underutilized allotment sites. Higher urban densities might lead to a reduction in the amount of urban green space. This is precisely the issue in New York City where the City Council is claiming there is a shortage of land for housing and are closing community gardens (Ferris *et al.* 2001).

What we can say on the basis of our work to date is that urban green spaces and community gardens (allotments in Europe) can be very positively linked to the implementation of Local Agenda 21 and sustainability policies and at the same time used to promote environmental equity. There is considerable evidence that poor and disadvantaged people not only suffer from low incomes but many also have to live in environmentally degraded environments that are threatened by polluting industry and the consequences of toxic waste dumping. This is not simply a US experience but is now a global phenomenon (Sachs 1995; Beck 1992).

References

Bass Warner, Jr, S. (1987), *To Dwell is to Garden*, Boston: North Eastern University Press.

Beck, U. (1992), *Risk Society: Towards a New Modernity*, London: Sage.

Bullard, R. D. (ed.) (1994), *Unequal Protection; Environmental Justice and Communities of Colour*, San Francisco: Sierra Club Books.

Chavis, M. E. (1997), *Altars in the Street: A Neighbourhood Fights to Survive*, New York: Bell Tower.

Cooper-Marcus, C. and Barnes, M. (1995), *Gardens in Healthcare Facilities: Uses, Therapeutic Benefits, and Design Recommendations*, Center for Health Design, CA, USA.

Environmental Politics (1993), Vol. 2, No. 4, Winter, Special Issue, ed. Caroline Thomas, London: Frank Cass.

Ferris, J. S., Morris, M., Norman, C. and Sempik, J. (eds) (2001), *People, Land and Sustainability: A Global View of Community Gardening*, Nottingham: PLS.

Garreau, J. (1991), *Edge City: Life on the New Frontier*, New York: Anchor Books.

Gottlieb, R. (1993), *Forcing the Spring: The Transformation of the American Environmental Movement*, Covello, USA: Island Press.

HC (1998), *The Future for Allotments*, Report of the Environment Transport and Regional Affairs Committee, HC 560, London: House of Commons.

Ladipo, D. (2001), Imprisoned America, *New Left Review*, 7, Second Series, January/ February, London, UK.

Roddick, J. and Dodds, F. (1993), Agenda 21's political strategy, *Environmental Politics*, 2, 4, Winter, London: Frank Cass.

Sachs, A. (1995), Eco-Justice: linking human rights and the environment. Worldwatch Paper 127, December, Washington DC.

Spriggs, N., Kaufman R. E. and Bass Warner, Jr, S. (1998), *Restorative Gardens: The Healing Landscape*, New Haven CT: Yale University Press.

Waters, A. (1996), *Chez Panisse Vegetables*, New York: HarperCollins.

CHAPTER 8

Turning the Car Inside Out:
Transport, Equity and Environment

Juliet Jain and Jo Guiver

Abstract

"Turning the car inside out" describes how the environmental damage and social exclusion inflicted by the car can only be seen from outside the car. It explains how car use has reshaped land, time use, social relations and economic patterns. It creates ever more pressures for increased car use, yet inevitably leaves the people temporarily or permanently excluded from cars having to negotiate car distances and times. The worst scenario of car saturation is rejected as untenable both because of the permanent social and environmental impact, but also the self-defeating nature of the quest for mobility.

Keywords

Car; Equity; Environment; Social practice

Introduction

Turning the car inside out refers to our contention that the car must be seen from outside if its detrimental effects on both the environment and social equity are to be recognized and tackled. Although car travel and ownership appear to offer individuals opportunities, choice and freedom, they come with a large price tag that is picked up by society as a whole and often disproportionately by those without access to car travel. This paper outlines the way in which cars not only create environmental problems and social exclusion but progressively re-order time and spatial relations, committing society to a spiral of ever more car use. "Motorized vehicles create remoteness which they alone can shrink. They create distances for all and shrink them for only a few" (Illich 1974: 42).

An environmental perspective is by necessity one from outside the car, but frequently the solution for problems of social exclusion related to transport is

Address for correspondence: *Juliet Jain, Centre for Science Studies, Department of Sociology, Lancaster University, Bailrigg, Lancaster, LA1 4TL. Email: j.jain@lancaster.ac.uk.*

to grant the "excluded" more mobility, therefore positioning individual needs over wider social and environmental considerations. In this paper we suggest that if more attention were focused on the excluding practices and consequences of car use, we would have more chance of countering environmental degradation and social exclusion in a number of time frames.

Lay discourses about transport and everyday activities presented in this paper indicate the complexities in addressing the social embeddedness of the car. The quotations used to illustrate our arguments come from research conducted, independently, for our Masters' dissertations. The quotation reference indicates the research source and any directly relevant contextual information. For the most part, the words of the respondents/participants need no introduction but serve as examples of lay discourse on the relevant issues and empirical evidence to support our arguments.

The quotations from focus groups come from research undertaken by one of the authors (Guiver 1998). This used the transcripts of nine focus groups, two conducted by the author (one of car users in Leeds, the other of 16- and 17-year-old car-dependent pupils at Lancaster Girls Grammar School) and the rest by Lancashire County Council's Planning Department in 1996 and 1997, for an exercise into "Perceptions of Travel". These were undertaken at various locations in Lancashire and included groups with different travel patterns, of different socioeconomic groups, ages and both genders.

Quotes from interviews and questionnaires are taken from a study of people who had actively chosen to become (or remain) "car-free" (Jain 1998). This research investigated motivations for living without a car and the lifestyle choices that were part of the decision. The data were collected via a postal questionnaire and 10 follow-up semi-structured interviews. The questionnaire respondents consisted of mainly professional people in full- or part-time employment (73 per cent) between the ages of 26 and 55 (74 per cent). However, the interviews were selected to represent a range of household types, e.g. families with young children, and single working and retired people of different genders, in different geographic locations across England.

The policy focus of this paper relates to recent initiatives by the UK government to change the future trajectory of travel in Britain, specifically arising from the 1998 White Paper on Transport, *A New Deal for Transport: Better for Everyone* (DETR 1998). While this document seeks to forward a relationship between the environment, economy and transport with individual choice, we argue that the interface between individual choice and policy initiatives requires further examination. We see the White Paper as promoting individual choice of access to destinations while reducing or denying choice of lifestyle or environment.

Definitions

Because of its emphasis on the relative nature of social exclusion, we have chosen to use the definition of social exclusion formulated by Burchardt *et al.* (1999: 230): "An individual is socially excluded if (a) he or she is geographically resident in a society but (b) he or she does not participate in the normal activities of citizens in that society."

Social exclusion is a relative, rather than an absolute, terminology that measures "difference" between groups of people, and we would argue that ownership or access to a car changes the context of inclusion and exclusion. As Harvey (2000: 78) argues, difference is constantly being "reproduced, sustained, undermined, and reconfigured by the political-economic and socio-ecological processes . . ." often with unexpected or uncalculated consequences.

The Brundtland definition of sustainability provides our frame of reference for "environment": "Sustainable development is development that meets the needs of the present without compromising the abilities of future generations." This definition itself emphasizes the temporal social inequalities produced by "unenvironmental" behaviour. Today's actions shape the future for the environment *and* society, although the exact outcomes are rarely predictable through linear "cause and effect" assumptions (Adam 1998a).

Environmental Impacts of Car Travel

The arguments about the direct impacts of motorized transport upon fauna, flora, climate and human habitat have been well rehearsed at Kyoto, Rio and other venues (see also Adams 1995; Whitelegg 1993, 1997), yet motorized travel continues to grow in defiance of commitments to sustainable growth (Tengstrøm 1998). For example, the 1998 White Paper on Transport estimated an increase of traffic in the UK by one-third in the next 20 years, and hence its policy aim to reduce this projected rate of growth in recognition of known consequences.

The global problem

The burning of fossil fuels has led to a build-up of carbon dioxide in the atmosphere, which is thought to cause warming of the world's surface environment because heat from the sun's rays is less able to escape. The exact mechanisms are yet to be understood and there will be many debates about the extent of the change, but there is a wide consensus that releasing carbon dioxide from fossil fuels contributes to freak weather conditions, which are likely to endanger human and other life. The release of carbon dioxide and the use of finite energy sources creates geographical and temporal inequalities (Adams 1995).

The parts of the globe most likely to suffer the consequences of climate change are those nearest to sea level, and already sensitive societies. Although wealthier nations like the Netherlands are at risk, climate change is most likely to affect poorer nations reliant on agriculture, particularly if they are situated near sea level or lack the social structures to organize preventative or remedial measures to deal with climate change and "natural" emergencies (Whitelegg 1997). Yet carbon dioxide emissions are most likely to come from the transport of richer industrial nations (only 8 per cent of the world's population are car owners—Elkin *et al.* 1991). However, the inequality is too easily portrayed as the "haves" inflicting trouble on the "have nots", when many of those affected by climate change also aspire to cars and the mobility they provide. Temporal inequality is caused by the actions of current generations imposing predicted problems upon future generations, of both climate change and resource consumption, which Adam (1998b) urges should be placed equally alongside other interests, e.g. economic gain, in transport planning.

The more local problem

Environmental degradation is evident at a local level. Air pollution and traffic noise are suffered by many of us on a daily basis. While road "danger" to humans may be considered a social problem, the carnage of wildlife is an environmental consequence. (For instance, Harris *et al.* (1992; quoted in Friends of the Earth 1997: 16) estimated that 47,000 badgers and 4,000 barn owls are killed each year.) Animal and plant habitats become isolated and non-viable where roads and traffic act as barriers, further reducing biodiversity (Friends of the Earth 1997). Land dedicated to moving and static vehicles is surfaced, contributing to the rapid run-off of water and exacerbating the risk of flooding (Elkin *et al.* 1991).

These environmental consequences, inflicted by car use, impact upon people who live, work, play, walk, cycle, etc. in affected areas regardless of whether they are car users or not.

The Social Impacts of Car Travel

The social impacts of the car interconnect with the environmental impacts. The car creates differences in lifestyle practices around time and space, excluding many temporary or permanent non-users from participating in a variety of activities, denying "citizenship" (Church *et al.* 2000; Hine and Mitchell 2001; Levitas 1998). In Britain, a third of all households are without a car, and while 45 per cent of households have one car, different household members' use may be limited to specific times (Potter 1997; DETR 1998). Only 57 per cent of women have a driving licence compared with 81 per cent of men (Hamilton and Jenkins 2000). Children, unless escorted passengers, are excluded from car travel, and low-income households, single parents, single elderly people and those with specific disabilities are least likely to own a car (Erskine 1996). Where more cars are available in a household other transport modes are used less, and more journeys are made compared to households without a car (Hamilton and Jenkins 2000).

Parallel to the growth in car use, other social changes have occurred, such as demographic changes, different work patterns including increases in women's employment and subsequent changes to childcare, and the rise of electronically transmitted information and mobile technologies. These have placed new demands on transport and expectations around individual schedules, and have extended the debate about where exclusion may occur and solutions may be found (see, for example, the visioning process in Lyons *et al.* 2000). New demand for car travel can only aggravate social difference through the direct and indirect effects on quality of life and the use of time and space.

The 1998 White Paper on Transport (DETR 1998) acknowledges a number of these points. It suggests policy solutions should take into account the various limitations that can exclude people from choices related to location, distance and time, as well as indicating the need to integrate transport policy to other areas that affect travel, such as education, health and land-use planning.

Direct social effects

Transport has many implications for the quality of life and health. Notably, childhood asthma has been linked to air pollution, and there is increasing evidence of heart problems being attributed to different air-borne pollutants from petrol and diesel combustion (Whitelegg 1997). The car itself offers little protection from air pollution as "the air inside the car can be more polluted than for the pedestrian on the pavement" (DETR 1998: 3). Meanwhile, the push toward reducing emissions by technological solutions can help only if traffic growth is reduced or reversed (DETR 1998: 23).

Traffic noise is intrusive, interfering with social activity and causing health problems related to stress and sleep disturbance, especially in urban areas (Whitelegg 1997). The use of cars also affects health in substituting a stressful, but sedentary way of travelling for walking and cycling, which may contribute to obesity and heart disease (Freund and Martin 1993).

Road traffic danger, through injuries and mortality, has important personal and economic consequences, particularly on the health and emergency services, and the cost of sick pay and temporary staff for employers (Davis 1992/3). UK national travel statistics (DETR 2000) show that 3,404 people (children and adults) were killed in road "accidents" in 1999 (of which 870 were pedestrians and 172 pedal cyclists), and nearly 38,400 were seriously injured (of which 8,955 were pedestrians and 3,004 were pedal cyclists). Those outside the car, i.e. cyclists and pedestrians, suffer higher risks of death and injury than those inside because they do not have the physical protection of the car (Erskine 1996; Freund and Martin 1993). Fear of "accidents" has shaped people's travel decisions away from cycling and walking to become car drivers, passengers or public transport users (Potter 1997). The road as a dangerous place therefore curtails the activities of a large section of society, e.g. children, who are permanently excluded from driving, and use more environmentally sustainable forms of transport. Hillman *et al.* (1990) found the space available to British children had decreased considerably between 1971 and 1990 and concluded "the increase in personal freedom and choice arising from widening car ownership has been gained at the cost of freedom and choice for children". Transport engineers have also spatially ordered the road to reduce exposure of pedestrians to the danger of motorized mobility, but in this process have removed pedestrian "desire lines", which creates time–space priority differentials between car users and pedestrians (Davis 1992/3; Freund and Martin 1993).

"Nowhere really to cross, you have got to walk up the street. If you were on one side of the road, say the post office, and you wanted to use the pedestrian crossing, you

have to walk to the top of town, use the pedestrian crossing and back on towards Woolies." (Fleetwood focus group)

Communities have been severed by roads and road danger affecting people differentially. Like a river, a road can deny access to an area and create islands. Those who can swim and who are not intimidated by the flow of water will have more access than the non-swimmers, the weak or weak-hearted. Children, elderly people, those with luggage, visual impairment or the less nimble are more likely to be denied access by roads, to be forced to make detours to bridging points, than young adults, the fit, unencumbered and confident. Appleyard (1981) researched three streets in San Francisco, and discovered that the streets with higher density and fast-moving traffic reduced the community interaction of the street as people crossed the road in a less random manner than on quieter streets. He also showed that individual home occupiers in the busiest street felt they had less "possession" of the street space in front of their homes. New urban motorways have also cut through existing communities, severing space much like the railways in the nineteenth century, often where communities are too disempowered to protest (Murray 1998). Space has therefore become redistributed away from those moving around local communities to those travelling through the space of others. As well as travelling through places with which they are unconnected, motorized travellers consume greater distance because of their greater speed and discourage other established sustainable spatial practices such as walking to the shops or cycling to work.

Understanding this spatial severance was part of the motivation for remaining car-free for one particular respondent, but more people reflected on the effect of car users on their own spatial practices and environment.

> *"I find it unacceptable that people who live in leafy environs—as we do—pollute, blight and endanger areas of lower income, where they would not live themselves precisely because of the traffic which they bring (and its noise and pollution)."* (Car-free questionnaire)

> *"I enjoy my car-free lifestyle, but it is made more difficult by the number of people who seem hell-bent on using their car for even short distances, degrading the environment I live in."* (Car-free questionnaire)

Cars occupy land, even when they are not being used, so that vast areas of our townscapes are locked away from other uses. Effectively, public space becomes "privatized" by car use (Beckmann, forthcoming). However, moving cars require more room than parked cars, and their space requirement increases with faster speeds (Engwicht 1992). Also, fast-moving vehicles prohibit other, simultaneous, use of road space, e.g. for play, due to the danger. Navarro (1985, in Whitelegg 1993) estimates that a single person in a car travelling at 10 kilometres per hour requires 18.7 square metres of road, and at 40 kph requires 60 square metres, while a pedestrian travelling at five kilometres per hour only requires 0.8 square metres, which highlights the inequalities in space consumption.

Indirect social effects

There has been a steady change in the spatial arrangements of locations since nineteenth-century industrialization and urbanization, aided by the developments in rail, tram, bus, car and air travel. The rapid growth in car ownership over the last 30 years has been reflected in the location choices of large retail units, business parks and in the centralizing of services and related land-use planning, while smaller local retail outlets and services have declined (Sheller and Urry 2000). This has caused a fragmentation of space. However land-use patterns favourably geared towards the car create differentials in access between car users and others, for example allowing greater choice of locations for living based on other "quality of life" factors while avoiding constraint by other transport networks. This spatial relationship is important to those without a car when making lifestyle choices, where destination decisions are often compromised by the type of transport available (Jain 1998), as this retired married woman, whose household had never had a car, describes:

> "Occasionally the vagueness of public transport, a shrinking of the railway system (now thankfully reversed) has made us long for our own transport! We understand why people who have it are reluctant to be without! Being car-less has restricted my life in some respects—and still does. Most activities and facilities are geared to car ownership! I know there are many places I haven't visited or things I haven't done through lack of own transport but whether that is loss or gain I can't quite calculate."
> (Car-free questionnaire)

The point of view that the car has become a necessity rather than a choice is held in the 1998 White Paper on Transport, yet the choice the car offers is based on increasing opportunities for more time spent on the move. Public transport policies deployed to replicate this do not challenge the assumption that mobility is a necessity:

> automobilization has opened up the urban fabric and freed the individual from some of his or her former physical boundaries . . . it simultaneously moulded another, more dangerous and dispersed structure that continually forces people and goods to maintain their movement.
> (Beckmann, forthcoming)

Many of the car's impacts result from speed and the desire to compress time and space. In accommodating speed, two sets of landscape have emerged. The walking landscape has been overlain with one ordered around conduits of speed and continuous movement, often justified in economic terms and time savings. While this change occurred with the railways, roads upgraded and specifically dedicated to motorized mobility have etched a dense network across Britain, and elsewhere in the world. People not equipped for the motorized landscape are therefore in a constant state of negotiation between the old and the new interpretations of time and space.

Public transport requires the user to comply with its timetables and routes, frequently requiring complex planning and sometimes demanding much greater time for each journey. Those without cars find access at certain times of the day, week or year denied to them, whether through service limitations or fear of certain spaces or modes of transport at specific times. Individual time poverty may be intensified when public transport networks cannot compete with the car's temporal and spatial flexibility, or where road congestion delays buses. Women are more likely to have complex routes linking multiple destinations, but have greater dependency on public transport than men, creating time inequalities (Hamilton and Jenkins 2000). Men, who tend to have single-destination journeys, historically have chosen more individual modes of travel, whether a bicycle or a car (Pooley and Turnbull 1999). In such differentiated landscapes those without a car have become excluded, not just through lack of spatial access in their choices of employment, education and retail, and of access to essential services such as health care, but also through time poverty (Church *et al.* 2000; Hine and Mitchell 2001).

"No buses where I live, none at all. Especially in school holidays—well they have the bus going to school but that's just the one going in and the one going out . . . it only goes to Kendal, it won't go anywhere else . . . it'll go further out so it's, you're just, completely cut off without a car unless you get a taxi and they're a lot more expensive where I live than anywhere else." (Lancaster Girls Grammar School focus group)

Rather than considering the longevity of the environment and the social effects of increasing mobility, the dominant discourse of "time = money" frames efforts towards immediate time-savings, often through provision for speed. This economic discourse is reproduced in the 1998 White Paper on Transport where a key aim is to improve traffic flow and reduce the cost of "time-wasting" congestion to the economy. It can be argued that individual and business time schedules, in the free-flowing movement of motorized traffic, have been prioritized in the cost–benefit calculations of road schemes, where variables are valued in monetary terms. This has added to the political legitimacy of constructing controversial routes such as the Newbury bypass to save travel time and relieve urban congestion, as it is more difficult to place economic values on habitats or quality of life than on time-savings to business (Adam 1998b).

Maintaining the relative speed of car travel has also enabled a growth in distance travelled, but without actually reducing time spent travelling, especially for commuting (Potter 1997; Pooley and Turnbull 1999). The car's time-space compression has enabled people to consume mobility in exercising their "right" to choose their place of work, their home and where they send their children to school. The consequences are highlighted by Engwicht (1992). He uses this example: a person living in location x taking up a new job in location y due to the opening of new road that provides a time-saving; a few weeks later a second person takes up a job in location x and travels from location y. This criss-crossing of journeys exemplifies how location becomes less important through access to faster mobility, except once more for those without a car, and it ignores the environmental consequences. This embedding of travel over increasing distances has little benefit to society.

"Well, on work days I spend two-three hours I would guess, travelling, because I have to drop my wife at Leyland, she works in Leyland, and I come back into Preston, so that's two-three hours in one day, every day. It gets on my nerves." (County Hall focus group)

Speed as a social problem also directly links to the environment. Car-based travel once epitomized an elitist human relationship with nature and the countryside, but has been transformed into an apparent indifference to the landscape it passes through (Liniado 1996; Rose 1993). Not only has speed channelled the urban space, it has also demanded the removal of roadside trees and hedges that impede the driver's sightlines, under the guise of safety.

"Motorways sprung all over the country. I know they need them for the amount of cars, but even so, by the time we're finished that's all we're going to have, motorways. There'll be no fields or no nothing. No trees."

"No fields, no trees, no nowt." (Colne focus group)

Again, this spatial domination through speed excludes other, slower forms of mobility such as cycling, horse riding or walking, although the driver and passenger have also excluded themselves from a different kind of relationship with the environment (Macnaghton and Urry 1998). Therefore, speed, via the socio-technical assemblages of car technologies, transport engineering and political decision making, has disembedded the individual from the natural and social environments, as roads slice through the landscape with little respect for sense of place (Lefebvre 1991; Sheller and Urry 2000). Several car-free people recounted differences between their relationship with the local environment and that of other car drivers they knew:

"I find not having a car makes me more appreciative of my local surroundings— Norwich and Norfolk. In the years that I've been cycling regularly I have seen more of Norfolk than most car drivers, since I travel at a pace that lets me see my surroundings properly." (Car-free questionnaire)

Individual Sense, Social Madness!

From the individual's point of view, a car offers freedom to move rapidly over a distance. This means the driver can, in an hour, access locations within a 50–60 mile radius, while as a cyclist they would be restricted to 10–15 miles, or as a pedestrian 3–4 miles. Even if distance is not sought, the car grants distances at much lower costs of time and effort and provides shelter from the elements as well as the power to carry loads much heavier than would be possible using muscle power.

Car use is widely associated with discourses of freedom and choice, freedom over distance, over one's own time-planning, and political freedom. This suggests that more individual mobility would aid liberation from "social exclusion" by providing access to a greater number of destinations. Indeed, the Thatcher government in the 1980s saw car ownership as a positive social aspiration, where the car embodied the sentiment of a democratic "right" of

citizenship through the political process. This was promoted by powerful motor organizations such as the AA (Urry 1999; Sheller and Urry 2000): "... greatest mobile force for freedom in the rich democracies ... A liberator of women, and a device that transformed a locally bound worker into a free yeoman" (*Economist* 1986: 14).

> *"More freedom having a car, more choice. You can just sit there and say 'let's go to "so and so" today', and just get in the car and go."* (Fleetwood focus group)

> *"Freedom, and you don't have to wait for anybody, you can go when you want to ... it's instantly accessible as well isn't it, if it's in your drive, you just jump in it."* (Preston focus group)

These discourses from "inside the car" also are ever-popular with the media, advertising, film and literature, constructing a whole culture around the car (Urry 1999). A number of images prevail, particularly with the portrayal in advertising of cars granting their owners access to unchanging landscapes/townscapes in a machine that guarantees them sex-appeal, style and/or protection for their children from a dangerous world (Bailey 1986; Wernick 1991). The car is imaged and practised as a "quasi-private space", extending the home out to a mobile, personalized protective cocoon that provides sensuous pleasure in the act of driving (Urry 1999).

Learning to drive is seen as a rite of passage into adulthood, and an essential skill for participation in the workforce, as well as a skill that provides pleasure (Freund and Martin 1993; Urry 1999). For young people it has reached the point where having a driving licence can be perceived as more important than the right to vote, if it were a choice between the two (Solomon 1998). Driving appears to offer social relations that are "lifted out" of the local contexts of interaction (Giddens 1990: 21); it is associated with self-improvement and the betterment of the individual through the experience of other places (Urry 1999). Not learning to drive, or being car-free sets the individual outside of the concept of full social participation, which was frequently articulated by interviewees and on questionnaires in Jain's (1998) study of people living without a car.

> *"The problem has been living in an affluent area. The other women feel guilty and obliged to offer us lifts, and others think we're eccentric, and others look down on you ... You've got to be motivated to be different."* (Car-free interview)

The freedom and spontaneity offered to the first motorists, travelling in a landscape moulded by pre-car transport, is no longer available since the car has "democratized" travel. Fellow car travellers create severe constraints on scheduling and journey times, and the distances imposed by the dispersal of land use commit millions of commuters every day to hours of sitting in traffic jams. Most driving is based on mundane routine, where growing congestion and competition for parking has transformed the car from an object providing freedom to an encumbrance, as time and energy become wasted in traffic jams and searching for a parking space.

"You set off earlier and you set off later so your working day's longer. Just to avoid rush hours and things like that."

"You certainly do plan your day round busy periods." (Preston focus group)

As Beckmann (forthcoming) points out, the liberalizing effects of the car have become muted by its mass use. New social relations now embed the motorist, and attempts to avoid the congestion of other motorists by devices such as intelligent transport systems are, if widely adopted, doomed to failure. The freedom of mobility becomes a battle between people exerting their greater "right" over particular space-time coordinates on a landscape that bears little resemblance to those suggested by car adverts. The government has responded by announcing initiatives to explore mechanisms such as road pricing and work-place charging to reduce numbers of cars travelling into urban centres where congestion is most serious. Proposals for restricting car access promoted by the 1998 White Paper have been followed by specific legislation in the 2000 Transport Act and pilot schemes to be delivered by Local Transport Plans (2000–5).

Nor does the car give freedom from danger. The car is subject to crime, leaving owners stranded by missing or "disabled" vehicles. Its ability to protect the human contents against accidents is reliant on the behaviour of other drivers. Equally, in depopulated spaces the initial security provided by the car is removed when it breaks down on the motorway, or when accessing isolated parking lots (Whitelegg 1997).

While the car is represented by an idealized concept of individual freedom on the open road, the reality is about collective practice—a mobility that is likely to be found locked into its own collective manifestation, namely a traffic jam. Road space is shared and limited, controlled by collective observation of rules and regulations. A collective trend towards yet more car ownership and use will only exacerbate the social differentials and increase the environmental pressures outlined above, and will extend the need for increased regulation of its use. Although the individual may see no other way of tackling their own inequities of mobility except by purchasing and using a car, it is clear that this "arms race" of mobility will not provide a solution for society as a whole. However, individuals are not the only agents involved in the proliferation of car use.

A collection of political and economic arrangements constitute car travel, from the agents involved in the spatial landscape design which exerts power over the individual destination choice to the information provided about the options open to drivers. For example, organizations may only provide information about accessing their site by car, leaving the individual struggling to find out about alternatives, as transport is not central to the organization's business. Large companies and other institutions would be unwilling to lose the economies of scale produced when customers and employees can be drawn from a 50-mile radius rather than a 5-mile one. Employers may also be reluctant to move away from the image of the company car, or not be able to envisage work being carried out without a car.

"The company has pool cars, but I try to use the train as much as possible. They were resistant at first because they preferred to pay for petrol than the train fare, so I had to make excuses like I was working on the train. My colleagues think travelling on the train is a bit of an endurance test." (Car-free interview)

"I was turned down as a manager in the offices of a nursing agency because 'a non-driver could not pick up the carers if they had a break-down in their cars' (infrequent) and 'if the manageress of the whole group was not available (rare), a non-driver would be unable to call out to visit clients if they requested this.' It amazes me that people think I'm helpless without a car, or that I'm not independent." (Car-free questionnaire)

Lutzenhiser and Shove (1996) indicate that travel is rarely "individual" at all, and is dependent on an array of networked agents. This suggests the car is socially embedded not just through its cultural meanings for individuals, but through the institutions that overtly and covertly support its survival. As Bauman (1993) argues, the large number of jobs that connect to the car as a means of mass transport, from car mechanics to oil refinery workers, demand political support if their positions are threatened. (The political response to the British "fuel crisis" in 2000 and the "saving" of jobs in closing car factories exemplify Bauman's point.) Some industries (car and component manufacture, petrol refineries and distributors) are directly dependent upon increasing car sales and use, and so promote the positive aspects while ignoring or downplaying the negative aspects of car travel.

"These companies are just in it for profit and all this advertising on the telly, I just think they are trying to make us feel good. I don't believe them for one minute." (Fleetwood focus group)

The association of the car with political freedom was exemplified by Mawhinney (1995), the former Conservative transport minister, in a speech as part of his attempts to encourage debate about the role of transport in society. Easy freedom of movement defines a free society. Discourses of choice are also associated with mobility, but as with political freedom, the focus is always on the advantages to the traveller.

> In some respects we can view the 1950s as an era of greater choice. This was an age of local shopping when it was rarely necessary to travel more than a mile or two to find all basic consumer goods. But of course, the range of goods was much smaller. You would not have found Kiwi fruits or fresh yoghurt at the corner shop, nor the vast range of electrical goods and toys from which consumers can choose today. (Mawhinney 1995: 43)

However, this choice is only offered to those with cars, and by taking way local custom creates a diminishing range of services available to all. The *freedoms to* and choice gained by the car user have been at the expense of numerous *freedoms from* (e.g. danger, noise, air pollution), with community, locally available goods and services being lost to everyone. When viewed from the perspective of society as a whole, rather than the individual car user, the move towards greater mobility can be seen as largely self-defeating, as increased traffic prevents individuals realizing the potential speed of their vehicles, and land use and social practices require increasing dependence upon motorized transport.

Discourse for Change

A focus on traffic or mobility, rather than access, has further entrenched car travel in land-use planning. Litman (2001) illustrates how a decision on where to build a school made on traffic grounds would favour a major artery with abundant parking; on mobility, a site with public transport and cycle ways; and on access within a neighbourhood, with short walking distances. He also suggests that the wealth of information about traffic behaviour skews planning decisions towards improvements for car travel and against other modes, for which there is a dearth of information.

As society continues to adjust to increasing levels of car use, so institutions, social practices, land use and common discourses make a reduction in car use appear less and less plausible. New generations find themselves living in places where they need a car to function in society, with no experience of other ways of travelling and in a climate where being able to drive is a sign of adulthood. While it is essential that the arguments for reduction on social and environmental grounds are acted upon, there are multiple reasons for the resistance to lifestyle change.

Individuals may view their priorities through the car windscreen rather than by standing on the roadside, despite some knowledge of environmental arguments. This is because lifestyles are constructed around a range of conflicting decisions, some of which might be perceived as outside the control of the individual. The sheer scale of climate change geographically (and its unquantified future effects) has made it difficult for people to feel that changing their lifestyles or activities on an individual basis would make any difference, especially when they perceive there is little support from governments or other agents (Harrison *et al.* 1996). Hence, understanding the global environmental effects of the car may provide little incentive to individuals to change daily travel decisions. This is particularly problematic for schemes that focus on individual travel choices such as the local authority-led "Travelwise" initiatives. While Burningham and O'Brien (1994) propose that a more useful approach is to localize the global, they recognize that people constantly manage lifestyle contradictions, e.g. not linking environmental knowledge with their own actions. However, even recognizing local environmental problems, for example experiencing the effect of air pollution on your child's asthma, may fail to engage behavioural change for the wider benefit of society (Hinchliffe 1997). Individual agency is powerless to incorporate the larger comprehension of environmental effects, as travel behaviour is compromised by other lifestyle choices (Tengstrøm 1998).

The Lex Report on Motoring (1999) indicates that few motorists understand the full-scale effect of driving on the environment, and many see the move towards reducing car travel as an infringement of their freedom to participate in social networks. Solomon (1998b) picks up this point to argue that recognizing the pleasure and social power people gain from driving and "whizzing around" is important in the blurring of the boundary between travel needs and desires. What persuades people to retain their car, and use it is a complex negotiation between individual perceptions and the social context, which emphasizes the conflict of interests between equity, society and the environment.

Jain's (1998) research on people choosing a car-free lifestyle echoes this. The research demonstrated that although 70 per cent of respondents indicated that global environmental concerns were a factor in deciding to live without a car, few were totally persuaded to be car-free purely on environmental grounds. The large range of "other" reasons given, which included finance and the stress of driving, suggest a complex approach to making lifestyle changes. Some respondents commented that it was only when the lifestyle change had occurred that their environmental awareness grew. As the earlier quotes indicated, not having a car can require quite a dogmatic mindset to counter social expectations. While the reasons for reducing car use can only be appreciated from the perspective of "outside the car", the process of change will only be possible by understanding the "insider's" point of view.

"Somewhere along the way we gradually became aware of the environment (large and small) problems involved in car ownership, and our situation made it easy to resist any desires and pressures to become car owners." (Car-free questionnaire)

"I gave up driving before I joined FOE and I only really understood my motives after I'd given up. Although financial considerations played a part in giving up driving they no longer apply. I was just recently offered an expensive company car, which I declined: my rail fare is paid instead." (Car-free questionnaire)

These car-free individuals articulated the environmental problems caused by the car as something they wanted to influence, but the social problems were mainly acknowledged in the way they had to adapt their routines to a car-orientated spatial and temporal landscape. The focus on the environment has also dominated transport planning discourses in the past, although the effect of the car on social differentials is now beginning to be explored, and has been translated into policy discourses via the 1998 White Paper on Transport. However, this is set in a context where trends in car travel still dominate the social and physical landscapes. For example, Hine and Mitchell (2001), in their exploration of the barriers to using public transport that exclude specific groups, discuss lay discourses that exemplify problems such as crossing busy roads to access bus stops, yet do not challenge the role that the infrastructure provided for cars plays in creating the initial social differentials or sustaining the spatial and temporal barriers discussed in their data.

The "outside" perspectives of environmental and social impacts of the car need to be placed centrally across the discourse of policy, business and the academy, and acted upon. Many individuals do not feel empowered to change and look to others in authority to make the changes (see Guiver 1998), although some are willing to take a stronger stance (see Jain 1998). However, the majority are locked into the tunnel vision from "inside the car". Lutzenhiser and Shove (1996) correctly indicate that it is necessary to address the wider network of agents that hold considerable power over "individual" choice. For instance, government policy has a key role in encouraging lifestyle changes that acknowledge the environment (Harrison *et al.* 1996). The 1998 White Paper on Transport acknowledges this but is tentative in its approach to invoking change for the individual: "We have had to make hard choices on how to combat congestion and pollution while persuading people to use their cars a little less—and public transport a little more" (DETR 1998: 3). However, the democratic right to drive has subsequently shifted the political emphasis, notably in fuel price cuts and commitments to road-building programmes. The trust relationship between policy and the individual, both complying with the same objectives, that Bauman suggests is essential (1993) has appeared to be lacking in current policy delivery.

While policy initiatives are emerging through new approaches to transport and land-use planning, e.g. the guidance for Local Transport Plans, and through pilot schemes of green travel plans, homezones, and car-free estates, these are only spatially contained enclaves of change. There needs to be a much wider debate about how and where destinations are created, which may lead to radical changes to working arrangements, the re-emergence of community-based facilities, and a re-culturalization of different or new modes of mobility that incorporate social *and* environmental equity. The 1998 White Paper on Transport takes steps towards this through the notion of integration of transport and environmental issues with other policy areas, but is still working within a car-based framework. For example, the "safe routes to school" programme aims to encourage walking to school, but does not challenge how a policy enabling parental choice encourages the travelling of greater distances to school, which are less suitable for walking.

Conclusions

The car can only remain a socially divisive technology. With continued car use the car will still demand more space, extend the consumption of distance and continue time differentials, unless its speed is reduced to walking pace. Nor will there be a reduction in danger or community severance, or the re-emergence of local facilities. Individuals can solve their own mobility problems with more car use, and remove their individual social inequalities through access to a wider set of destinations, employment opportunities and services, but this can only extend the collective problems. A scenario of equal and universal car access would ensure that even more land is covered in roads and cars for greater numbers of hours, until gridlock occurs, and is likely to leave still socially excluded a small pool of people who would never be able to drive. The alternative, to reduce car use, would be preferable for society, the environment and equity.

For individuals to reduce their personal mobility in a landscape and timescape still based on car mobility will be difficult. The problem is bigger than their individual actions. Only the agents with an overview of the problems from "outside the car" can start the move to less mobility. The discourses and actions that sustain and promote car mobility need to be addressed in order to create equitable transport visions for the future. This will require a strong lead from government policies, and a trust that corporate interest will not override social and environmental concerns so that individuals can feel that changes to their travel behaviour are worthwhile. Negotiating with those who benefit economically from car travel will require multiple strategies that work towards a common goal, embedding a true interpretation of integration. Mapping the relationships between the agents involved in continuing a trend towards more car mobility, and the discourses that arise in this process may be one way to addressing the complex nature of organizing policy directives. (These agents include the individual, government and business.) Looking at the interface between these different discourses may illuminate the difficulties in translating policy goals into individual actions. What is clear is that the common goal to reduce the impact on the environment and increase social equity should focus on how to reconfigure a landscape of conflicting social, economic, political and environmental interests around the human rather than the machine.

Acknowledgement

The authors would like to thank Lancashire County Council for giving permission to use quotations from focus groups conducted by them.

References

Adam, B. (1998a), *Timescapes of Modernity: The Environment and Invisible Hazards*, London: Routledge.

Adam, B. (1998b) [R(8)] *Relevance of Time Dimension: Time, Common Transport Policy and the Environment*, EURO-TENASSESS Contract No. ST-96-AM .601.

Adams, J. (1995), *Risk*, London: UCL Press.

Appleyard, D. (1981), *Liveable Streets*, Berkeley: University of California Press.

Bailey, S. (1986), *Sex, Drink and Fast Cars: The Consumption of Images*, London: Faber and Faber.

Bauman, Z. (1993), *Postmodern Ethics*, Oxford: Blackwell.

Beckmann, J. (forthcoming), Automobility—a social problem and theoretical concept, *Environment and Planning, D: Society and Space*.

Burchardt, T., Le Grand, J. and Piachaud, D. (1999), Social exclusion in Britain 1991–1995, *Social Policy and Administration*, 33, 3: 227–44.

Burningham, K. and O'Brien, M. (1994), Global environmental values and local contexts of action, *Sociology*, 28: 913–32.

Brundtland Report (1987), *World Commission on Environment and Development, Our Common Future*, Oxford: Oxford University Press.

Church, A., Frost, M. and Sullivan, K. (2000), Transport and social exclusion in London, *Transport Policy*, 7: 195–205.

Davis, R. (1992/3), *Death on the Streets*, Hawes, North Yorkshire: Leading Edge Press.

DETR (1998), *A New Deal for Transport: Better for Everyone*, London: HMSO.

DETR (2000), *Road Accidents in Great Britain: 1999. The casualty report.* http:\\www.transtat.detr.gov.uk/tables/2000/ragb/ragb00_1.pdf

Economist, The (1986), The unfinished revolution, 25 January: 14–15.

Elkin, T., McLaren, D. and Hillman, M. (1991), *Reviving the City: Towards Sustainable Urban Development*, London: Friends of the Earth.

Engwicht, D. (1992), *Towards an Eco-City: Calming the Traffic*, Sydney: Envirobook.

Erskine, T. (1996), The burden of risk: who dies because of cars? *Social Policy and Administration*, 30, 2: 143–57.

Freund, P. and Martin, G. (1993), *The Ecology of the Automobile*, London: Black and Rose Books.

Friends of the Earth (1997), *Unlocking the Gridlock: A Key to a New Transport Policy*, London: Friends of the Earth.

Giddens, A. (1990), *The Consequences of Modernity*, Cambridge: Polity Press.

Guiver, J. (1998), *The Trouble with Buses . . .* MA dissertation, Independent Studies, University of Lancaster.

Hamilton, K. and Jenkins, L. (2000), A gender audit for public transport: a new policy tool in the tackling of social exclusion, *Urban Studies*, 37, 10: 1793–1800.

Harrison, C., Burgess, J. and Filius, P. (1996), A comparison of lay publics in the UK and the Netherlands, *Global Environmental Change*, 6, 3: 215–34.

Harvey, D. (2000), *Space of Hope*, Edinburgh: Edinburgh University Press.

Hillman, M., Adams, J. and Whitelegg, J. (1990), *One False Move—A Study of Children's Independent Mobility*, London: Policy Studies Institute.

Hinchliffe, S. (1997), Locating risk: energy use, the "ideal" home and the non-ideal world, *Transactions of the Institute of British Geographers*, 22: 197–209.

Hine, J. and Mitchell, F. (2001), Better for everyone? Travel experiences and transport exclusion, *Urban Studies*, 38, 2: 319–32.

Illich, I. (1974), *Energy and Equity*, London: Marion Boyars.

Jain, J. (1998), *Responding to the Risks of a Car-Driven Society: Motivations and Practices of Car-free Lifestyles*, MSc dissertation, Geography Department, University of Bristol.

Lefebvre, H. (1991), *The Production of Space*, Oxford: Blackwell.

Levitas, R. (1998), *The Inclusive Society*, Bristol and London: Macmillan.

Lex Report on Motoring (1999), *Driving for the Future: The Authoritative Research on the Attitudes and Behaviour of Britain's Motorists*, 11th edn, Bourne End: Lex Service Plc.

Liniado, M. (1996), *Car Culture and Countryside Change*, MSc dissertation, Geography Department, University of Bristol.

Litman, T. (2001), *What's it Worth? Lifecycle and Benefit Cost Analysis for Evaluating Economic Value*, Symposium on Benefit–Cost Analysis, Transport Association of Canada, *www.tac-atc.ca.* (*www.vtpi.org* accessed 13/6/01).

Lutzenhiser, L. and Shove, E. (1996), *Individual Travel Behaviour: The Very Idea.* Discussion paper for OECD Project on Individual Travel Behaviour: Workshop on "Choice, Culture and Technology", Brighton, 17–19 July.

Lyons, G., Chatterjee, K., Marsden, G. and Beecroft, M. (2000), *Transport Visions: Society and Lifestyles*, London: Landor Publishing.

Macnaghton, P. and Urry, J. (1998), *Contested Natures*, London: Sage.

Mawhinney, B. (1995), *Transport: The Way Ahead*, London: Department of Transport.

Murray, S. (1998), *Social Exclusion and Integrated Transport*, http://www.art_man.ac.uk/transres/socexclus5.htm.

Pooley, C. and Turnbull, J. (1999), The journey to work: a century of change, *Area*, 31, 2: 281–92.

Potter, S. (1997), *Transport Statistics*, London: Landor Publishing.

Rose, G. (1993), *Feminist Geography: The Limits to Geographical Knowledge*, Cambridge: Polity Press.

Sheller, M. and Urry, J. (2000), The city and the car, *International Journal of Urban and Regional Research*, 24, 4: 737–57.

Solomon, J. (1998a), *To Drive or to Vote? Young Adults' Culture and Priorities 1998: A Discussion Paper*, London: Chartered Institute of Transport.

Solomon, J. (1998b), *Reaching hearts and minds*. Proceedings of Seminar C, European Transport Conference, 41–51, Loughborough University.

Tengstrøm, E. (1998), *Policies for a Sustainable Transport—Why Do They Fail?* Proceedings of Seminar C, European Transport Conference, Loughborough University, September, pp. 55–61.

Urry, J. (1999), *Automobility, Car Culture and Weightless Travel: A Discussion Paper*. Project ScenSusTech Scenarios for a sustainable society: car transport systems and the sociology of embedded technologies, Sociology Department, Trinity College, Dublin.

Wernick, A. (1991), *Promotional Culture: Advertising, Ideology, and Symbolic Expression*, London: Sage.

Whitelegg, J. (ed.) (1993), *Transport for a Sustainable Future: The Case for Europe*, London and New York: Belhaven Press.

Whitelegg, J. (1997), *Critical Mass: Transport, Environment and Society in the Twenty First Century*, London: Pluto Press.

CHAPTER 9

The Greens and Social Policy:
Movements, Politics and Practice?

John Barry and Brian Doherty

Abstract

The central aim of this paper is to show how different types of green movement respond to questions of social policy. An important factor in this is a difference in attitudes to the state between more anarchistic greens and those greens that are prepared to accept a permanent and/or strategic role for the state. The paper is divided into two parts. In part one, after defining the green movement, it outlines how different green social movements from local groups, direct action protestors, established environmental groups and green political parties, have developed analyses, responses and alternatives to social policy issues. Part two of the paper looks at some of the ideological/theoretical debates within green politics with regard to social policy, with particular regard to the role of the state. It goes on to look at some of the ways in which European green parties have viewed social policy, and at proposals they have advanced for moving the aim of social policy from "welfare" to "well-being". It concludes with suggesting that the "post-materialist" characterization of green politics is very wide of the mark in terms of the range of analyses and policy alternatives greens have put forward, from health, education and drugs to transport. The central and long-standing green concern with lessening socioeconomic inequalities (but without relying on indiscriminate and unsustainable "economic growth") means that in terms of social policy, green politics can be seen as an "environmentalism of the poor", concerned with "materialist" issues.

Keywords

Green movement; The state; Green political parties; Sustainability; Social justice; Inequality; Environmentalism of the poor

Introduction

When people think of the green movement they think principally of groups that are concerned with protecting the environment. Yet greens have always been concerned with broader political, social and economic issues, too. The

Address for correspondence: *John Barry, School of Politics, Queen's University Belfast, 19–21 University Square, Belfast, BT7 1PA. Email: j.barry@qub.ac.uk.*

rise of green parties, green direct action networks and the transformation of previously small campaigning groups such as Greenpeace into large organizations with a mass base of paying supporters have increased the heterogeneity within the green movement and political and organizational differences between these groups have raised the question of whether it is still accurate to speak of the green movement, as distinct from green movements. We also tend to speak of the green movement as a social movement, like feminism, the peace movement or the labour movement, which has its roots in civil society and has some autonomy from the state. And yet, at the time of writing, greens are or have been part of the government in Germany, France, Belgium, Finland and Italy.

One aim of this article is to show how different types of green movement respond to questions of social policy. An important factor in this is a difference in attitudes to the state between more anarchistic greens and those greens that are prepared to accept a permanent role for the state. This will be tackled further in the second part of the paper.

Defining the green movement

First, however, we need to define the green movement. The green movement is a social movement in so far as the various kinds of greens share the following characteristics.

(1)   A collective identity. In order to take sustained action together greens must have some sense of solidarity and common purpose. They must be able to define what is at stake in their actions, identify adversaries and frame the issues in such a way as to make their actions meaningful. This identity only emerges gradually as a product of experience and collective action. Social movements generally emerge from existing social or political groups and new movement identities are built from older ones. For many of the first activists in new green movements in Europe and North America in the 1970s the influence of the New Left was important in shaping their commitments to equality and social justice, and struggles over nuclear power and the influence of other movements such as feminism also had a significant impact on green identity and practice. Thus green identity emerged as a result of the experience of greens in a variety of movements and conflicts.

The nature of a social movement's collective identity is therefore always fluid and provisional, having to be continually reaffirmed and renegotiated. The principles underlining green identity will be explored more fully in the second part of the article, but broadly, the green identity is based upon interdependent commitments to ecological rationality/sustainability, social equality and a radical grassroots democracy. But the identities of movements are not only based upon these cognitive commitments, however. The fabric of the green movement is also made up by cultural practices, such as green lifestyles and the emotions of friendship, anger and pride, which provide important elements of motivation. Much green praxis is based on taken-for-granted assumptions that only become apparent as such when compared with the practices in different types of campaign. For instance, Lichterman

(1996) compared the culture of mainly white green activists and mainly African American and Hispanic anti-toxics activists. Where the culture of the latter was based on an assumed organic bond the greens saw themselves as individuals without any necessary bond, and concentrated on processes such as encouraging participation and consensus as ends in themselves because they saw empowerment of individuals as an important end in itself. Greens tended to regard all aspects of life as potentially political; for them the balance between home life and activism and the nature of occupations were political choices, whereas the anti-toxics activists tended to see them as separable spheres. Moreover, whereas greens regarded activism as having transformed their identities, the anti-toxics activists saw their activism as an expression of their community obligations. Lichterman shows how in each case different culture thus made collective action possible, but it also reflected cultural differences which made alliances between the different types of groups difficult.

(2)   A second feature of a social movement is that the groups and individuals involved within it are linked in a loose network. A social movement network is always broader than any one organization within it, since it includes informal as well as formal ties between individuals and groups. To show that this network exists we need to show that the movement interacts internally, even if its adherents sometimes disagree about strategy.

One example of this was during the protests against fuel prices in Britain in September 2000 (Doherty *et al.* 2000). Activists from Friends of the Earth, the Green Party, Transport 2000 and direct action networks debated collectively on e-mail lists and in strategy meetings how greens should respond to the fuel protests. A clear split emerged between most people in formally organized mainstream groups such as Friends of the Earth, Greenpeace and the Green Party and the more anarchistic networks of green direct activists. While some from the mainstream green groups organized counter-demonstrations, the individuals from the direct action groups regarded protests against the fuel protesters as misplaced. For them the structural causes of the crisis for farmers and hauliers could not be dealt with effectively by government because they were systemic and would require revolutionary changes in food production and transport. Yet, despite these disagreements the discussion rested on a sense that the movement as a whole shared enough common ground to be able to debate a collective strategy. Both sides in this argument agreed that high fuel taxes were not the best way to achieve a reduction in fuel consumption and both accepted that wider issues of rural governance and the economic pressures created by industrialized agriculture underlay farmers' grievances. In the aftermath of the fuel protests a number of conferences were held and an e-mail discussion list was formed bringing together farmers open to green critiques of industrialized agriculture and greens prepared to work with farmers. It is in these kinds of ties that we can see evidence of the network character of the green movement.

(3)   Involvement in protest and challenges to opponents. Protest is the form of action that we most associate with social movements (although not all

protests are carried out by social movements). It is through public protest actions that social movements challenge, cause disruption and uncertainty for their opponents and create conflicts in which others are forced to take sides. Protest is a resource of those without power and a means of expressing the intensity of commitment to a cause.

While some suggest that there has been a decline in green protest, this is difficult to substantiate. The best efforts at measurement (Rootes 1999) indicate that while levels of protest declined in the 1990s in some countries such as France, Italy and Sweden, in others they either remained stable (Germany and Spain) or rose (Britain). Moreover, types of protest action also varied, with the earlier, more confrontational and mass actions characteristic of the movement against nuclear energy declining in some cases, but remaining in others such as Germany. In Britain and the USA environmental direct action appears to be increasing.

However, with the exception of protest against nuclear energy, mass demonstrations by environmentalists have been rare. One reason for this is a more general change in protest in which spectacular or emotionally powerful actions by small numbers can reach large numbers through the media. This tendency is increased as the debate between political parties has become less openly ideological, leaving more space for movements to take the initiative. There are fewer national protests targeted at government policy, the new locus of mass protest is against unaccountable transnational power. Although greens played an important role in building the networks that mobilize such protest, they are now part of a much more diffuse coalition which shares very little in tactics, identity or culture. Another important change affecting the movement is the entry of the greens into government. While green parties in governments still take part in protest, and express their support for actions of civil disobedience, as the French greens did for the symbolic destruction of the site of a MacDonald's store by Jose Bové in Millau in France in 1999, there have also been splits within the movement, as in Germany where the Green environment minister backed the transport of nuclear waste in 2001 to a storage site against the protests of other parts of the movement.

(4) Posing a challenge to existing forms of power. Green analysis of the environmental crisis, social inequality, violence and the weakness of current forms of democracy suggests that a radical restructuring of existing society is required. They challenge the power of large business in their opposition to wasteful and unjust forms of trade and consumption, they call for major redistribution of wealth, not only within but also between countries; in their support for non-militaristic defence and their concern to reduce the power of bureaucracies and experts and increase the scope of local and participatory decision making, they pose a challenge to technocratic and political elites.

Again, however, there are degrees of radicalism. Greens in government retain these values and speak for them, but some such as Joschka Fischer, the German foreign minister, have also supported military involvement in Kosovo, albeit in the face of strong opposition from within his party. As political parties prepared to take part in government the greens have had to adjust to their role as part movement and part institutionalized party. Along with some of the formally organized NGOs, institutionalization has made the actions of these greens less radical even as it has increased their influence on questions of policy.

As Tarrow (1998) says, the challenge of social movements is abated when they have become routinized, meaning that they participate in the rules of the political game, and no longer threaten the elites with uncertainty. But, even if part of the green movement has been institutionalized, the movement as a whole has not, and new waves of grassroots activism have emerged through local environmental campaigns and direct action networks.

Taken together, these four characteristics constitute an ideal type. Some green groups are closer than others to this model, while some environmental groups cannot be defined as part of the green movement *qua* social movement. The most obvious examples are conservation groups such as WWF, the RSPB and the National Trust. These do not engage in protest, do not challenge the system and are not generally committed to the green collective identity based upon the interdependence of ecological rationality, social equality and grassroots democracy. They see their role much more narrowly as concerned with specific policy issues and as achievable within the existing structures of society. In this sense their concerns are more narrowly environmental than those of green groups.

There are three types of green social movement groups: the green parties, the more radical of the environmental movement organizations (EMOs) such as the various national branches of Friends of the Earth International, and the green direct action groups such as Earth First! Although they vary greatly between different countries and between these different types of group they do all share a green identity, are linked by network ties, take part in protest actions and demand a radical restructuring of the social and political order. However, the question of who is and who is not a green is not settled. Groups change over time and new groups become part of the movement. For instance, in some countries such as the Netherlands and Italy there are close ties and much shared identity with the animal protection movement, but not in others, such as Britain (Rootes and Miller 2000). Also, mainly for reasons of space, the analysis in this article deals only with greens in the wealthy industrialized countries. There are certainly environmental social movements in the South and the increasing ties linking them with Northern greens mean that a transnational green movement is beginning to take shape, but this is beyond the scope of the present article. In one sense, measured by their conformity to the ideal type there is an identifiable single green movement in the industrialized countries. Yet because, when green groups are measured against this ideal type there is also much heterogeneity, it is also legitimate to speak of green movements in the plural. A fourth type of environmental group considered in this article is local environmental groups. Although not part of the green movement in the sense that they do not necessarily share a green identity, they still often have some features of a social movement.

How, then, do greens engage with questions of social policy? We can divide *engagement* into two types. The first is implicit and reflected principally in the practices, including protest actions, of groups. Here we are talking primarily of local environmental campaigns and direct action groups. The second is more explicitly related to questions of policy and is reflected in the campaigns and policy initiatives of the more radical green non-government organizations (NGOs) and the green parties. We will deal first with issues of social policy raised by local environmental groups and direct action networks.

Local Environmental Campaigns

Local environmental groups are sometimes defined as Nimby (Not in my backyard), suggesting that they are only motivated by a parochial and selfish concern with local interests. As interviews with activists show, this is true of some, but these groups are too varied in character and discourse for the Nimby label to be a taken-for-granted starting point for analysing their motives. Moreover, the Nimby label distracts from the common transformation in identity, which occurs as local campaigners expand their knowledge and discourse and begin to analyse the structural causes of conflicts and possible alternatives, and shift from a Nimby position to a Niaby (Not in anyone's backyard) or Nope (Not on planet earth).

Most local environmental conflicts occur because a group organizes against a perceived hazard, often one with implications for health. In the 1970s many conflicts were over nuclear power; more recently waste disposal, whether of toxic chemicals in landfills or waste in incinerators, has been a major focus of conflict. At stake in these conflicts are competing conceptions of risk. Government regulators and industry operate with quantifiable calculations of acceptable risk. Local environmental campaigners are rarely reassured by this kind of knowledge. Building a new site, or revealing new information about an existing site, introduces a new risk in their lives. Since the science of chemicals such as dioxins emitted from incinerators is so uncertain, the risk appears unquantifiable. Moreover, new risks of any kind threaten the predictability and sense of routine that makes us ontologically secure. When industry and governments behave arrogantly, or deny access to information, this heightens the distrust felt by locals.

Some local environmental campaigns are begun by people with little or no campaigning experience. The Love Canal campaign begun by Lois Gibbs in Niagara in 1978 is an important example of this. When health problems began to multiply among school children in Love Canal, evidence emerged that the local school was built over a toxic waste site. After being patronized and ignored by state and health officials Gibbs led a campaign of lower-middle-class women which succeeded in having the school demolished, getting compensation for blighted homeowners and bringing the issue of toxic waste to national attention.

Gibbs's campaign led to the formation of a national network of anti-toxic campaigns which provided support to other relatively novice groups. These networks were critical of the mainstream environmental organizations in the USA for their over-concentration on the protection of non-human nature and the lack of attention to the environmental hazards suffered by the poor.

As Gottleib (1993) and Pulido (1996) have shown, the USA, like other countries, has a long tradition of environmentalism based on issues such as workplace environmental hazards, sanitation and water quality, which has rarely been acknowledged in the mainstream histories of the movement. In the 1980s and 1990s as evidence emerged showing that toxic waste and other environmental hazards were disproportionately sited near communities of colour, environmental racism became a major focus of protest and political debate (see Schlosberg 1999).

Local environmental campaigns raise issues relevant to social policy in a number of ways. Those involved in such struggles are engaged in a struggle over who has the right to speak for the local community, and this involves definitions of what the community and its interests are. Sometimes this is geographical and based on shared hazards or loss of amenity, at other times it is more explicit in addressing issues of power, such as environmental racism, or inequality. The discursive conflict between technocratic conceptions of power, whose apparent objectivity is reinforced by existing social structures, and other forms of knowledge such as local knowledge, which are not valued in policy making and which challenge the basis on which technical decisions are made (Fischer 2000), are a common element in local environmental campaigns.

Direct Action Groups

The direct action networks are the most radical wing of the green movement and their informal character and lack of concern with defining collective policy mean that it is difficult to discern collective positions regarding social policy. Nevertheless, issues of social policy are relevant to understanding the movement's practice. In the 1990s in Britain, for instance, green direct action groups have taken joint action with the Disabled Activist Network and in support of asylum seekers.

When speaking of direct action networks in Britain we are referring to local groups of mainly young activists, some but not all with middle-class backgrounds and higher education, who organize under a variety of overlapping labels such as Earth First! or Reclaim the Streets. Similar networks exist in the USA, Australia, Ireland and the Netherlands. Although in the past Earth First! in the USA was often associated with an anti-human, pro-wilderness position, this is no longer the case. Proponents of such ideas left the network at the beginning of the 1990s after failing to convince other activists that social justice and feminism were not relevant issues for Earth First! activists. This is a good example of how the collective identity of the movement has evolved, based on negotiating the interrelationship between commitments to social and environmental goals.

The British direct action networks are rooted in the long-standing green alternative milieu, and much of the culture and many of the practices of the network have a history that can be traced back to groups such as the Torness alliance in the late 1970s and the peace camps of the 1980s. Individuals involved in each of these earlier campaigns passed on skills and ideas to later groups and these were also sustained in the less visible local alternative networks based around communal houses, wholefood and permaculture networks.

One sign of this continuity is that the issues that activists argued over in the 1970s and 1980s were also argued over in the 1990s, and still are. These include the justifiability of damage to property, what counts as violence, how to manage power relationships within small groups and the politics of gender on camps. Having said this, while the issues are the same, the discourse has shifted as a result of experience. As Purkis's (2001) analysis of collective leadership in Manchester Earth First! shows, one contrast with earlier attempts to work non-hierarchically is that there is now a more realistic acceptance and tolerance of imperfections.

Protest camps have been a particular site of tensions of interest to social policy makers. Throughout the 1990s they attracted a diverse mix including many with mental health problems. The occupation of a derelict site owned by the Guinness company in Wandsworth by The Land is Ours, a land rights movement, was intended to provide an exemplary model of sustainable land reclamation and use, and to draw in the local community. While much of this was achieved prior to the eviction of the "Pure Genius" camp by Guinness, a continuing point of tension was what some campaigners regarded as the exploitation of the camp by local agencies who they believed were using the camp as a fall-back when other facilities were overstretched. Wandsworth was a Conservative-controlled council which prided itself on its low spending. Direct action campaigners have agonized over how to deal with this problem. In so far as camps are meant to embody principles of alternative society, activists feel that they should be able to integrate those with social problems. Yet camps also have a strategic and practical purpose and do not in practice work as perfect alternative communities, and so at times activists have agreed to exclude individuals whom they cannot accommodate effectively.

Through their roots in the wider alternative milieu those involved in direct action networks often move from public protest action to involvement with alternative projects such as permaculture communities, local community gardens and alternative health projects. In Manchester, for instance, activists combine involvement with Earth First! direct action and community initiatives on the "Redbricks" estate in Hulme, which has a strong countercultural presence. These include collective efforts to manage drugs-related crime without involving the police, which have included a "reclaim the night" march, a permaculture community garden, which provides food for a cheap weekly "People's Kitchen" in the local community pub, and an intranet within the estate, providing low-cost internet access.

Social Policy in Green Parties and Green NGOs

In general, green parties adopt a holistic and integrated view of social policy, seeing it not as a set of discrete policies or policy areas but as interrelated and mutually determining. For example, housing policy is related to transport and health (including mental health) policies, since housing affects health. The building of new housing stock is often affected by transport policy, road building programmes and land use and planning, as well as having a significant impact on individual health and well-being and on the natural world.

Equally, however, it is important to point out that green parties have proposed, and support, policies which are connected not to environmental issues narrowly understood, but to their broader emancipatory and progressive political goals. For example, the German Greens succeeded in achieving a change in German nationality law making German citizenship (traditionally based on ethnic descent) more easily available to non-"Germans" born in Germany. This had been a major priority for the Greens, though opposition from all the other parties forced Greens to accept some major compromises. In France, the French greens (Les Verts) initiated the debate which led to the legislation on the 35-hour week, by making it a major feature of their 1993 election campaign. They now propose the shortening of the working week to 32 hours (with the long-term goal to reduce it to 28 hours). They also, like the German Greens, seek to disconnect citizenship from nationality, and speak of "Reviving the revolutionary and republican ideal, we think that all who inhabit a territory are citizens and part of that collectivity, regardless of their race, religion or . . . their nationality" (Les Verts 2001).

At the same time, greens are explicit in regarding much of social policy as "defensive" forms of public spending, in the sense that social policies in areas such as health care are often "negative costs" of the organization of the economy aimed at securing increases in economic growth. The increase in the volume of road transport, for example (an integral aspect of the drive for economic growth), has massive implications for health policy. From the number of people killed or injured on roads each year, to the increase in childhood asthma (Jacobs 1996), from a green perspective one cannot sensibly isolate transport from health.

Equally, other social policy areas are, from a green perspective, unduly focused on a narrow set of aims and objectives dominated by the economic growth agenda. A glaring example of this is the way education policy has been (and is increasingly) dominated by the needs of the leading sectors of the global economy, where the main aim of education seems to be the production of literate, numerate, mobile, ICT-skilled members of the workforce. In contrast, the UK Green Party's *Manifesto for a Sustainable Society* suggests that

> We are still living in an age of mass education, which is a product of nineteenth century industrial society's demand for a numerate and literate workforce. The "one size fits all" model still dominates, with increasing standardisation of a knowledge-based curriculum, and national testing . . . The link between the education system and the economy means that certification is overemphasised, implying learning has no value for its own sake, but only in relation to its contribution to the material wealth of society or that of the individual learner. (1997, 2000: ED 110, 111)

In terms of health, the expansive definition and understanding of health used by the British Green Party is very typical of how green parties in general and the wider green movement views health. Rather than the usual focus on physical health, the Green Party's manifesto states that

> Health is the condition in which individuals and communities achieve their full physical, intellectual, social and spiritual potential. Health for individuals is only possible in the context of a healthy environment and society. The healthy society is one which guarantees a safe and clean environment, material security for all its citizens; good work; adequate housing; a balanced and unpolluted diet and clean water; appropriate education; a safe transport system; accessible and sensitive public services; equality of opportunity; a secure present and hope for the future. All Green Party policies are designed to promote the health of individuals, communities and society. (1997, 2000: H100)

This extremely wide conception of health basically covers all the main areas of social policy from a green perspective, to the extent that simply put, the "sustainable society" can be simply called the "healthy society" (which of course has the direct implication that modern society is "unhealthy"). Going beyond even the preventative-curative balance within health policy (in which from a green perspective increased resources should be put to promote *health* and preventing rather than simply dealing with *illness*), this radical view of health offers a challenging view of this central area of social policy.[1]

From a green viewpoint, health is understood in a way in which almost all the other areas of social policy—from housing and education to transport, but also including economic and public policy—are directly related to it. Increasing the resources of the NHS (more doctors, nurses, equipment, etc.) without also altering transport, housing, food policy, is less effective than taking a holistic view of health in which all the main determinants of health are included as part of the policy initiative. To take but a small example, significantly altering the transport system in the UK towards a more integrated version, which would decrease the number of car journeys, would do more to improve the health and save the lives of some of the most vulnerable members of society (children and the elderly) than reducing NHS waiting lists. According to Cahill, "Road accidents are the major cause of death and injury to children, accounting for a quarter of all deaths of school children and two thirds of all accidental deaths" (1994: 91). Thus, as the green position makes clear, it is an obvious area in which government transport policy has a potentially positive public health benefit.[2]

Transport represents a policy area upon which many other green social (and public) policy proposals fall. While the short- to medium-term goal of a green transport policy would be the creation of a truly integrated transport system, with an emphasis on decreasing car ownership and use, the long-term goal would be the radical reduction of the need to travel long distances in the first place. As Henderson puts it, "we seldom take the transport debate to its logical terminus: how to reduce the need to travel in the first place . . . If one considers the goal here as minimizing the number of movements required to deliver quality of life, then localization of much of the economy makes mainstream sense" (2001: 32). Linking transport policy to the localization agenda (in which the siting and building of housing, places of work, education, recreation, shopping and other amenities would be designed so as to minimize the need to travel) is at the heart of the alternative the green movement proposes to the current transport system dominated by both the "car economy", with its demand for speed, more roads and priority over all other road users, and the dominant "car culture" in which individual freedom, comfort and social status are expressed or realized in and through owning and using cars.

It is also a policy area upon which there is widespread agreement between green parties and the broader green movement, thus offering a focus for concerted and effective common action for the green movement as a whole, green parties, direct action environmentalism and environmental non-governmental organizations.

The Green Critique of and Alternatives to the Welfare State

The state and social policy

The green attitude to the state is absolutely central in discussion of the relationship between the green movement and social policy debates. This is because any discussion of social policy involves the state and its agencies, institutions and procedures (both central and local) in some way, shape or form. Thus, more anarchistic parts of the movement reject the idea of "social policy" as a central or important aspect of the green political agenda since this implies accepting a legitimate and continuing role for the state, which they see as part of the ecological problem rather than an element in the creation of a more sustainable society. In this way, green views of social policy are related to views about the state.

What unites most green perspectives are:

1. A critical view of the state which does not see it as a "neutral" instrument for the achievement of political ends, although pragmatic greens adopt an instrumental attitude towards it for strategic purposes (often expressed as the green strategy of "marching through the institutions"). Even here, "pro-state" greens such as Barry (1999) and Jacobs (1999), including of course green political parties, do not privilege the state as the pre-eminent, dominant or most appropriate political institution for the achievement of green ends. As Doherty puts it: "The greens have responded to new conditions and issues with a distinctively modern strategy based on accepting the limits of the state in guaranteeing social and political change" (1992: 102).[3] Rather pragmatic greens view the state as one combination of institutional mechanisms or means to achieve green political ends, the others being more community-based initiatives within civil society, and the market.

2. More positive views of the state can be found when the focus is at the local state level, which is seen (for a variety of ecological, democratic, participatory reasons) as more in keeping with the green preference for

decentralized, bottom-up forms of political and socioeconomic organization. This is particularly so when one looks at the Local Agenda 21 initiative, and the focus on developing and implementing local sustainability plans.

Begg, writing from an activist's perspective, and describing the existing welfare state as embodying "power-over" (rather than a more emancipatory "power to") writes:

> working at the interface between systems of power is effectively opening up a conduit between the two. You are allowing a flow of energy or resources from one to the other (or more often a combination of both) . . . Anyone seeking to work for empowerment, equality or social change will have relationships with many bodies shaped and governed by power-over . . . However, it is not the case that every connection with the dynamics of power-over weakens the process of social change. (2000: 211)

And as he pragmatically states, "At the end of the day, the question is not whether or not to sup with the devil, but rather whether the spoon is long enough" (Begg 2000: 214).

At the same time, many within the green movement would see that the achievement of or the transition to a more sustainable society would in and of itself lessen the need for state-centred social policy as conventionally understood. An example of this is the UK Green Party's social welfare policy which states that, "We believe that a sustainable society would remove many of the causes of present day social problems. A return to smaller, more caring communities would reduce the need for both volunteers and social workers. The current role of welfare agencies would change and diminish; they would no longer carry the main responsibility for those in need" (1997, 2000: SW204).

The state, the market and community

While, ideologically, most greens are committed to privileging non-state and non-market forms of socioeconomic organization, and community-based forms of welfare provision, from a pragmatic point of view they often adopt a pro-state position in order to use the resources of the state to foster and support community-based practices and to prevent these from being undermined by the unregulated or under-regulated free market. While favouring community, grassroots, self-reliant forms of welfare provision, greens generally support the welfare state and seek to reform it so that (1) it can prevent welfare and other parts of individual and collective life from being commodified and privatized by the market, and (2) it becomes more supportive of community-based modes of organization of social, political and economic life. Like left-wing defenders of the welfare state, the green position is that basic human needs such as education and health should be distributed according to need and not ability to pay. As the UK Green Party's *Manifesto for a Sustainable*

Society puts it: "While not opposed to private health provision in principle, Greens are opposed to a transfer of resources away from the public health system which is available to all. Private Health Insurance should be a taxable employment benefit where offered" (Green Party 1997, 2000: H324), while it also advocates the abolition of the internal market and NHS trusts together with GP fundholding (*ibid.*: H321).

This green focus on community and the centrality of it within green social policy proposals is a logical extension of some of its core principles and values. The emphasis on "acting local, thinking global" and the resolute defence of the local, the human-scale and the familiar against the centralizing, indifferent and non-democratic consequences of political and economic organization from above and outside the local area is one of the hallmarks of green political ideology (Barry 1999). It fits with its aim of the progressive decentralization and democratization of more and more areas of people's lives, of "appropriate scale", that is, reducing the level of decision making or service delivery to the lowest level possible. These twin themes, democratization and decentralization, are the heart of many green social policies. For example, the UK Green Party's view is that "increased and protected funding of community services will enable health care as far as possible to be provided at home or in community-based facilities" (Green Party 1997, 2000: H302); education should be democratically organized such that students have an input into the education they receive (1997, 2000: ED331), and the same principle goes for the provision of residential care for the elderly (SW533) and rationing within the National Health Service (H323).

This community focus within the green movement's view of social policy makes it very critical of the state-centred, centralized, overly bureaucratic, impersonal and standardized provision of welfare services, which many on both the left and right have also criticized. While in keeping with green ideology, this critique of the welfare state also has another dimension in that many of the activists and/or supporters of the green movement and green parties are drawn from the public sector (Cotgrove and Duff 1980; Kriesi 1989; Rüdig *et al.* 1991), especially those working in the provision of health care, health promotion, education, social services, probation services, local government, those whom sociologists have classed as the "new middle class". In this sense, then, the type of social policies greens suggest are supported by some of those who are actually employed by the welfare state in the provision of those services, and to this extent, one can view green social policies as a form of "institutional reflexivity" and self-criticism, of welfare state workers criticizing and offering alternative and supplementary modes of welfare provision.

It is important to note that the focus on community-based modes of welfare provision is regarded not as suggesting the erosion of the welfare state, but rather as supplementing existing modes and institutions, thereby increasing the variety, range and choice of welfare available to individuals, as well as giving them more say in what, how and when welfare services are provided.[4] Alongside democratization and decentralization, the other important green principle in the shift from exclusive state welfare to more community-based modes of provision is self-reliance—and a break with a view of welfare which is overly centred around the possession of material things and money and in which formal employment in the cash economy is seen as the dominant and most important social and economic role and contributor to welfare. Ultimately, and in the long term, from a green perspective, informal, non-cash modes of economic activity and work ought to be seen as at least equally important as remunerated formal employment (if not more). Hence the ubiquity of support within the green movement for such innovative forms of community-based socioeconomic activity as "time banks", local exchange trading systems (LETS), "green currency schemes", community gardens and allotments, bartering and skills exchange, and other forms of community-based, informal, non-cash forms of socioeconomic activity. At the same time, greens have long integrated the feminist argument concerning the obscene anomaly of "reproductive" work in the domestic sphere being at one and the same time "dis-valued" (by not receiving a cash figure or being included in official government GDP measurements), while also constituting some of the most important work and activity which goes on in society, and without which the current socioeconomic order could not sustain itself. In this sense, the green focus on the community should also be understood to include the domestic sphere, as a site of work, valued activity and well-being.

The community focus of green social policy integrates its decentralist, democratic, local and self-reliant aims in that a green social policy agenda would seek to allow people in communities to decide themselves how and in what way "their" welfare ought to be provided, with the explicit goal of enabling and encouraging as many people as possible to become less reliant on either formally paid employment or welfare benefits and services. Or rather, the aim of green social policy is to enable and empower individuals to choose from a wider range of welfare options than is currently provided (paid employment or state benefits).

Jacobs's suggestion that "publicly-raised funds should be directed into local, voluntary and community-based enterprises and organisations, with the twin aims of raising long-term employment and meeting social needs" (1996: 96), is a good example of a broad green approach to social policy. Whereas traditional left and right social policy debate is largely confined to finding the appropriate mix of state and market mechanisms, an ecological approach to social policy grounds itself in the "social economy" or what is sometimes called the "third sector", with the public or state and the private or market sectors, being the other two.[5] Part of this new perspective finds expression in the increasing "partnership approach" to local social provision. For greens the advantage of partnerships between state, voluntary and private sectors locally is that this should strengthen the local and informal economies, and foster genuine community economic development. However, the hard question here is the extent to which the informal, local, community focus becomes the end and driving force of these partnerships, rather than being cynically used for "good PR" by the private sector, and as a cheap way of delivering statutory services by the state.

The importance of this has to do with the green aim of rebuilding local communities. Thus the green preference for centring social policy on the social economy is not simply that the latter provides services and activities which neither state nor market sector can, although this is of course important. It is also the preferred focus because encouraging the delivery of social policy through the third sector will greatly facilitate the reinvigoration of communities. As Jacobs puts it: "Community-based organisations tangibly raise levels of hope and self-confidence and a sense of social participation. By enabling people to work together for one another, they give expression to feelings of altruism and mutuality, and thereby help to regenerate a sense of community" (1996: 100). The recovery of community as a central plank in the overarching aim and method of social policy from a green position does not (as some critics of community have suggested) mean a return to closed, intolerant communities. Rather, the green appeal to community ought to be viewed as calling for the nation to be seen as a network (or community) of communities, coordinated by central state agencies but with local government and the third sector having increased autonomy and competence in the design and implementation of social policies. "Meeting local needs locally" is thus a central objective of green social policy.

While this community focus is central to green policy proposals and is common to most manifestos and policy programmes of green parties, as noted above the green movement has also initiated a bewildering variety of community-based experiments, enterprises, groups and organizations most of which have some direct or indirect social policy dimension. From these various permanent, transitory, historical and current community experiments and community-based, ecologically motivated practices we can discern the outlines of what a green, community-based social policy agenda may look like.

Sustainability, Inequality and Social Policy

While recognizing the reality of socioeconomic inequality and the poverty, powerlessness and other associated social, psychological, health, family/ domestic and socioeconomic problems (crime and public disorder), that come from the fundamental, unequal distribution of wealth and opportunity in society (as well as globally between societies), the green movement/s also recognize the limits of existing social policy responses to this. In general terms, rather than investing energy, time and resources into simply ameliorating the worst effects of inequality, greens seek to address the root causes of it. However, given the centrality of the critique of conventional economic growth within all sections of the green movement (this "limits to growth" position is a defining feature of the movement), greens reject the dominant view that only by redistributing the fruits of a growing capitalist, competitive economy can equality, social inclusion and environmental improvement be achieved. Rather, the green path to tackling inequality is premised on redistribution (of existing social wealth) without the commitment to unsustainable and undifferentiated economic growth, alongside a radical shift from money- and commodity-based measurements of welfare to a focus on well-being, quality of life and free time. In directly linking the achievement of a sustainable society to social justice, greens recognize that redistribution from the better-off to the most vulnerable members of society is absolutely essential, both practically and morally.

The basic green argument with regard to lessening socioeconomic inequalities is that linking this social goal to redistributing economic growth merely entrenches inequality rather than lessening it. The reason for this is that in societies such as the welfare states of the west, state legitimacy is, in part, dependent upon a commitment to lessen inequalities via redistributive measures. However, co-existing with this is the standard defence of economic inequality which claims that it is necessary for creating the conditions for economic growth. In other words, an unequal distribution of the benefits of socially produced wealth is a necessary condition of a growing, successful economy (less is said about the unequal distribution of the social, economic and environmental costs and risks of economic growth). Wealth and income inequalities are argued to be economic incentives that are absolutely essential for encouraging employment of the best individuals, which contributes to overall economic productivity and growth. The basic argument is that while some gain more than others, everybody does gain. Thus the green critique of economic growth can also be regarded as an argument against the social inequalities that are a structural component of contemporary social and economic policies. The increase in inequality in the United Kingdom over the last twenty years can be interpreted as evidence of this relationship between economic growth and socioeconomic inequality—as the economy has grown (as measured by conventional GDP/GNP accounting), so has inequality. While having unequal slices of a growing cake means that in absolute terms everyone is gaining—or is "better-off" using the conventional (and misleading) measure of disposal income—the reality is that the existence of relative inequality detrimentally affects people's quality of life. For example, even though economic growth may mean the car-less can buy more things, and also benefits car-owners by enabling them to buy new and more expensive cars, the reality of persistent relative inequality between the two groups highlights the problem. As Levett points out: "The more the well-off drive, the more amenities move to sites with plentiful parking, and the fewer remain accessible without a car" (2001: 30). Improving the quality of life of individuals and communities requires shifting attention away from income and benefit measurements alone (the fruits of economic growth) towards the non-income (and non-employment) components of quality of life and well-being. As Levett again succinctly puts it: "The key is to target well-being directly, and stop treating economic growth as a proxy for it" (2001: 31). Thus, from a green point of view government social (and public) policy should be aimed at improving the quality of life of individuals, families and communities, and this requires a shift from a focus on ensuring economic growth, competitiveness and employment.

The green argument for a "steady-state economy", or an economy in which maximizing output, profits or paid employment would not be the dominant imperative, can thus be seen as a strong egalitarian argument for decreasing social and economic inequality. With an economy not geared towards maximizing production, income and formally paid employment, the justification of an unequal distribution of socially produced wealth cannot be that it is required for procuring greater wealth production. In short, with the shift to a less growth-orientated society, the normative basis for social co-operation needs to be renegotiated, as does social policy. The implications of this are dramatic for social policy, given that one of the central justifications for social policy is the lessening of socioeconomic inequalities via the redistribution of income, goods and services generated from a growing economy (Huby 1998: 15). The green argument is that if one wishes to reduce inequalities, then abandoning the exclusive focus on a growing economy as the way to do this may be a more realistic way of achieving it, since an inegalitarian distribution of social wealth is less morally and politically justifiable within the context of a non-growing economy. However, such talk of a principled rejection or downplaying of the traditional commitment to economic growth would obviously lead to strong resistance from both labour and capital interests, since it spells nothing less than the radical transformation of industrial society and the welfare state system which has developed alongside and with it.

Equally, greens are committed to a more egalitarian society on the grounds that this is a more effective way to increase general well-being or quality of life. As Boardman *et al.* note, reducing inequalities "not only benefits the poorest in society, but society as a whole, for there is growing evidence that narrowing income inequality in a society adds to the overall social quality of life. The benefits for the poorest households go substantially beyond the direct effects of extra income. There is strong evidence that in the developed world, it is not the richest countries which have the best health but the most egalitarian" (Boardman *et al.* 1999: 11).

One interpretation of the green critique of orthodox economic growth and the commitment to establishing a more egalitarian distribution of income and wealth is that economic *security* rather than economic *affluence* is important for a more equal social order within modern democracies and is a better way to increase overall social well-being, as suggested above. The green view is that it is the *distribution* of wealth within society, not the *absolute level* of wealth, which is important in a democratic political system. Similarly, the lessons for social policy are that what is important is the distribution of work (not just waged employment in the formal economy), free time, and other "public good" dimensions of a decent quality of life, such as a quiet, pleasant, clean work and living environment, and personal security. A key green policy designed to ensure socioeconomic security and decrease inequality as well as to improve quality of life, is the basic income or citizens' scheme which is a non-means-tested income distributed by the state to all eligible citizens. The importance of economic security to quality of life cannot be overemphasized, since security of livelihood with a guaranteed decent standard of living, rather than increases in material consumption of commodities and the increases in income needed to afford that level of consumption, seem to be more important to people and would link the meeting of needs, social justice and environmental sustainability. In the increasingly insecure world of the global economy, where a "job for life" is a thing of the past, economic security rather than economic affluence (dependent as it is on the fickleness and unpredictability of the global economy) is a safer bet for most people

135

(apart from those for whom "risk-taking" and insecurity are not things to be avoided, but are rather "business opportunities" and incentives).

Jacobs (1996), from what can be called a "green welfare" position, makes an important distinction between economic growth understood as year on year increases in personal disposable income (which is the dominant view) and economic growth understood as implying greater public, as opposed to private, spending and investment. A more sustainable society is likely to mean one in which available resources are invested in public services and institutions (education, welfare, health, transport), rather than increases in personal disposable income.

Given the high profile of improving public services as the dominant issue in the 2001 UK election, perhaps the ground is ready for the linking of this demand to a critique of the dominance of the economic growth agenda, and a shift towards making "well-being" and "quality of life" central to what governments are for and the dominant aim towards which they should be orientated.

The point is that public consumption of the fruits of economic growth does seem to imply less overall consumption (and potential ecological damage) than private consumption. Jacobs also points out that, "As many people have realized over recent years (if only by default), consumption of public goods can make a higher contribution to well-being than equivalent spending on private goods" (1996: 35). Examples of this would be a shift to collective forms of provisioning: from large-scale issues such as a shift towards greater use of public rather than private transport, to more micro-level issues (e.g. shared services such as clothes washing rather than individual washing machines and dryers). In terms of the latter, as was indicated earlier, the green movement has demonstrated ways in which maximizing individual benefits from scarce resources can be done if these resources are shared and used collectively. To offset inevitable reactions to this shift towards collective modes of consumption as unnecessarily draconian, there is also an argument for the continuation of individual consumption patterns premised on technological improvements in the "ecological efficiency" of production. Thus one could imagine a "green" social policy in which the aim was to provide goods and services which were produced and distributed in an ecologically sustainable manner and/or produced and consumed by a variety of units ranging from the individual to the household and various collectivities of individuals and family groups.

However, for most greens the aim of social policy (and all government policy) should be the enhancement of well-being and improving the quality of life of individuals, families and communities directly, rather than focusing on "welfare" and the latter's dependence upon a growing economy and its cash and commodity components. Thus, what is required is a shift from economic growth to social/sustainable development. And in terms of social policy provision, the green position is to focus more on investment in public services together with a greater emphasis on community-based forms of need-meeting, and away from providing people with additional income (which is usually no more than either a "stop-gap" measure—as in winter fuel allowances—or compensatory or defensive rather than dealing with the root causes of inequality and diminishing quality of life).

Conclusion

An important consequence of the integration of social policy issues and problems into the green movement's political agenda is that this makes it less likely for it to be viewed as a single issue movement. While concern for the environment and the aim of ecological sustainability remain central to the green movement, it has never been the case that "saving the planet" was its only or primary aim and objective. The plight of deprived peoples and communities in the developed and developing world, the socioeconomic inequalities and their effects on the lives of millions of people, the reality of "environmental injustices" where people from marginalized groups tend to live in worse environments, and disproportionately bear the "environmental costs" of an economic system which produces benefits from which they are also disproportionately excluded, have all been at the heart of the green movement since its origins the 1960s.

While green politics is often presented as "post-materialist", the politics of a middle class concerned with aesthetic matters of local environmental destruction, the extinction of some specific animal or plant or forest, which have little direct bearing on human welfare or needs-provision, the analysis here points to the fact that in addressing social policy concerns, green politics is a "materialist" politics in the sense of addressing the real concerns and needs of people, a politics in which justice and sustainability and the meeting of human needs are all necessary elements. In dealing with the socioeconomic causes which give rise to the need for social policy, the green movement in welfare state societies articulates a view of green politics as, in part, an "environmentalism of the poor" (Guha 1997). The green movement does address and deal with issues of socioeconomic inequality, poverty, ill health, insecurity and social exclusion, and offers both an analysis (rooted in the structural dynamics of the capitalist organization of the economy and centralized state organization of politics and society) and a solution whose defining character is in seeing all these problems as interrelated and as impossible to deal with in isolation from one another. For "sustainable development" to be anything more than an abstract term used by various elites and minority groups and to have some real, direct and positive connection to people's everyday lives and ambitions, it must engage with these issues of the transformation of social policy and the enhancement of social well-being, especially that of the poorest and most vulnerable members of society.

Notes

1. Les Verts, the French Green Party, have a similar radical view of health care: "The right to health for all, a vital achievement of social struggles, is too often confused with that to consume medicine . . . Our priority is to reduce this excessive medicalization of health . . . This presupposes that each citizen takes responsibility for their own health" (Les Verts 2001).
2. Other positive benefits of an integrated transport policy would be to improve the health of schoolchildren by enabling them to walk to school, as well as allowing streets to return to being safe places for children to play by redressing the balance of road design and use away from car-users towards non-car-users (through

traffic-calming measures, to banning cars to lowering speed limits) and decreasing childhood asthma caused by car emissions.

3. The growing acceptance of the necessity and desirability for a more "positive" attitude towards the state from an ecological perspective, and the need to elaborate the potentials (and obstacles) of the "greening of the state", are particularly acute at the international level, where it is becoming increasingly obvious that a rejection of the state, particularly in terms of its capacity to regulate the ecological and other socioeconomic consequences of globalized and globalizing markets, is, to say the least, problematic.

4. Indeed, in some versions of green politics (particularly those we can describe as "ecosocialist") there is a strong place for the local state as part of the democratization and decentralization of society which are regarded as central to the sustainability transition of society. This "green municipalism" with its echoes of "municipal socialism" is described by Mellor (1996).

5. The social economy includes businesses and voluntary organizations whose primary aim is to meet social needs rather than to make profits. Examples of such entities include community businesses, housing associations, food cooperatives, and community financial organizations such as credit unions. A recent and growing dimension of the social economy is LETS (local exchange trading systems), which create a "local currency" to facilitate local barter exchange of goods and services between local people without the use of sterling (Barry and Proops 2000).

References

Barry, J. (1999), *Rethinking Green Politics: Nature, Virtue, Progress*, London: Sage.

Barry, J. and Proops, J. (2000), *Citizenship, Sustainability and Environmental Research*, Cheltenham: Edward Elgar.

Begg, A. (2000), *Empowering the Earth: Strategies for Social Change*, Devon: Green Books.

Boardman, B. with Bullock, S. and McLaren, D. (1999), *Equity and the Environment: Guidelines for Green and Socially Just Government*, London: Catalyst and Friends of the Earth.

Bündnis 90/Die Grünen (1998), *New Majorities Only with Us*, Bonn. (*www.gruene.de/aktuell/english*)

Cahill, M. (1994), *The New Social Policy*, Oxford: Blackwell.

Cotgrove, S. and Duff, A. (1980), Environmentalism, middle-class radicalism and politics, *Sociological Review*, 28: 333–51.

Davis, A. (1997), The public health impact of motor transport in the UK, Health and Transport Research Group, School of Health and Social Welfare, Open University, Milton Keynes.

Diani, M. and Donati, P. (1999), Organisational change in western European environmental groups, *Environmental Politics*, 8, 1: 13–34.

Doherty, B. (1992), The Fundi-Realo controversy: an analysis of four European Green parties, *Environmental Politics*, 1, 1.

Doherty, B. (2002), *Green Movements*, London: Routledge.

Doherty, B., Paterson, M., Plows, A. and Wall, D. (2000), Constructing the fuel protests: new populist movements in British politics. Paper presented at the ISA/BSA Conference on Social Movements at Manchester University, 4–6 November.

Fischer, F. (2000), *The Politics of Local Knowledge: Citizens, Experts and the Environment*, Durham, NC: Duke University Press.

Gottlieb, R. (1993), *Forcing the Spring: The Transformation of the American Environmental Movement*, Washington, DC: Island Press.

Green Party (1997, 2000), *Manifesto for a Sustainable Society*, London: UK Green Party, *http://www.greenparty.org.uk/policy.mfss*

Green Party (2001), *Reach for the Future*, Manifesto for General Election, London: UK Green Party.

Guha, R. (1997), The environmentalism of the poor. In R. Guha and J. Martinez-Alier, *Varieties of Environmentalism: Essays North and South*, London: Earthscan.

Henderson, C. (2001), The sublime virtue of staying put, *Green Futures*, 28, May/June: 32–4.

Huby, M. (1998), *Social Policy and the Environment*, Buckingham: Open University Press.

Jacobs, M. (1996), *The Politics of the Real World*, London: Earthscan.

Jacobs, M. (1999), *Environmental Modernization*, London: Fabian Society.

Kriesi, H. (1989), New social movements and the "New Class", *American Journal of Sociology*, 94, 1: 1078–1116.

Les Verts (2001), La responsabilité planétaire; La solidarité; La citoyenneté, *www.les-verts.org/*

Levett, R. (2001), What quality? Whose lives? *Green Futures*, 28, May/June: 28–31.

Lichterman, P. (1996), *The Search for Political Community: American Activists Reinventing Tradition*, Cambridge: Cambridge University Press.

Mellor, M. (1996), Getting from there to here. In J. Stanyer and P. Dunleavy (eds), *Contemporary Political Studies*, Belfast: Political Studies Association.

Pulido, L. (1996), *Environmentalism and Economic Justice: Two Chicano Struggles in the Southwest*, Tucson, AZ: University of Arizona Press.

Purkis, J. (2001), Leaderless cultures: the problems of authority in a radical environmental group. In C. Barker and M. Lavalette (eds), *Leadership in Social Movements*, Manchester: Manchester University Press.

Putnam, R. (2000), *Bowling Alone: The Collapse and Revival of American Community*, New York: Simon and Schuster.

Rootes, C. (ed.) (1999), *Environmental Protest in Seven European States, EC Environment and Climate Change Research Programme: The Transformation of Environmental Activism* (preliminary report: unpublished papers), University of Kent.

Rootes, C. and Miller, A. (2000), The British environmental movement: organizational field and network of organizations. Paper presented at the ECPR Joint Sessions, Copenhagen, 14–19 April.

Rüdig, W., Bennie, L. G. and Franklin, M. N. (1991), *Green Party Members: A Profile*, Glasgow: Delta Publications.

Schlosberg, D. (1999), *Environment Justice and the New Pluralism*, Oxford: Oxford University Press.

Tarrow, S. (1998), *Power in Movement*, 2nd edn, Cambridge: Cambridge University Press.

Wainwright, H. (2001), Space of waste, *Guardian*, 25 April.

CHAPTER 10

Democracy, Social Relations and Ecowelfare

Paul Hoggett

Abstract

Like Marxists before, greens are trenchant critics of the commodification of human life by consumer capitalism. They have been persistent advocates of less materialistic ways of living but, as such, have been easily dismissed as champions of frugal, small-scale community living. This essay argues that a society which fostered non-materialistic ways of living could offer more rather than less to its citizens if it put at the centre of its vision the quality of human and social relations. A relational perspective insists that human capacities—aesthetic, spiritual, practical/intellectual, ethical and convivial—are developed through our relations to others and to nature, including the nature and otherness in ourselves. The primary aim of an ecowelfare society should be to create the conditions for such human capacities to flourish in a balanced way. The essay first describes four areas of our everyday social relations where qualitative change is necessary if a democratic culture is to flourish. Capitalism privileges the development of the practical/intellectual and, in consequence, our over-extended technical powers now put the world at risk. Green democracy must be approached in this light. Participation in political discussion and decision making at all levels of society enhances individual and collective ethical and convivial capacities and therefore fosters citizens who have the capacity to respond to social and ecological insecurity. To be convincing, green democracy needs to recognize the actual complexity of society, a complexity that direct, face-to-face models of democracy cannot deal with. In opposition to the markets and managerialism of existing governments greens should develop a vision of the extended democratization of all levels and institutions of society, from housing estates and health centres to universities and non-departmental public bodies like the Arts Council. In doing so it must recognize the differences, tensions and conflicts in all communities irrespective of whether these are generated around place, identity or lifestyle. It must therefore promote the maximum diversity of democratic forms.

Keywords

Relational; Capacities; Complexity; Conflictual

Address for correspondence: *Paul Hoggett, Faculty of Economics and Social Science, University of the West of England, Frenchay Campus, Coldharbour Lane, Bristol, BS16 1QY.*

Are Greens Naturally Democratic?

Cahill (1999) notes that the social policy community has been reluctant to face up to the grip that consumerism has on the population. Many years ago E. P. Thompson in his wonderful essay "Writing by Candlelight" (Thompson 1970) illustrated how consumerism pits consumers against producers and encourages a ruthless attitude towards the human and natural resources which are needed to keep consumers in the manner to which they are accustomed. It therefore provides for individual satisfaction in a way which is at odds with the value of interdependency with fellow humans and the natural world. But what makes people change their minds and look for an alternative? One body of opinion suggests that we are faced with a number of imperatives (e.g. unsustainable economic and population growth) that we must respond to before it is too late (Ophuls 1977). This perspective assumes that people will only change if they are forced to. It relies on fear as a motivator and the green future it envisages is often perceived as austere and unattractive—a necessary medicine rather than something exciting or fulfilling. To those living in the West it prescribes "less" but says little about an alternative vision of "more". Torgerson (in this volume) describes this as "green frugality". It is probably latently anti-democratic. It says that, given the imperatives we face, strong government may at times be needed to impose rules on recalcitrant citizens (setting limits, for example, to a range of human behaviours from car use to choice of family size). This kind of green democracy may therefore be less respectful of human autonomy than liberal democracy; certainly, the claim for some natural affinity between green and democratic politics seems undermined (Saward 1993).

In contrast, following Kovel, I believe that "non-repressiveness should be an authentic ecosocialist ideal" (Kovel 2000: 13). It follows that in this essay I want to focus on the "more" that a green society can offer beyond what a liberal capitalist society can provide. And I think that the idea of an ecowelfare society, considered in its expansive and positive sense as that which provides the conditions for human development, is central to this vision. I also think that such a society would generate forms of strong democracy built around a politics of interdependency that is unrecognizable to prevailing liberal notions of democracy.

Why should greens be more democratic than liberals, social democrats or socialists? We tend to think of greens as heavily participatory, into consensual decision making, etc., but is there a natural affinity between green and democratic thought? I have already noted the latent authoritarianism in some catastrophist versions of green thought. But even within more mainstream elements of the green movement there are strong grounds to suggest that some of the greens' existing democratic credentials are built upon a vision of the future which is both untenable and oppressive. As Saward (1993) notes, "most visions of green democracy are . . . variants . . . on a model of direct democracy in small, often rural, face-to-face communities, characterised by labour intensive production, self-reliance if not self-sufficiency, a related minimisation of trade and travel between communities, and decision-making by face-to-face assemblies" (p. 71). In other words, this is dangerously close to a vision of a network of homogeneous *gemeinschaft* communities located in a society stripped of complexity where there is no need for the state and probably no need for welfare institutions (one often gets a strong sense that care, education, etc. would be informalized in a green utopia, and we know what that probably means in terms of gender relations). There are striking parallels between this notion of "return to community" and the old Marxist idea that in the post-revolutionary epoch there would be a withering away of class society and therefore of the need for government and judiciary, "for as institutions they are based on the assumption that there will be severe conflicts of interest in society and that these must be ordered and regulated" (Held 1996: 147). The idea of a people living in unity and harmony is a recurring theme in radical movements, as if a desirable future would be one without difference, conflict or antagonism, that is, where there would be no need for politics (Polan 1984; Kenny 1996).

So, if we kick away these two props, catastrophism and crude communitarianism, what is left of green democracy? I suggest that actually a great deal is left if we link green politics to a positive vision of an emancipatory society. To do this we need a concept of the human agent which is not the rational, self-seeking, instrumental actor of conventional economics nor the harmonious cooperator of some green utopias. What I seek to achieve in this essay is to outline a fundamentally relational view of the human being in which both solidarity and conflict are viewed as inevitable and vital dimensions of a facilitating environment in which human capacities can flourish.

A Relational Perspective

Human beings are fundamentally relational beings, that is, they find fulfilment primarily by virtue of their relations with others and with nature. This simple idea, if pursued consistently, has radical implications both for our vision of a "good society" and for our concept of what politics is.

I see human capacities as having four essential dimensions—the relational, expressive, practical-intellectual and spiritual. These are not culturally or historically specific but an aspect of our ontological status. I make no apology for saying that they are part of our nature, though clearly the form in which they are realized will be historically and culturally specific. I see these four dimensions related to each other in the way outlined in figure 1, that is, as overlapping spheres in which the relational is primary.

In giving primacy to the relational sphere I am arguing that all human powers, including spiritual, are developed in relation to other humans and to nature. In other words, we are dependent upon others and upon nature for our fulfilment. And, in an identical fashion, others are dependent upon us. Such a simple idea and how hard we rebel against it! The narcissism of contemporary culture pitches us against the very ideas of humility and respect that interdependency implies. But I also want to take issue with the view of some greens that interdependency equals cooperation and harmony (Mathews 1996). Our relational capacities are developed through the experience of difference and conflict as much as through solidarity and empathy (Simmel 1955; Coser 1957; Gilmore 1987). The child develops not just because

Figure 1

Human capacities

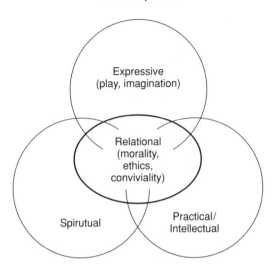

its parents love it but because they inevitably frustrate, disappoint and disillusion it. And they do this because ultimately they have their own lives to lead.

Our relational capacities find expression in two core aspects of everyday life—morality and conviviality. While Piaget and developmental psychologists have charted the development of moral reasoning, Melanie Klein (Klein and Riviere 1937; Klein 1957) developed a specifically relational account of the development of moral feeling or, as Winnicott put it, our capacity for concern (Winnicott 1963). Winnicott (1971) also developed a relational account of the development of the child's capacity for play, a capacity that he saw lying at the heart of the development of culture. Play contributes both to our expressivity (in music, art, sport and other areas where we put our imagination to work) and to our conviviality. But at its root conviviality relates not to what we do with others but to our capacity to be with others— to derive pleasure from companionship, conversation and play with others (Maffesoli 1996). Anyone who looks at the organizations of civil society only from an instrumental perspective, seeing them simply as a means to an end, misses out on half of what they are about. People derive tremendous fulfilment from being with others and the ostensible purpose of group activity often almost becomes secondary (Bishop and Hoggett 1986).

I propose to deploy the term "development" to refer to the realization of human powers and capacities. This might seem as if I am privileging the notion of human autonomy, a core liberal value. Eckersley (1996) has argued cogently for the integration of liberal and green values and when she says "humans, both individually and collectively, have a moral responsibility to

143

live their lives in ways that permit the flourishing and well-being of both human and non-human life" (1996: 223) I find myself in broad agreement. But I am more concerned for the "flourishing" than for the autonomy and in this, like David Pepper (1993: 118ff.), I take my starting point from Marx rather than J. S. Mill, and specifically Marx's early theory of alienation (which included alienation from nature as well as from self and others—Mezaros 1970). Whereas liberals are preoccupied with the problematic relation between autonomy and the state, libertarian socialists have been preoccupied with the problematic relation between the development or distortion of human capacities on the one hand and the organization of work and consumption on the other. Whereas liberals have been concerned with "freedom from" (the state, etc.), libertarian socialists have been concerned with "freedom to" (enjoy, create and imagine independently of the accumulation, consumption or regulation machines). Moreover, whereas liberal discourse pitches autonomy against community, a libertarian socialist discourse sees freedom as a relational phenomenon—whereas for the former the other is a potential threat to self's autonomy, for the latter the other is the essential means by which self's capacities can flourish. By appropriating this libertarian socialist tradition green politics can recover a set of values which are both relational and hedonistic, concerned for nature, people and pleasure.

In speaking of "powers" and "capacities" I have in mind a potential which may or may not be realized. Thus whilst a newborn child has the latent capacity for conviviality this capacity has to be developed through life if it is to enjoy play with others and participate in family, group and cultural ritual. The development of this capacity depends considerably upon its environment; indeed Winnicott (1965) coined the phrase "the facilitating environment" precisely to describe the role of the environment, and the quality of the social relations that constitute it, in enabling this potential to be realized. It is the facilitating environment which enables us to flourish. However, under certain conditions some of our capacities may flourish at the expense of others. Adorno and Horkheimer (1979), for example, perceived in capitalism the ultimate realization of an instrumental rationality which enabled our practical/intellectual powers to flourish while our ethical, spiritual and expressive capacities remained undernourished.

I am aware that in the literature on developing countries the concept of development has itself become deeply problematic (Adams 1990; Esteva 1992). Nevertheless, I believe it is worth persevering with, particularly if we can free it from some of its modernist inflections. Speaking of development from quite different terrains, from that of "developing countries" on the one hand and "child and individual development" on the other, Esteva (1992) and Rustin (1991) respectively indicate the way in which "development" has acquired teleological connotations as if some endpoint of development were known against which societies or individuals could be judged. If we free the concept from its modernist scaffolding then I believe many of the objections which might otherwise be made against it, especially its failure to recognize the actuality of individual and social diversity, would fall. Following the thinking of my colleague Robert French, I see development in non-linear terms (French 1999). In other words it is not a question of the stages that an individual, group or society passes through (from lower to higher), for this reduces the qualitative to the quantitative. Development then becomes a process of arriving at a definable state which is already known and can be pinned down, predicted and measured. In contrast I see the transformation of the internal social relations of a society, organization, group or individual as that which facilitates its development, i.e. the realization of its capacities.

Ecowelfare and the Quality of Social Relations

A relational perspective can help us understand more clearly how an ecowelfare society would differ from, and offer more than, either consumerist or traditional welfarist models. These three different visions of the "good society" are summarized below:

Consumerism   well-being originates in the quantity and variety of material goods and services purchasable as commodities by consumers.

Welfare-statism well-being originates in the quantity (if not variety) of public goods and services received as a right by citizens.

Ecowelfarism   well-being resides in the quality of the relations between people and between people and nature.

Consumerist and welfare-statist ideologies are primarily concerned with issues of quantity and the concept of "standard of living" is central to this. Welfare-statism traditionally assumed that economic growth was necessary to generate the surplus that reforming governments then redistributed in terms of public goods and services (Offe 1994). In contrast Ecosocialism, with its focus on the *quality* of social and environmental relations, privileges qualitative development—both individual and social—rather than quantitative growth.

A society whose primary aim was to enhance the quality of social relations in order to facilitate the development of human powers and capacities would be a society without an itch to consume and without an anxiety to constantly improve its standard of living. In this essay I want to focus on those local social relations which contribute primarily to people's emotional well-being—the relation of the individual to his/her embodied self, social relations within households and families, "community relations" including relations between and within different communities sharing the same space, and social relations between employed providers and receivers of welfare. It is this "texture" of human relationships (Titmuss 1974) that should be the primary concern of an ecowelfare society. Each of these four sites constitutes both an arena for political action and for the development of relational welfare policies. Many accounts of participatory democracy, including green variants, operate within narrowly restricted notions of the sphere of politics. In the following section I argue that struggles around the quality of social relations lead us towards the democratization of everyday life. With the decline of democratic labour movements it is to this area that we must now look for the soil from which an extended formal democracy can be grown and sustained.

The Politics of Interdependency

Through his concept of "strong democracy" Benjamin Barber (1984) provided not only a critique of the dull maximum of liberal democracy but also offered a participatory, self-governing alternative. Strongly influenced by the people's assemblies of small New England towns, Barber's largely philosophical work nevertheless offered a practical vision of democratic neighbourhood government. There are many strengths to his argument. It clearly positions itself in opposition to those unitarist forms of communitarianism which, as we have seen, underpin some green versions of direct democracy. It celebrates difference, conflict and the power of "talk" (which it sees having affective and cognitive dimensions), and offers a picture of direct democracy as an ongoing local process of moral/political argumentation in a way which has subsequently figured strongly in debates about deliberative democracy (Benhabib 1992).

However, in a rather unreflexive way Barber (1984: 117) announces that strong democracy is consonant with "the separation of private and public realms of action". For Barber not all action is political, only "public action: i.e. . . . action that is both undertaken by a public and intended to have public consequences" (1984: 123). Barber is immediately aware of the difficulty this use of "and" is going to get him into and over the next page he steadily backtracks so that he ends up conceding that private actions which have public consequences can also be considered political. He gives the example of tobacco smoking but could more usefully have mentioned sexual abuse, domestic violence and all those other private actions which express the poverty of social relations between genders and generations and which have both individual and public consequences. One gets the feeling that the old feminist slogan "the personal is the political" rests rather uneasily in Barber's psyche. In some respects Barber still operates with a rather traditional, liberal conception that the proper sphere of politics is in political and not civil society. This is a view I disagree with strongly, for it separates politics and democracy from the culture of everyday life.

Our relation to our embodied selves, relations between people of different sexuality, gender and generation particularly as they are enacted in households and families, community relations and relations between the providers and users of welfare services all describe different facets of interdependency which cross the private/public boundary. In what follows I will sketch some of the political struggles and relational welfare policies which arise within these four sites.

Respect for the nature in ourselves

Most perspectives on human empowerment give emphasis to the active subject. But it would be a mistake to believe that we only develop ourselves, and specifically our moral and spiritual capacities, as active beings; there will always be times in our lives when we face nature passively, as the object of what fate throws at us, particularly, for the vast majority of us, in sickness and death. Even as the object of misfortune and fate, indeed some would say particularly then, we can find new strengths. But a people in revolt against their interdependency with the natural world are also in revolt against the nature in them, that is, their nature as dependent beings. We remain in flight from death, ageing, illness, disability and madness, as if these things have no proper place in our lives, tarred with the scornful brush of the so-called "dependency culture" (Hoggett 2000). An ecowelfare society would be a society in which the passive and tragic voice of nature—the random and accidental way in which physical and emotional incapacity typically falls upon us—would be respected. Under conditions of capitalist modernity the passive and tragic voice in ourselves has been disavowed and externalized— the sick, the dying, the frail, the mad, those with physical and learning disabilities find themselves and their experiences removed from shared everyday living, kept at a distance, and this despite the rhetoric of "normalization" that dominates much of European social policy (Entwhistle and Hoggett 1998). Green welfare would promote the utmost respect for human dependency and would champion the development of a new generation of human-scale institutions and integrated, community-based models of support in which holistic models of health, social care and education would flourish. We do not have to engage in abstract thought experiments, such an approach is already prefigured in some third-sector innovations throughout Europe and the UK, many of which are outlined in the recent ten-country European Foundation report (Pillinger 2000). Many such projects are experimenting with user- and worker-based cooperatives, they emphasize both user involvement and the development of a mutually respectful relationship between workers and users.

A democracy of the emotions

This useful phrase from Giddens (1994) draws our attention to the impact of detraditionalization in the sphere of our most intimate social relations —between parents, children, friends, lovers. Processes of modernization have started to release citizens from pre-given roles and as a result the sphere of our most intimate relations has become a site for struggles around sexuality, gender and generational relations, leading to reflexive learning and the development of our relational capacities. Our roles and characters, the way in which we behave towards others, are no longer a pre-given destiny but the raw material for reflexive action through which we can develop our capacity to play, care and love. Indeed, we no longer see our character as immutable, we can take up different relations towards ourselves as well as towards others. There is no longer any excuse for the things that we do to others as husbands or fathers, we are confronted with our own responsibility even in the most intimate relations that we participate in. Social policy would be geared towards supporting this incipient democratization of everyday social relations in a way which has been comprehensively outlined by Fiona Williams (2000) through her concept of "good enough principles for welfare".

Emancipatory welfare practices

In recent years the social relations of formal welfare provision have become an arena for political struggle by a whole range of groups from schoolchildren to survivors of psychiatric treatment. Under social democracy the state exacted a price for becoming the guarantor of welfare. The social relations of welfare, specifically the relations between the producers and users of welfare services, became fundamentally undemocratic and objectivizing. The same rationality which sees external nature as something to be mastered and controlled has been turned upon human nature, where it came to saturate medicine, psychiatry, education and other practices. However, the accumulated practices embodied in health, education, social work, planning, etc. cannot simply be abandoned in favour of anti-professional, lay ones (Illich 1977). Instead, we require a resocialization of welfare so that the citizen is related to as a co-determining subject rather than object of such practices. There is already research evidence to suggest that treatment outcomes for patients with cancer, HIV, etc. are enhanced if the subjects of such treatments do not experience themselves as passive recipients but are encouraged to mobilize their inner resources in the treatment process (Greer 1999; Jensen *et al.* 2000). Clearly, complementary therapies would also have a much greater role to play precisely because of the way in which they require the subject of such practices to play an active role in the treatment (Faulkner 1997; Wallcraft 1998). Such holistic practices pose a head-on challenge to the hegemony of positivistic, asocial and rationalistic models of the human subject (Taylor *et al.* 1998).

Convivialization of community life

Spatial communities—the village, the neighbourhood, the town, the city— are the primary site for the realization of our expressivity and conviviality. Here we join clubs, drink and eat together, dance, listen to music, hang out and play games. Here we encounter each other in our differences of taste, style, ritual and habit. Here also we harass, attack and abuse others and destroy the physical environment we all share. I do not want to say much here other than to indicate the key role that policies for cultural development (Nystrom 1999), urban design, community safety and the promotion of respectful community relations have in maximizing the convivial and expressive possibilities of everyday life in public spaces.

To summarize, ecowelfarism should fight for qualitative change in social relations in four areas of life:

- the recognition and valuation of our dependency upon the nature in ourselves and in others
- the resocialization of welfare practices
- a democracy of the emotions
- the convivialization of community life

Taken together, such changes could contribute considerably to individual and social development, but they would also contribute to the consolidation of democratic principles and practices in everyday life, something Pateman (1970) refers to as "socialization for democracy" (p. 42) or the development of "democratic character" (p. 103). In contrast to liberalism, ecosocialism understands the interpenetration of public and private spheres and therefore sees democratization as something which should penetrate institutional practices, our shared encounters in spatial, ethnic and elective communities and our relations with family and friends. Only this would provide the necessary context or soil in which Barber's strong democracy could flourish—to have a truly democratic political society you have to have a democratic culture, one rooted in the activities of everyday life.

Decentralization and Democracy

Let us now move from the soil to the plant—i.e. the public sphere as normally recognized by many variants of liberal and green democracy. The relational perspective that I have developed complements the argument of Torgerson (see above, this volume) in that it enables us to see that political democracy is not simply a just means of decision making. Nor does its value lie only in its role as a possible means of challenging existing power relations. While democratic participation may achieve these results, from a relational perspective it is the process of political participation itself which has value to the extent that it develops human powers and capacities. Unlike much of the politics of the past many of the new forms of politics have a strongly expressive dimension. Politics does become a performing art, fused with imagination (Jowers *et al.* 1999; Wall 1999). But perhaps more importantly, the democratization of political society at national and local levels is essential to the development of our moral and ethical capacities. For too long governments have tried to exclude citizens from participation in the complex ethical and moral questions that saturate collective everyday living. Our ethical powers are undernourished and puny in comparison to our technical abilities. And as a result we live in a risk-saturated world endangered at all levels by technique which has been developed as a means to control nature, including the nature within us. Involvement in decision making at all levels of society—from the very local to the global, from the governance of institutions and facilities to the governance of spatial areas—is vital if technique is to be resocialized, that is, put in the service of nature, including human nature, rather than deployed for the subjugation of it.

But there are real tensions between representative, deliberative, direct and participative principles of democracy which must be worked through, and local democracy would be the crucible for experimentation in an ecowelfare society. Moreover, by muting the strident instrumentality of capitalist modernity, the links between democratic participation and our expressive and convivial capacities would begin to flourish (Hoggett and Thompson 2002). The imagination that many contemporary social movements bring to the organization of decision making would infect mainstream democratic life— who knows, meetings could even become enjoyable!

So what might a local green democracy look like? Here I want to draw upon twenty years' experience as researcher, consultant and adviser around issues of community development, local democracy and stakeholder governance (Hambleton and Hoggett 1984, 1987; Burns *et al.* 1994; Hoggett 1997). I will start from the building blocks of a democratic polity—the individual citizens—and work up.

Facilitating individual participation

Existing research (Parry *et al.* 1992) indicates that citizens participate unequally in public life because they have unequal access to material resources and unequal amounts of cultural capital. The convivialization of community life would help redress such issues. Community schools would become the norm rather than the exception, convivial tools from recording studios to networked workstations would become part of a new local "commons". One of the main barriers to participation for poorer people concerns the costs of participation—time, travel, care of dependent relatives. The introduction of a taxable and conditional Participation Income based upon the existing precedent of jury service, could be a transitional step towards a full and unconditional Basic Income.

Concepts of participation must be informed by recognition of the different identities that all citizens have—of place, culture, gender, sexuality, and so on. A vibrant democracy would give emphasis to people's differences as much as it would to what people have in common. Thus a democratic political society would foster a plurality of participatory mechanisms and structures. We have argued elsewhere (Hoggett and Thompson 1998) that self-governing associations giving both voice and exit rights to their members could provide a key avenue for the realization of particularist identities. There are already many examples of such organizational forms, from the Stockholm Cooperative for Independent Living which has spawned a network of disability service cooperatives in Sweden (Entwhistle and Hoggett 1998) to a huge variety of user-owned and user-controlled organizations in the UK, such as the Creative Living Centre in Manchester. One of the key challenges for the future is to find effective means of combining universalist and particularist structures for participation (i.e. how do particular interests find expression on democratic general interest bodies?). We need to develop hybridized forms. Among the different possibilities we can include reserved places for underrepresented groups on otherwise directly elected bodies (Phillips 1995), election by lot (Fishkin 1991) and stakeholder models of representation (Hutton 1999). Ellison's concept of local policy communities (Ellison 1998) would also provide a possible model for participation for those with particular interests in policy areas such as education, primary care, etc.

Direct and participatory democracy

Moving up a level, I believe the green model of direct, face-to-face citizens' assemblies is untenable on an extended basis for several reasons. First, as I have already argued, it is based on the assumption of homogeneous *gemeinschaft* communities operating in a society stripped of complexity. Second, it flies in the face of all that we know about the dynamics of large groups (Kreeger

1994)—that the larger the assembly the more likely it is to be undermined by the operation of uncontainable emotional forces such as anger, hatred and despair (Hoggett and Miller 2000; Thompson and Hoggett 2001). Third, it "resolves" the complex but necessary problem of representation by wishing it away. Representation is not just an issue bound up with the sordid lives of "general interest" political parties; it is central to the organization of all forms of particularist community action—trade unions, tenants' groups, self-help groups, housing cooperatives; none of these can work in the absence of some kind of elected organizing body. The question is not "how can we do without representatives" but "how can representatives be made properly accountable to those they represent" and "how can we ensure that those without a strong voice find proper representation"? So, if direct democracy is untenable in all but exceptional circumstances, what local democratic bodies can give expression to general and particular interests and identities during "normal times"?

Perhaps one can glimpse the outlines of what might be possible in some of the new Regeneration Partnership Boards in the UK. The Hartcliffe and Withywood Partnership Board in South Bristol, which manages a regeneration budget of £15 million for a working-class community of 22,000 people, will have 17 members, 10 of whom will be directly elected by 5 neighbourhoods based upon administrative boundaries within the area. In addition, 2 members will be nominated by local community organizations, 1 place will be reserved for a local councillor and 4 places will be reserved for nominees from major local agencies such as health and the police. Early experiments with direct elections in other regeneration projects suggest that local people seem much more prepared to vote than in elections for local government (*Guardian*, 23 May 2001). The Partnership has also given consideration to the underrepresentation of certain groups. It intends, for instance, to extend the vote to all local citizens of secondary school age and above and is considering the best way of ensuring a voice for groups like ethnic minorities and people with disabilities. So, we could imagine a self-governing body in the future with reserved places for ethnic minorities or people caring for dependent relatives etc., along the lines that the London Borough of Islington pioneered in the late 1980s. Now imagine that home care, nursery education, housing repair, environmental maintenance, adult education and training and some other public services were provided by self-governing associations each of which sent representatives to the local board. At the moment Withywood Secondary and Teyfant Primary schools are community schools, now imagine the other local secondary and primary schools were also community schools, and together all of these school governing bodies, local head teachers and other educational interest groups formed a very local version of one of Ellison's (1999) local policy communities, and they sent two representatives to the board. Now do the same for local primary care services; imagine the local health centres were run by patients' councils.

Now we come across a real tension. The larger the assembly the more inclusive it can become of all possible local interests and identities. But the greater the number of different interests represented and the greater the size of the deliberative body the more inefficient it will become (Greer *et al.* 2001).

In other words there is a tension between representativeness and deliberative capacity. It's no use saying "ah yes, but in the long run the decisions that are made will be of a much greater quality", because experience does not bear this out. It is just as likely that the larger the range of interests, the greater the propensity to move towards a lowest common denominator type of decision. Moreover, decision making will certainly become a slow process, and the legitimacy of the assembly may be undermined if it is seen to be too slow to sort out problems before they become crises. So the assembly will have to construct some kind of core executive group which will need to develop a symbiotic relationship with the main body of the assembly. The point I am trying to make is that whoever says democracy says complexity; those who seek to evade this either have a low tolerance level for reality (as Freud noted, preferring "wish fulfilment" instead) or are latently authoritarian (preferring the "tyranny of unstructurelessness" to the formalization of rights and responsibilities).

The decentralization of government

Moving on, what about the powers available to such assemblies? This brings us to questions of scale and the need for radical decentralization. The regeneration budget available to Hartcliffe and Withywood is a small fraction of the total amount of public resources presently being spent in the area that local people have no control over. One of the consequences is that local people, particularly younger people, do not share the perception that these are their resources, they belong to someone else, "the council", and are fair game. The local housing office looks like an army bunker from Northern Ireland and is covered in razor wire; parks, gardens, youth centres, playgrounds, all-weather sports pitches, trees, open spaces, etc. are subject to unremitting desecration and attack. Local youth workers and environmental workers sometimes throw up their hands in despair.

Imagine now that the local board had a budget of £100 million and was responsible for all environmental, housing and transport management and the provision of education, primary care, social care, personal social services, 'beat' policing, leisure, employment, social security and training services. It exercised its responsibilities via a mixture of grant funding (of self-governing welfare associations, community schools), commissioning (of specialist services such as primary care) and by being the management agent for services provided by the local authority (e.g. personal social services). The disaggregation of the relevant budgets on a formula (i.e. needs-driven) basis is perfectly possible. In the UK central government more or less does this already for schools (albeit according to a formula which is very weakly needs-oriented) and several local authorities have already accomplished such a disaggregation for planning, street lighting, environmental maintenance, social care and other services. If we look around beyond the UK we realize that anything is possible—the city of Oslo, for example, has happily organized all social care, personal social services and primary health care on a completely integrated and decentralized basis for over a decade. Now imagine, in addition, that Hartcliffe and Withywood had some revenue-raising powers of its own. Even now, the law relating to urban parishes allows for rates to be levied of up to two pence in the pound. And now imagine that every year the local board—which we could call a Neighbourhood Assembly (although it would be very different to the rather vague proposals with similar names that Benjamin Barber (1984: 267–73) and Murray Bookchin (1992, ch. 8) propose) organizes a citizens' budget-making process along the lines of that which has been pioneered in the Porto Alegre district in Brazil. Here, then, would be some direct democracy in action alongside the highly decentralized but representative local assembly.

Democratizing institutions

On to scale: many things cannot be decentralized to this level. Yet again, greens must face the actual complexity of government and public services in contemporary society. Wishful thinking about constructing government and public services piece by piece from neighbourhood building blocks is naive—it would be impossible to run post-16 education or most forms of specialist health care on this basis, let alone environmental protection or transport strategy. The need for large, specialist institutions such as hospitals and universities will persist until technical change removes the conditions which make such phenomena necessary. The same holds for the rest of the apparatus of the state at local, regional and national levels. In the UK the problem of the lack of accountability and responsiveness of this apparatus has been tackled by recourse to markets and, more recently, by recourse to managerialist regulation. The one thing that has not been tried is extended democracy. Indeed, the centralization of state power via the emasculation of local government and the spread of the quangocracy has proceeded apace under Labour (Skelcher et al. 2000; Kitchen 2001); this was depressingly predictable. The problem with quangos is not that they are unaccountable but that they are accountable only upwards and in this sense they epitomize the process of centralized decentralization (Hoggett 1996) which has been such a feature of the British state over the last decade. So, what can be done?

Starting at the very centre, I disagree with the view of some reformers (Skelcher et al. 2000: 9) that Non-departmental Public Bodies such as the Environment Agency, BBC, etc. are best left as appointed bodies. The governing bodies of all such agencies should be subject to the democratic principle. Different democratic principles could apply to different bodies. For example, the BBC and the Radio Authority could effectively become membership associations where payment of one's TV licence granted membership of the association. The boards of such bodies would then be subject to direct election by the body of members. In contrast, bodies such as the Environment Agency would be best subject to forms of stakeholder democracy where each of the major constituencies—conservation, agriculture, recreation, etc.—sent representatives to the governing body. Many of these bodies such as the Environment Agency already have embryonic regional structures which would themselves be subject to the same democratic principles. Another model is that of the elected single-purpose authority such as an elected national health authority recommended by the recent Hutton Commission on the future of democracy in the NHS (Hutton 2000); one could imagine, for example, that if we ever had a rail transport system back under public control it could be organized at regional and national levels along the lines of an elected single-purpose authority. All of these models would also be compatible with the principle that some members of the governing body should be elected by lot.

Democratizing representative democracy

Moving down a level, the Hutton Commission suggests that the strategic responsibilities of the now-defunct regional tier within the NHS, once revived, could be incorporated into elected regional assemblies. Regional Development Agencies, a new tier within the quangocracy, have already accrued to themselves a substantial resource base (particularly regarding transport and regeneration). Existing national services such as social security and employment are ripe for decentralization to this level (indeed, in Germany social security has always been the responsibility of local government; Clarke and Hoggett 2000). Applying the principle of subsidiarity, that political decisions "should only be taken at a higher level when absolutely necessary" (Burns *et al.* 1994: 257), functions should always be discharged at the lowest possible level.

Finally, to local government. Deep democracy requires strong local government. This is not a call for the return of local councils as service providers, though economies of scale are such that some specialist services will always have to be provided at a municipal level, but there is no reason why even many of these services could not be supplied by specialist service cooperatives. Imagine, then, a city largely run through a network of self-governing neighbourhood citizens' assemblies, membership-based civic associations, user and producer cooperatives, and locally elected single-purpose authorities (governing non-primary forms of health care, for example). Local authorities would then have three key functions—for strategic initiatives, coordination and conflict resolution, and resource distribution. Strong local government is impossible without the removal of central controls over local spending and the power to generate local transport, energy and business taxes. But the allocation of resources to neighbourhoods and to non-spatial communities such as those based on a shared minority cultural identity, while being the responsibility of the local authority, would obviously be subject to continuous processes of contestation and negotiation. Many strategic initiatives, for light rail or other public transport systems, for example, could clearly only be undertaken by municipal authorities with effective financial autonomy. Finally, many decisions made at the very local level will have knock-on effects for other neighbourhoods or interest groups; the local authority would play a key role in resolving such coordination problems.

Beyond party politics

Local government lies on the boundary between representative and participatory forms of democracy. Green politics turns its back on competitive party politics, raising its colours firmly on the terrain of participatory demo-cracy—a terrain which has been inhabited by generations of labour move-ment activists, anarchists, feminists and cooperators. It follows that in a green democracy political society would no longer be the primary preserve of competitive parties. Local, regional and central government bodies would become progressively hybridized. Take local government. Inititially, perhaps 50 per cent of the elected members of such bodies would be returned by political parties; the other seats would be occupied by representatives of neighbourhood citizens' assemblies and directly elected representatives of particularist constituencies such as young people, people with disabilities, and some could be elected by lot.

Developing new deliberative techniques

Finally, given the tension between participation and deliberation, attention would have to be given to maximizing the deliberative potential of the new decision-making bodies at all levels of society. Contemporary social move-ments have been at the forefront of developing new "deliberative technolo-gies" (Thompson and Hoggett 2001) such as consensus decision making, conflict mediation, the use of moderators and facilitators, small break-out groups, and so on (Schlosberg 1995). If a society based upon extended forms of democracy is not to collapse into discursive chaos, then the development, dissemination and evaluation of such technologies (and other innovations such as the election to deliberative bodies by "lot" along the lines of citizens' juries, the use of tele-democracy, referenda, etc.) would become a key priority for central government. A green government, having scrapped the panoply of regulation and inspection through which successive governments have sought to exercise central control could do no worse than build a Democracy Commission on the ashes of the old audit society.

Conclusion

In the space available I have tried to give a reasonably concrete picture of what an extensively democratized green society might look like. In contrast to many existing models I see the impulse for green democracy rooted in the need to realize our moral and ethical capacities in a complex modern society beset by both social and ecological insecurity. But the democratization of political society has to be situated in the broader context of the development of a democratic culture the preconditions for which lie in a changed relation-ship to nature, including the nature in ourselves, the democratization of relations between genders and generations, the development of emancip-atory welfare practices and the convivialization of community life. Such a society would, I believe, go a considerable way to offering a vision of human fulfilment based on the development of our relational, practical, expressive and spiritual capacities, which is a viable and attractive alternative to con-sumerism and productivism. It is precisely people who want more out of life who should be attracted to a green alternative.

References

Adams, W. (1990), *Green Development: Environment and Sustainability in the Third World*, London: Routledge.

Adorno, T. and Horkheimer, M. (1979), *Dialectic of Enlightenment*, London: Verso.

Barber, B. (1984), *Strong Democracy: Participatory Politics for a New Age*, Berkeley: University of California Press.

Benhabib, S. (1992), *Situating the Self: Gender, Community and Postmodernism in Contemporary Ethics*, Cambridge: Polity Press.

Bishop, J. and Hoggett, P. (1986), *Organising around Enthusiasms: Mutual Aid in Leisure*, London: Comedia.

Bookchin, M. (1992), *Urbanization without Cities*, Montreal: Black Rose Books.

Burns, D., Hambleton, R. and Hoggett, P. (1994), *The Politics of Decentralization*, Basingstoke: Macmillan.

Cahill, M. (1999), Sustainability: the twenty-first century challenge for social policy. In H. Dean and R. Woods (eds), *Social Policy Review, No. 11*, Luton: Social Policy Association.

Clarke, J. and Hoggett, P. (2000), Regressive modernisation? The changing pattern of social services delivery in the UK. In H. Wollmann and E. Schroter (eds), *Comparing Public Sector Reform in Britain and Germany*, Aldershot: Ashgate.

Coser, L. (1957), *The functions of social conflict*, London: Routledge and Kegan Paul.

Dryzek, J. (1992), Ecology and discursive democracy: beyond liberal capitalism and the administrative state, *Capitalism, Nature, Socialism*, 3, 2: 18–42.

Eckersley, R. (1996), Greening liberal democracy: the rights discourse. In B. Doherty and M. de Geus (eds), *Democracy and Green Political Thought*, London: Routledge.

Ellison, N. (1999), Beyond universalism and particularism: rethinking contemporary welfare theory, *Critical Social Policy*, 58: 57–85.

Entwhistle, T. and Hoggett, P. (1998), The Changing Needs and Preferences of the Users of Social Public Services in Europe. Unpublished report to the European Foundation for the Improvement of Living and Working Conditions: Dublin.

Esteva, G. (1992), Development. In W. Sachs (ed.), *The Development Dictionary: A Guide to Knowledge as Power*, London and New Jersey: Zed Books.

Faulkner, A. (1997), *Knowing Our Own Minds*, London: Mental Health Foundation.

Fishkin, J. (1991), *Democracy and Deliberation: New Directions for Democratic Reform*, New Haven, CT: Yale University Press.

French, R. (1999), The importance of *capacities* in psychoanalysis and the language of human development, *International Journal of Psychoanalysis*, 80, 6: 1215–26.

Giddens, A. (1994), *Beyond Left and Right: The Future for Radical Politics*, Cambridge: Polity Press.

Gilmore, D. (1987), *Aggression and Community: Paradoxes of Andalusian Culture*, New Haven, CT: Yale University Press.

Greer, S. (1999), Mind-body research in psychooncology, *Advances in Mind-Body Medicine*, 15: 236–81.

Greer, A. and Hoggett, P. (1999), Contemporary governance and local public spending bodies, *Public Administration*, 78, 3: 513–29.

Greer, A., Hoggett, P. and Maile, S. (2001), Quasi-governmental organisations—Effective and democratic? In C. Cornforth (ed.), *What Do Boards Do?* London: Routledge.

Hambleton, R. and Hoggett, P. (eds) (1984), *The Politics of Decentralisation: Theory and Practice of a Radical Local Government Initiative*, Bristol: School for Advanced Urban Studies.

Held, D. (1996), *Models of Democracy*, 2nd edn, Cambridge: Polity Press.

Hoggett, P. (1996), New modes of control in the public services, *Public Administration*, 74, 1: 9–32.

Hoggett, P. (ed.) (1997), *Contested Communities*, Bristol: Policy Press.

Hoggett, P. (2000), *Emotional Life and the Politics of Welfare*, Basingstoke: Macmillan.

Hoggett, P. and Hambleton, R. (1987), *Decentralisation and Democracy*, Bristol: School for Advanced Urban Studies.

Hoggett, P. and Miller, C. (2000), Emotions and community organisations, *Community Development Journal*, 35, 4: 352–64.

Hoggett, P. and Thompson, S. (1998), The delivery of welfare: the associationist vision. In J. Carter (ed.), *Postmodernity and the Fragmentation of Welfare*, London: Routledge.

Hoggett, P. and Thompson, S. (2002), Towards a democracy of the emotions, *Constellations* (forthcoming).

Hutton, W. (1999), *The Stakeholding Society*, Cambridge: Polity Press.

Hutton, W. (2000), *Commission on the NHS: New Life for Health* (the Hutton Commission), London: Vintage.

Illich, I. (1977), *Disabling Professions*, London: Marion Boyars.

Illich, I. (1992), *In the Mirror of the Past*, London: Marion Boyars.

Jensen, K., Back-Pettersson, S. and Segesten, K. (2000), The meaning of "not giving in": lived experiences among women with breast cancer, *Cancer Nursing*, 23, 1: 6–11.

Jowers, P., Purdue, D., Durrschmidt, J. and O'Doherty, R. (1999), DIY culture and extended milieux: LETS, veggie boxes and festivals, *Innovation*, 12, 1: 99–118.

Kenny, M. (1996), Paradoxes of community. In B. Doherty and M. de Geus (eds), *Democracy and Green Political Thought*, London: Routledge.

Kitchen, H. (2001), *A Democratic Future*, London: Local Government Information Unit.

Klein, M. (1957), *Envy and Gratitude*, London: Tavistock.

Klein, M. and Riviere, I. (1937), *Love, Hate and Reparation*, London: Hogarth Press.

Kovel, I. (2000), The struggle for use value: thoughts about the transition, *Capitalism, Nature, Socialism*, 11, 2: 3–19.

Kreeger, L. (1994), *The Large Group*, London: Karnac.

Maffesoli, M. (1996), *The Time of the Tribes: The Decline of Individualism in Mass Society*, London: Sage.

Mathews, F. (1996), Communitarianism and the ecological self. In F. Mathews (ed.), *Ecology and Democracy*, London: Frank Cass.

Mezaros, I. (1970), *Marx's Theory of Alienation*, London: Merlin Press.

Nystrom, L. (1999), *City and Culture: Cultural Processes and Urban Sustainability*, Stockholm: Swedish Urban Environment Council.

Offe, C. (1994), *Disorganised Capitalism: Contemporary Transformations of Work and Politics*, Cambridge: Polity Press.

Ophuls, W. (1977), *Ecology and the Politics of Scarcity*, San Francisco: W. H. Freeman.

Parry, G., Moyser, G. and Day, N. (1992), *Political Participation and Democracy in Britain*, Cambridge: Cambridge University Press.

Pateman, C. (1970), *Participation and Democratic Theory*, Cambridge: Cambridge University Press.

Pepper, D. (1993), *EcoSocialism: From Deep Ecology to Social Justice*, London: Routledge.

Phillips, A. (1995), *The Politics of Presence*, Oxford: Oxford University Press.

Pillinger, I. (2000), *Quality in Social Public Services*, Dublin: European Foundation for the Improvement of Living and Working Conditions.

Polan, T. (1984), *Lenin and the End of Politics*, London: Methuen.

Rustin, M. (1991), Post-Kleinian psychoanalysis and the postmodern. In *The Good Society and the Inner World*, London: Verso.

Saward, M. (1993), Green democracy? In A. Dobson and P. Lucardie (eds), *The Politics of Nature*, London: Routledge.

Schlosberg, D. (1995), Communicative action in practice: intersubjectivity and new social movements, *Political Studies*, 43: 291–311.

Simmel, G. (1955), *Conflict and the Web of Group-Affiliations*, tr. from German by R. Bendix, London: Collier-Macmillan.

Skelcher, C., Weir, S. and Wilson, L. (2000), *Advance of the Quango State*, London: Local Government Information Unit.

Taylor, P., Peckham, S. and Turton, P. (1998), *A Public Health Model of Primary Care*, London: Public Health Alliance.

Thompson, E. P. (1970), Writing by candlelight, *New Society*, 24 December.

Thompson, S. and Hoggett, P. (2001), Group dynamics and deliberative democracy, *Policy and Politics*, 29, 3: 351–64.

Titmuss, R. (1974), *Social Policy: An Introduction*, London: Allen and Unwin.

Wall, D. (1999), *Earth First! and the Anti-Roads Movement*, London: Routledge.

Wallcraft, J. (1998), *Healing Minds*, London: Mental Health Foundation.

Williams, F. (2000), *New Principles for Welfare*, Cambridge: Polity Press.

Winnicott, D. W. (1963), The development of the capacity for concern, *Bulletin of the Menninger Clinic*, 27: 167–76.

Winnicott, D. W. (1965), *The Maturational Processes and the Facilitating Environment*, London: Hogarth Press.

Winnicott, D. W. (1971), *Playing and Reality*, London: Tavistock.

CHAPTER 11

The Implications of Consumerism
for the Transition to a Sustainable Society

Michael Cahill

Abstract

An exploration of the nature of consumerism in rich societies, noting the damaging impact on the environment and the loss of interest in public life. The challenge of moving towards sustainable lifestyles is explored with reference to household labour and the use of the car.

Keywords

Consumerism; Lifestyles; Sustainability; Housework; Cars

Introduction

The central paradox which this article explores is that the world now experiences a high level of consumption for citizens based on advanced technology and infrastructure, so that wealth is at an all-time high but the gains which have accrued from this are threatened by environmental degradation, global warming and climate change. For three decades the consumption patterns of citizens in the West, with high waste and obsolescence, have been identified as a major factor in environmental problems. At the Rio Summit in 1992 consumption patterns in the rich world were identified as a problem in the move to a more sustainable society (Michaelis 2000). Yet in the following decade, so far from the economies and societies of the rich world moving towards more sustainable consumption, there has been an acceleration in consumer spending.

The appeal of consumer culture is undeniable. It is said to have been one of the principal reasons why the Eastern bloc collapsed, as its citizens wanted the commodities freely available in the West. Similarly the consumer culture of the rich world is viewed with envy by many in the poor world today. Within rich-world societies consumption has become a central feature of

Address for correspondence: *Michael Cahill, School of Applied Social Science, University of Brighton, Falmer, Brighton, BN1 9PH. Email: m.cahill@bton.ac.uk.*

identity, including attitudes to social and political life. Those apologists for the Western world order were so wrong when they declared that with the fall of the Berlin Wall and the abandonment of state socialism in Eastern Europe there had been an end to ideology. For consumerism was as potent an ideology as communism ever had been—the more so because it had no political expression but was implicitly subscribed to by all mainstream political parties. But there has been a profound reaction. In Seattle, Prague and Genoa at the major protests against globalization it is anti-consumerism which is one of the themes that unites the great variety of demonstrators who come to these events. The literature which is now appearing to make the case of the anti-globalization protests is likewise firm in its identification of consumerism as one of the foremost ills of our age (Klein 2000; Hertz 2001). Given this context this article makes the following assumptions: that present-day modes of production and consumption in the rich world are unsustainable for future generations and will be unsustainable if adopted by the poor world; that ecologists and others who wish to effect a transition to a more sustainable society have to acknowledge the profound attachment to consumption which has pervaded culture and society in the rich world and its undeniable appeal to the poor world. Social policy can be one of the ways in which sustainable patterns of consumption can emerge, but this will entail the creation of a welfare society informed by ecological principles. In order to pursue these themes I will outline the environmental impact of consumerism before reviewing the literature on consumer society and then examining the feasibility of sustainable consumption.

The Environmental Impact of Consumerism

The environmental impact of consumerism on the planet became apparent in the last 30 years of the twentieth century. Between 1970 and 1995 global income per capita rose by one-third and in the rich world more food, energy and transportation was consumed. Energy consumption increased rapidly and water shortages became more apparent. Globalization and the implications of a car-dependent lifestyle increased the strain on the earth's resources. A World Wide Fund for Nature report published in 1998 concluded that humans had destroyed 30 per cent of the natural world since 1970, involving serious depletion of the forest, and freshwater and marine systems. Analysing global consumption patterns to produce a measure of the burden placed on the natural environment by human beings, the report stated: "People put pressure on forest, freshwater and marine ecosystems through the production and consumption of resources such as grain, fish, wood, and freshwater, and the emission of pollutants such as carbon dioxide" (WWF 1998: 1). As material indices of wealth rose, so environmental indices fell. Individual consumption was dramatically skewed, with the average North American consuming ten times as much as the average Bangladeshi (WWF 1998). This was "overconsumption" on a vast scale. Through the mass media and the process of globalization this "over-consumption society" has become an ideal for people all over the planet—a way of life to which millions aspire.

Private Lives and Private Pleasures

The ideology of consumerism has been developing for some time in the UK but it is in the 30 years since 1970 that it has assumed a dominant form. Although consumerism is often discussed as a facet of postmodern society it is the result of a long-term process with the decline of manufacturing industry and the rise of the consumer market. In the interwar period the UK domestic economy expanded, putting purchasing power into the hands of working-class people and leading to a marked increase in spending on household durables, transportation and communication goods (Bowden 1994). If consumerism is discussed in terms of its ability to enable people to achieve identities, it could be argued that it was in the late 1950s that it was recognized as a force which would influence the aspirations and attitudes of the British people—the age of affluence had a transforming impact on the working class, especially as it led to three successive general election victories for the Conservative Party (Marwick 2000).

In the 1950s the home became a much more attractive place for working-class people with the drudgery having been removed from a number of household tasks and television greatly enhancing domestic leisure. The postwar full-employment and welfare-state consensus witnessed the emergence of a consumer society for the working class. These years saw the rise and rise of the work-and-spend ethic in which work would be valued for the opportunities it gave to purchase goods and participate in consumer society rather than, as many social reformers had believed, more affluence enabling greater free time and leisure (Cross 1993). That process did not go unnoticed by social scientists (Galbraith, Riesman) or cultural critics (Hoggart, Williams), leading in the UK to fierce debates on the "Americanization" of culture, the proper role of advertising and the impact of commercial television on society.

Martin Pawley in his book *The Private Future: Causes and Consequences of Community Collapse in the West*, published in 1973, provided an acute diagnosis of the problems which face a society where individual consumption and privatized lifestyles are prevalent.

> In a sense choices made by peoples of the West—for the private car and against public transport, for suburban life and against urban or rural community, for owner occupation and against tenancy, for the nuclear and against the extended family, for television and against the cinema and the theatre, for social mobility and against class solidarity, for private affluence and against community life, for machine politicians and against charismatic leaders, for orgasm and against conception, for eroticism and against reproduction, for pollution and against regulation—all these are choices in favour of privacy, in favour of individual freedom, in favour of anonymity, but against the very idea of community. The triumph of consumer society is a triumph of all private goals over all public goals. (Pawley 1973: 60–1)

Although one can disagree over the details and dissent from his dystopian perspective, Pawley's central point, shorn of the exaggeration of polemic, remains valid: that privatized lifestyles lead to the erosion of community and participation in public life. In the thirty years since this book appeared there has been an intensification of technological change, with e-mail, fax machines and mobile phones, which has enabled privatized lifestyles to flourish.

Technology is intensifying individualization: the mobile phone is a very good example of this as it enables private one-to-one communication. Car-based mobility enables individualization to flourish.

Technology has promoted individualization. The persuasiveness of the television derives in part from the fact that advertising hails us as individuals. Convenience, freedom and choice are dominant ways of seeing the world. They are enshrined in the market with its promise of all three. Today we seem to be on the verge of an intensification of these trends made possible by fast-developing technologies.

Consumer society by its nature and by its assumptions tends to the private and personal. Individualization describes the process whereby we are encouraged to act as individuals and to behave as individuals rather than collectively. Over the past half century consumer goods have penetrated deep into the psychology of the population. As Erich Fromm remarked: "I am = what I have and what I consume" (Fromm 1976, cited in Dittmar 1987: 3). Self-expression is attained through the use of material possessions more clearly with some goods than others—clothing and the car assume key importance.

The influence of consumerism on individual life choices is profound. If we accept Bocock's definition of consumerism as "the active ideology that the meaning of life is to be found in buying things and pre-packaged experiences" (Bocock 1993: 50), then it affects many facets of society. If the ideal for the ambitious young person is to make a successful career, then caring responsibilities, including motherhood, appear much less appealing for they inhibit commitment to a full-time job. The falling birth rate, the high divorce rate, the fragility of partnerships between men and women: these are all indices which need to be set alongside the number of new cars on the roads or the number of foreign holidays taken. Single-person households with their attendant environmental problems are set to increase rapidly. "About 80 per cent of household increase will be accounted for by persons who live alone. By 2010 single person households will become the predominant household type in Britain" (Scase 1999: 15). Environmental objectives and individual preferences are set to collide as government attempts to ensure that 60 per cent of new building is on brownfield sites while housebuyers exhibit a preference for greenfield sites and country locations where an urban lifestyle is made possible by the car.

The Decline of the Public

Consumerism has downgraded the importance of democracy, with choices about products now regarded as much more important than choices about political parties.

There has been a marked disengagement from public life not only in the more obviously political areas such as membership of political parties, which had been declining in the UK since the mid-1950s, but in representative political institutions such as local government (Bentley *et al.* 2000). Hayes and Hudson in their recent study of Basildon reported "a profound detachment from all forms of collective political process or social agency. Local people are living their lives increasingly in the private sphere especially through family life" (2001: 11). Nationally, only one in ten young people aged 18 to 26 have any real involvement in politics compared with one in three of those aged 65 or more (Jowell *et al.* 2000). Hayes and Hudson observed: "All the evidence of our survey suggests a disengagement from the political sphere and perhaps more importantly from all the intermediary and mediating institutions through which public discussions about priorities used to be conducted" (2001: 67). This was clearly seen at the British General Election in June 2001 when voter turnout was the lowest since 1918.

The Sociology of Consumption

There have been numerous studies of the role of consumer goods in contemporary society. It is clear now that goods can be appropriated and used in unanticipated ways so that the consumer does not just receive the message but sometimes responds to it and sometimes ignores it. A great deal of time, effort and money goes into establishing what is likely to appeal to individual taste. Goods are used to create an identity and a style. Advertising and public relations are central both for business and politics in the moulding and handling of public opinion. Advertising increasingly aims not so much to provide information but to engage the emotions of individual consumers and enlist these emotions in the buying of products. A similar process occurs in politics where politicians sell their ideas on the grounds of their own essential niceness (Mestrovic 1997).

The expenditure of vast sums on psychological studies of consumer behaviour does enable more efficient manipulation of the emotions of the consumer. Emotions are packaged and fed back to consumers (Mestrovic 1997). Mestrovic has declared that we live in a post-emotional society, i.e. one where "synthetic, quasi-emotions become the basis for widespread manipulation by self, others, and the culture industry as a whole" (1997: xi). It is the hopes, fears and aspirations of the population which the corporations wish to tap into for then they can sell them back to us as a soft drink, a car or a pair of jeans. As Jim Brackin, creative director at Amherst has explained: "People are driven by their emotions, it's not about fact and logic. Increasingly, the only button you press is an emotional one. You find out what the needs are and you discover ways of reflecting those needs" (Booth 1999). Yet it is the accumulation of goods and the energy needed to produce them which is contributing to the chronic environmental burdens which confront our planet.

Recent work in the sociology of consumption has stressed the autonomy of the consumer. Bourdieu claimed that consumption is based upon the cultural capital of groups in the population who have differential access to "symbolic capital" resulting from their educational level. Consumer culture is a form of negotiation based upon the appropriation of signs and symbols and their use as a form of identity. In this sense they can be viewed as a form of liberation and expression (Miles 1998). That may well be, but there is evidence that major corporations now engage in "cool hunting", attempting to find out what is "cool" in the eyes of their target youth market (Klein 2000: 68).

Lifestyle is the pattern of social relations, the attitudes, the tastes and the material goods which mark out one group from another (Chaney 1996, 1998; Lury 1996). Those who read lifestyle the best are the most successful in business or in politics, whether that be Tesco or New Labour. Those who get it wrong can be seriously damaged as with Marks and Spencer or the Conservative Party. Business, politicians and all who are dependent on a market for their survival mould and tailor their message to appeal to the aspirations, hopes and fears of their customers. The extensive data collected via market research on people's attitudes enable consumers to be accurately targeted (Lansley 1994).

Sustainable Lifestyles

The post-Rio agenda of sustainable development has been played out at several levels—supranational, with the various treaties and agreements, national government with sustainable development plans and policies, and at the local level with Local Agenda 21. Running through all these sites of discussion has been a focus on the importance of individual change and individual responsibility in order to achieve sustainable practices. The foregoing account of consumer society is a bleak one for the prospects of sustainable development. If the transnational corporations have such a hold on the process of identity creation then the prospects for sustainability look gloomy. Alternative identities have a struggle to be recognized and always run the risk of being co-opted into a form of consumer iconography or product. Similarly, post-emotionalism suggests that there is little psychological space for individuals and communities to change their behaviour in everyday life when the demands of a work-and-spend society dominate their lives. Nonetheless, the moves to sustainable practices in everyday life have to take account of the constraints and opportunities afforded by patterns of life, family and work in contemporary society. Crucially, they need to take cognizance of the importance of consumer goods for self-identity and self-expression. If this does not occur, then sustainable lifestyles will remain stuck in a green ghetto.

Household practices and transportation are clearly going to be crucial in the next decade in the move towards more sustainable lifestyles. We can examine these in a number of different areas, but here we briefly consider housework and driving. If lifestyle is represented in choice of goods then the best showcase is the home. Homes need attention as cleaning, cooking, washing and ironing are regular tasks which must be performed, but they are also significant users of energy given their electrical supply, hot water systems, baths, showers, internal toilets and—for 80 per cent of homes in the UK—central heating. Energy used in the home now accounts for 30 per cent of the UK's total energy consumption (Stokes 1999). How we organize our daily lives and how we travel has a major impact upon the environment. Christensen has compared the lifestyles and use of energy of a dual-career, two-car family—which he dubs an "American" family; that is, two adults and two children—with three other family types, including a radical green-lifestyle family with two careers but no car. The American-style family caused eight times as much pollution as the radical green family (Christensen 1997).

Time-deprived households are a problem in moving towards sustainable lifestyles, as their reliance on time-saving products and their search for convenience increases environmental damage and waste. Consumer society accords a low value to household labour and household tasks. The improved status and increased economic power of women in the UK has been largely the result of much higher levels of participation in the labour market. Identity for women is usually seen in terms of position in the labour market, as that of the male has always been, while many traditional male identities have been fractured with the decline in unskilled labour. This has led to the reassessment and renegotiation of gender roles which is far more than the movement of women into what were once described as men's jobs and men into jobs previously reserved for women. The outcomes are often an intensification of time pressures which can hit families with children especially hard, with less time for parents and children to be together. Household labour traditionally associated with women has had a low valuation in the UK since the 1960s as has caring work whether carried out in families or in the labour market where home carers and residential care staff—who are overwhelmingly female—are on low wages.

Housework

A service economy has been created which serves the needs of the time-pressed affluent workers in our society. Women's position in the labour market has been transformed in the UK over the last 30 years. Although there is some shift in the distribution of household tasks between men and women, it is still the case that the main responsibility for this work falls on the woman. Attitudes among men would appear to have changed much more markedly than their behaviour (Jowell *et al.* 2000). Given female participation in the labour market, this leads to a premium being put on time-saving and convenience foods. More affluent women workers often use housework and other services to save the time that would be spent doing these jobs themselves. This growing housework role is often performed by low-paid women. A range of other personal service jobs have greatly expanded in number since the 1980s. This new service class is often part of the informal, black economy. The informal arrangements which characterize domestic employment have their downside when there is well-documented evidence of systematic abuse of migrant workers who are sometimes to be found in exploitative relations with their employers (Anderson 2000). More than 2.7 million households pay for some kind of help, a survey revealed (Norwich Union Insurance 2000).

A globalized economy and society is heavily reliant on high-speed transportation which permits the free flow of intellectual labour as well as goods. There is a global class of high income earners who maximize their income advantage by moving from country to country (Frank 1999). In their time-pressed lives they require servicing and there are eager (often migrant) workers ready to carry out these tasks. Douglas and Isherwood maintain that those who occupy or aspire to high-status posts will avoid "high-frequency-low-esteem tasks" which would reduce their personal availability for work (cited in Spaargarten and van Vliet 2000: 66). The energy consequences of the high-earning global class are alarming—their hypermobility with its frequent use of air travel and high car dependence is extremely damaging for the planet. Continuing growth of the service economy provides opportunities for unskilled or semi-skilled workers who have been displaced by the main-stream economy. Time-pressed dual-career families nowadays often rely on a cast of service workers to get through the week: nannies, gardeners, cleaners, supply the services. Innumerable sports clubs as well as child-minders occupy the time between the end of the school day and the end of the parents' working day. The questions raised for sustainable lifestyles by these trends tend to revolve around the energy implications and waste production of such households. (This is not to deny that these problems are encountered in other households who use no domestic help.) Dark green discourse which promotes self-reliance and equality would not agree that a low status should be given to household labour.

The complexity of domestic arrangements which enables these time-pressed affluent households to operate is usually centred around one item of modern technology.

Driving

The car is the essential technology to access consumer society. To be competent in the consumer society a car is essential. One might say that the driving licence is the badge of citizenship with non-car drivers as second-class citizens. The car is the most potent symbol of freedom in a consumer society (Mulgan 1994: 48). The perception of self which is held by the driver is changed by the view from the car (see Jain and Guiver in this issue). Advertising for cars is nowadays just as much about the kind of man or woman you aspire to be—for example, in control and secure in a dangerous world—as about the mechanical attributes of the vehicle. Many people's lives are held together by their car so that their sense of self—their job, their hobbies, their friendships—is all made possible by the automobile. This technology has transformed a nation's sense of the personal and its sense of time. The mobile privatization which is conferred on car drivers makes them much less likely to use public transport. Although the car transformed society and space in the twentieth century it seemed to have escaped the attention of generations of social scientists—as Urry has argued—so that there were studies of the lives of car workers or their work practices (Goldthorpe *et al.* 1969; Beynon 1973; Urry 2000) but none on the impact of the technology on social relations in the society. Urry has directed his comments on the inattention of social science to this transforming technology in the direction of sociology but, *mutatis mutandis*, the same could be said of social policy. It took the damage which the motor car has done to the environment before sociology and social policy awoke to the human consequences of a mobility-divided society in which one-third of households do not have access to a car.

As motorization increased, non-drivers found that their ability to participate in society was reduced because bus services and rail lines have closed. Children learn from an early age that to be a competent citizen is to be a car driver so that their environmental objections to car use are laid aside as adulthood and the prospect of taking the driving test at age 17 beckon. As Solomon has shown, it is the driving licence which is regarded by young people as the key attribute of citizenship in a consumer society, not the vote (Solomon 1998).

One of the principal identities for the majority of adults in this society is that of motorist, leading them to view the world through the perspective of car ownership and to think it natural that they should have this private space from which to view reality. This technology affects how we view distance and the world in general, making us assume that everyone else travels in the same way and has the same access to facilities.

There are clear environmental imperatives in relation to car use. The car has to be used less as it is such an important source of carbon emissions. Innumerable reports have documented the damage to the environment and human health. This, then, is a prime area for lifestyle change. As the environmental transport agenda laid out in the government's transport White Paper of 1998 made clear, measures such as workplace parking charges, home zones, lower speed limits in residential areas would all be designed to reduce use of the car and encourage use of alternative forms of transport, particularly rail and bus but also (in line with the public health agenda) to encourage more people to walk and cycle (DETR 1998).

"The case of the car" raises in an acute form the means by which sustainable development and lifestyle can be addressed. If cars are for the majority of adults increasingly part of their nature, then do they have the capacity to reduce their dependence on cars? Voluntary reduction in car use in a society so car-dependent as the UK would appear to be an option only to be chosen by a few while incentives and penalties will be required for the majority. This is a considerable challenge for government. In a review of the Blair government's transport policy Robinson came to the conclusion that "the public still rejects the view that the car needs to be restricted at all" (Robinson 2000: 248). He believes that restrictions on car use are seen as threats to the values of liberty, individuality and freedom which in other contexts New Labour espouses. The enormity of the cultural and individual shift required to achieve a sustainable transport policy with reduced use of the car has not been acknowledged by government either in the Transport White Paper or the Ten Year Plan for Transport (DETR 2000). Yet there are some encouraging signs of change in the discourse around cars. Voices previously ignored or indeed silent like the 15,000 or more in the UK each year who are bereaved because of road deaths and the numerous victims of road offences who are disabled for life are making their voice heard through such organizations as Roadpeace.

Consumer Exclusion

In a society where identity has to be constructed rather than inherited, where one has to construct one's identity because it is not pre-given by family or occupation, to be poor is to be unable to sustain a proper identity. Consumer society through its sophisticated media and advertising penetrates almost every single home and creates the aspiration to the consumer good life, but for some the wherewithal to achieve the good life is lacking. In a society where pleasure has been privatized, to be without the necessary goods creates frustration on a large scale. Crime and vandalism are obvious outcomes.

There have been a number of studies documenting the human problems which affect those who cannot handle the freedom (credit) that consumer society bestows upon us. The repercussions of the consumer society for those living on low incomes or benefits can have serious consequences. Shopaholics, for example, are people who are addicted to shopping which usually involves them in buying large amounts of goods beyond their ability to pay, and sometimes they resort to shoplifting. A recent estimate put the number of shopaholics in the UK at 700,000 (Edwards 2000: 124). Social policy studies have been slow to explore the repercussions of living in a consumer society for those on low incomes. Credit and debt are the subject of a number of important studies. What does this work show? That the movement of large retailers out of city-centre sites has increased the cost of living for those who cannot access these stores. Some inner-city and suburban estates have no food shops whatsoever—indeed, in some areas it is much easier to buy drugs than food.

The dominance of consumerism has meant that social comparisons have intensified at all levels of society. The impact of television advertising on young children is well attested. Consumer culture has penetrated the playground so that brands are identified at an early age by children. When there is a strong emphasis upon winning and making a success in the culture, then the majority of people by definition are going to be losers. The outcome of comparison based on people's ownership of consumer durables is that there have been some disturbing increases in personal unhappiness and anti-social behaviour. "Rates of depression, delinquency and substance abuse among children and adolescents have risen substantially since 1950" (James 1997: 356). The consequences of this are increasingly seen in the high referral rates for child psychiatric clinics and the rising suicide rates among young males.

The erosion of older forms of communal solidarity have left some areas unprotected against the consumer society. They are the parts of the country where once labour solidarity and working-class culture protected the community against the low self-esteem that otherwise would have been produced by the lack of money and resources. Without this protection these areas are suffering from collective low self-esteem (Davies 1997).

Micro-social Policy

It is at the "micro-social" level that environmental change must come about if it is to significantly improve the lives of the poorest. There are innumerable surveys which show that residents of deprived neighbourhoods are concerned about the state of their streets, stairwells and local play spaces. Those who are car-dependent evince less interest in these issues as they are much less frequent users of pavements or public transport. Clearly if the population are to be persuaded out of their cars and on to public transport or to use walking and cycling as transport modes, then the quality of the local environment becomes of paramount importance for all sections of society. This was recognized by the prime minister, Tony Blair, when he endorsed the "liveability" agenda in April 2001—endorsing small-scale measures to improve the quality of people's lives: "We need local parks which are well looked-after and easily reached with a push chair. We need streets to be free of litter, dog mess and mindless vandalism" (Blair 2001).

These measures fit in with an environmental transport agenda which prioritizes lower speed limits, the creation of home zones and speed restrictions which will save the lives of children, particularly those from social class 5 where there are the greatest number of deaths and serious injuries from traffic. Walking is a good way to keep fit, as is cycling, but these require a supportive infrastructure in towns and cities which will make them safe activities to undertake. These measures will benefit those whose major modes of transport are walking and public transport, most often the poorest, but the benefits are not confined to them for safer streets can be enjoyed by all. However, green policies of this local micro-social kind—in health, education, housing, social security—are insufficient. They need to be accompanied by a social philosophy which promotes communal and sustainable values. For sustainable consumption to become an integral part of people's lives then consumerism has to be countered. Environmental catastrophe—for example, the loss of one's home by flooding—is one way of making the connection between unsustainable lifestyles and environmental change, but a responsible environmental politics cannot wait upon this. The question is whether in a postmodern world of moral relativism and post-emotionalism the intellectual resources for sustainable consumption are available.

If we are to live in accordance with our knowledge of environmental limits then restraint, duty, care, saving and love need to take precedence over such values as hedonism, freedom, spending and greed. The former are some of the values of a sustainable good life which would inform behaviour; there have to be ways and means by which they can be inculcated or transmitted to future generations.

This is a big step: political sociology shows that very few people understand the basic terms of the political system, while the recent UK general election results reveal the extent of disengagement. In these circumstances governments need to lead public opinion on environmental issues as the systems of economic production will not—cannot—provide an alternative vision to that of the market.

A recent book on feminism and the environment concludes: "the ecological crisis may only be solved by changing individual lifestyles and behaviour and existing environmentally destructive modes of production and consumption" (Littig 2001: 152). The 1992 Rio Earth Summit put sustainable lifestyles on the world's environmental agenda but, as we have seen, the expansion of consumer capitalism has made this a more difficult task ten years later.

The transition from a consumer society to a sustainable society is going to be difficult and painful. Most proponents of sustainable development tend to underestimate this—consciously or not—but it will mean a major change in the way of life of most people in rich societies. One of the problems with the transition is that there is little vision which would motivate people towards making the necessary changes in their way of life. The central and the local state will need to be utilized to engender a revival of public life in which the socio-environmental agenda can be promoted. Sustainability by stealth is not an option.

References

Anderson, B. (2000), *Doing the Dirty Work*, London: Zed Books.
Bentley, T., Jupp, B. and Stedman Jones, D. (2000), *Getting to Grips with Depoliticisation*, London: Demos. (http://www.demos.co.uk.B-offers.htm)
Beynon, H. (1973), *Working for Ford*, London: Allen Lane.
Blair, T. (2001), Improving your local environment, 24 April. (http://www.number-10.gov.uk/news.asp?NewsId=2008)
Bocock, R. (1993), *Consumption*, London: Routledge.
Booth, E. (1999), Getting inside the shoppers' mind, *Marketing*, 3 June.
Bowden, S. (1994), The new consumerism. In Paul Johnson (ed.), *20th Century Britain: Economic, Social and Cultural Change*, London: Longman.
Bulmer, M., Lewis, J. and Piachaud, D. (eds) (1989), *The Goals of Social Policy*, London: Unwin Hyman.
Chaney, D. (1996), *Lifestyles*, London: Routledge.
Chaney, D. (1998), The new materialism? The challenge of consumption, *Work, Employment and Society*, 12, 3: 533–44.
Christensen, P. (1997), Different lifestyles and their impact on the environment, *Sustainable Development*, 5: 30–5.
Cross, G. (1993), *Time and Money: The Making of Consumer Culture*, London: Routledge.
Davies, N. (1997), *Dark Heart*, London: Chatto and Windus.
Department of the Environment, Transport and the Regions (DETR) (1998), *A New Deal for Transport: Better for Everyone*, Cm 3950, London: Stationery Office.
Department of the Environment, Transport and the Regions (DETR) (2000), *Transport 2010: The Ten Year Plan*, London: DETR.
Dittmar, H. (1987), *The Social Psychology of Material Possessions: To Have or to Be*, Brighton: Harvester Wheatsheaf.
Edwards, T. (2000), *Contradictions of Consumption*, Milton Keynes: Open University Press.
Frank, R. H. (1999), *Luxury Fever: Why Money Fails to Satisfy in an Age of Excess*, New York: Free Press.
Galbraith, J. K. (1958), *The Affluent Society*, Harmondsworth: Penguin.
Goldthorpe, J., Lockwood, D., Bechhoffer, F. and Platt, J. (1969), *The Affluent Worker*, Cambridge: Cambridge University Press.
Hayes, D. and Hudson, A. (2001), *Basildon Man*, London: Demos.
Hertz, N. (2001), *The Silent Takeover: Global Capitalism and the Death of Democracy*, London: William Heinemann.
Hoggart, R. (1957), *The Uses of Literacy*, London: Chatto and Windus.
James, O. (1997), *Britain on the Couch*, London: Century.
Johnson, P. (ed.) (1994), *Twentieth Century Britain: Economic, Social and Cultural Change*, London: Longman.
Jowell, R., Curtice, J., Park, A., Thompson, K., Jarvis, L., Bromley, C. and Stratford, N. (2000), *British Social Attitudes: The 17th Report*, London: Sage.
Klein, N. (2000), *No Logo*, London: Flamingo.

Lansley, S. (1994), *After the Gold Rush*, London: Century.
Littig, B. (2001), *Feminist Perspectives on Environment and Society*, Harlow: Pearson Education.
Lury, C. (1996), *Consumer Culture*, Cambridge: Polity Press.
Marwick, A. (2000), *A History of the Modern British Isles 1914–1999*, Oxford: Blackwell.
Mestrovic, S. (1997), *Post Emotional Society*, London: Sage.
Michaelis, L. in Dodds, F. (2000), *Earth Summit 2002*, London: Earthscan.
Miles, S. (1998), *Consumerism as a Way of Life*, London: Sage.
Mulgan, G. (1994), *Connexity*, London: Chatto and Windus.
Norwich Union Insurance (2000), *Clean Break: The Changing Face of Domestic Help*, Norwich: Norwich Union.
Paterson, M. (2000), *Understanding Global Environmental Politics: Domination, Accumulation, Resistance*, London: Macmillan.
Pawley, M. (1973), *The Private Future: Causes and Consequences of Community Collapse in the West*, London: Thames and Hudson.
Riesman, D. (1961), *The Lonely Crowd: A Study of the Changing American Character*, London: Yale University Press.
Robinson, N. (2000), *The Politics of Agenda Setting: The Car and the Shaping of Public Policy*, Aldershot: Ashgate.
Scase, R. (1999), *Britain towards 2010*, London: Department of Trade and Industry.
Solomon, J. (1998), *To Drive or to Vote? Young Adults' Culture and Priorities*, London: Chartered Institute of Transport.
Spaargarten, G. and van Vliet, B. (2000), Lifestyles, consumption and the environment: the ecological modernisation of domestic consumption, *Environmental Politics*, 9, 1: 50–76.
Stokes, R. (1999), Lagging behind, *Guardian* (Society), 24 March: 10.
Urry, J. (2000), *Sociology beyond Societies*, London: Routledge.
Williams, R. (1961), *The Long Revolution*, London: Chatto and Windus.
WWF (1998), *Living Planet Report 1998*, Godalming: World Wide Fund for Nature.

INDEX